DATE DUE			

GAYLORD M-2   PRINTED IN U.S.A.

The Measurement

of Readability

A review and summary of the research dealing with readability and its measurement, with implications for using such measures as an aid to increasing the effectiveness of writing and speaking.

The Measurement *of* Readability

GEORGE R. KLARE

Professor of Psychology
Ohio University

Iowa State University Press
Ames, **Iowa, U.S.A.**

About the Author . . .

GEORGE R. KLARE is Professor and former
Chairman of the Department of Psychology of
Ohio University where he has been since 1954.
He has been professionally interested in read-
ability since his work at the University of
Minnesota where he received the doctorate in
psychology in 1950, and the bachelor's and
master's degrees in 1946 and 1947, respectively.
Following an instructorship at the University of
Minnesota, and two years as staff psychologist
with the Test Division of the Psychological
Corporation, he became Research Associate at
the University of Illinois in 1952.

Dr. Klare has written numerous journal
articles, many on readability, and is co-author,
with Byron Buck, of an earlier book, *Know
Your Reader*.

From 1957 to 1959, he served as Consultant
and Instructor in the Written Communication
Training Program of the National Project in
Agricultural Communications. He is a member
of both the Midwestern and American Psychological Associations and the American Personnel and Guidance Association.

Developed for the
Association of State Universities
and Land-Grant Colleges by the
National Project in Agricultural Communications

Composed and printed by
The Iowa State University Press
Ames, Iowa, U.S.A.
Reprinted, 1964

Preface

THIS BOOK is one of a series of three dealing with research in human communication. Others in the current series include:

Adoption of New Ideas and Practices
 by Herbert F. Lionberger

Legibility of Print
 by Miles A. Tinker

The development of these books was sponsored by the National Project in Agricultural Communications, and published for the use of students, practitioners, and researchers in the several fields concerned with various aspects of communications.

NPAC operated under the auspices of the American Association of State Universities and Land-Grant Colleges and was supported financially by the W. K. Kellogg Foundation and the institutions and organizations that participated in its activities. Its program was one of research, training, and service activities designed to contribute to the improvement of communications in agriculture and home economics. Housed at Michigan State University throughout its life, it became a formal part of that institution's structure in March, 1960, and was closed officially in March, 1962. Continuation of the projects in this series was effected by the Iowa State University Press through publication and distribution of the valuable information thus derived.

Acknowledgments

I WISH TO THANK the following persons for their help at the various stages of this book's preparation:

- Mrs. Paul Hagensick, Mrs. William Sears, and Mrs. James Sheridan, who made almost all of the annotations and abstracts of the studies listed in the bibliography.

- Miss Catherine Nelson, of the Ohio University Library, and Dr. Edgar Dale, of Ohio State University, who made it possible for me to examine many hard-to-get references.

- Dr. John Parsey, formerly of the National Project in Agricultural Communications, for references, ideas, encouragement, and editorial assistance.

- The many writers in the field of readability whose work I drew upon, and my wife, Julia, whose strength I drew upon.

GEORGE R. KLARE

Table of Contents

ix

List of Tables

Introduction

THIS BOOK is primarily a review of research literature in the field of readability, together with an analysis of trends and conclusions that can be drawn from the existing data. The term "readability" has come to be used in three ways:

(1) To indicate legibility of either handwriting or typography.

(2) To indicate ease of reading due to either the interest-value or the pleasantness of writing.

(3) To indicate ease of understanding or comprehension due to the style of writing.

Essentially, these are the alternatives followed by most writers on the topic of readability. Research in each of these areas is legitimately referred to as readability research. Most of the recent research, however, has centered around the third part of the definition; this, plus the widespread publicity given to readability formulas designed to measure comprehensibility, has made the third use the most common. This book is restricted to the analysis of research stemming from the third meaning. Studies of the legibility and interest-value of writing have been excluded, except for occasional studies that also have some relevance to understandability. The reader may wish to check such references as those of Paterson and Tinker (11) and Burtt (3) on typography and readability, and Waples (17) and Bernstein (2) on the relation of subject-interests to actual reading, but no attempt has been made to cover these areas.

The references reviewed here include those directly concerned with readability theory; the construction and validation of readability formulas; and the application of readability principles and formulas to writing. In addition, others which provide new points of view on readability, review the existing literature, or serve as bibliographic sources, have been included. Articles and books which had only an indirect connection with readability, or made only passing reference to it, could not practicably be included unless they made some special contribution to the theory or use of readability. If this restriction had not been made, it seems probable that the 482 items in the Bibliography might have been doubled. Within the above limitations, however, all important references in the period up to and including 1957 are reviewed; in addition, all important 1958 references that could be located at the time of writing (1959) are reviewed, as are certain selected 1959 references. Since the original publication of a piece of research may have gone unnoticed, and since journals and articles which keep records of published research usually are a year or more behind the publication of the studies themselves, it is possible that some important recent work may have been missed unintentionally.

Perhaps the major feature of this book for most readers is the review and analysis of "readability formulas." But formulas are simply devices which provide a quantitative estimate of readability; they are too often emphasized at the expense of the *principles* behind them. In this review both principles and formulas are discussed with three purposes in mind:

To increase the reader's general background in the field of readability;

To point out practical methods and procedures for using readability principles and formulas; and

To provide a body of data useful for future research and the development of theory.

The first major part of this book draws together, for writers and editors, useful, practical information on applying readability principles and formulas. The topics include what the user should know about his reader; how he should take his "purpose for writing" into account; and a suggested method for his using readability formulas in writing and revising. The approach taken is that proper application may help the user gain the advantages of readable writing and yet avoid the criticism that formulas have harmful effects on writing. This approach can also be seen in the subsections discussing which formulas to use for particular purposes and the inherent limitations in each. Part I may be read without reference to the rest of the book by anyone who is concerned at the moment only with practical application.

The next major part is the research review itself. It begins with the historical precedents of readability and goes on to the development of formulas. Though interest in the general problem of readability can be traced back one thousand years or more, present-day interest seems to have sprung from the development and publicizing of the formulas. Writers have disagreed on just how to define formulas, so that counts of the number of measuring devices published, from Lively and Pressey's first in 1923, to the year 1954, have varied from 29 to 56. *In this book, "readability formula" refers to a method of measurement* intended as a predictive device *that will provide quantitative, objective estimates of the style difficulty of writing.* The method must be general enough to provide estimates over a range of applicability and difficulty, and must be capable of providing these estimates without involving the use of readers in any way. Using this

definition, 31 formulas and 10 variations of existing formulas
(excluding foreign language formulas) were found to have
been published during the years 1923 to 1959. There appear
to have been four general periods of development during
these years: (1) The development of early formulas, 1921–
1934; (2) The development of detailed formulas, 1934–1938;
(3) The development of efficient formulas, 1938–1953; and
(4) The development of specialized formulas, 1953 to date.
In addition to the readability formulas, a number of other
methods have been developed to measure readability. These
are generally of three kinds: the "clinical" method, the
method of reader judgments, and various testing methods.
Table 1, pages 75ff., presents a summary of the formulas developed to date.

Of the various methods of measuring readability used in
research, formulas are much the most common. Part II also
contains a brief picture of the major areas in which formulas
have been used: (1) *Education,* where the studies cover elementary, secondary, college, and adult education, and where
the largest number of applications has been made; (2) *Business and industry,* where communications intended both for
management and for workers have been analyzed; (3) *Journalism and mass communications,* where the influence of
readability has been much greater than even the large
number of published studies would indicate; (4) *Legal and
governmental writing,* often considered the area where increased readability is most needed; (5) *Psychological tests and
questionnaires,* where either special formulas or special rules
for applying regular formulas are necessary because of the
small units of context — sentences or less — to be analyzed;
(6) *Writing,* where special principles designed to help writers
produce more readable writing are described; (7) *Speech,*
where attempts have been made to apply formulas to orally
presented material much as they are applied to written ma-

terial; and (8) *Foreign languages,* where both special foreign-language formulas and regular English formulas have been applied. The major conclusion drawn by the many appliers of readability formulas is that much of the material analyzed is too difficult for its intended audience. Also in Part II is evaluative information on three aspects of readability formulas: sampling, analyst reliability, and validity.

The samples suggested by the developers of modern formulas appear generally adequate. There is, however, no single sample size that can be considered best for *all* situations. In general, sample size should be increased when (1) counts of *number* of different words or *percentage* within a given category are made; (2) a high degree of accuracy of measurement is desired; and (3) application time is not a matter of great concern. Studies show that there is high analyst reliability with the Flesch Reading Ease and Farr-Jenkins-Paterson formulas. Similar studies have not been made for other formulas, but are clearly needed, especially for formulas which use a word-list.

Evidence of formula validity comes from three sources. The first is the extent to which a formula can account for the variance (variability) in the original criterion passages on which it was developed. Recent formulas yield a maximum correlation coefficient of around .70 between formula scores and indices of difficulty in criterion passages, thus accounting for about 50% of the variance. In terms of prediction error, formulas are probably accurate to within about one grade level of a "true" rating. The second source of evidence on validity comes from comparisons of the readability scores of several formulas on the same reading material. Data are incomplete here, not only because all of the possible comparisons between formulas have not been made but also because the existing comparisons are difficult to interpret for technical reasons. Several clear-cut conclusions that can be drawn are: (1) the Dale-Chall and Flesch Reading Ease formulas yield the most nearly comparable scores; (2) the Dale-Chall formula is involved in more high intercorrelations with other formulas than any other single formula; (3) formulas may tend to disagree with each other in readability grade placements of material even though there is a high *correlation* between formula scores. The third source of validity evidence lies in studies which relate formula scores to some outside criterion of readability. For example, formula scores on a series of reading test passages may be correlated with comprehension scores on the passages. Or, in another type of study, a passage may be re-written at several different levels of readability, with formula scores compared to some outside criterion. In all, 65 studies were located, of which 39 gave positive evidence of validity, 16 gave negative evidence, and 10 gave results of such a nature that it was not possible to consider them one or the other. When the studies are broken down by criterion used, it can be seen that those involving reading efficiency, judgmental, and readership criteria give a strongly positive trend, while those using comprehension and retention (and listenability) criteria yield positive results only in certain circumstances. The results categorized in terms of criteria are found in greater detail in Tables 2 through 6, on pages 133, 137, 144, 149, and 152; a summary of all studies is presented in Table 7 on page 155. Though "human interest" is often considered an aspect of readability, it has not been included in the analyses because not enough validity studies have used it to make a reliable interpretation possible.

Part III of this book begins with a discussion of possible underlying reasons for the validity results found in the studies reviewed. These are examined under two main headings: basic readability factors present in written material, and basic considerations in the reader. In written material, two factors emerge from the several different analytic approaches, a word factor and a sentence factor. The word factor appears to be basically frequency of occurrence, but word length is also important; the sentence factor appears to be basically length, but redundancy is also important. As for the reader, the basic factors appear to operate in different ways. Speed of word recognition and memory span are directly affected by the word and sentence factors mentioned above. Skill factors represented in educational level and special reading experience with the topic being read, and the factors of "set to learn" * and the "principle of least effort," on the other hand, are basic factors in the reader that are *not* a direct function of the factors in the written material. All four of the reader factors, however, affect a person's reading behavior, i.e., his reading efficiency, his judgment of difficulty or acceptability, and his comprehension, learning, or retention of the material.

Chapter 11, Part III, considers future directions that readability research may profitably take. The first is basic research, with particular attention to setting up a theoretical framework for viewing the variables in language, the reader, and reading behavior involved in the study of readability. Table 8, on page 188, presents a first crude attempt to set up such a framework. A second direction possible is the attempt to discover new factors useful in the measurement of readability, both quantitative and qualitative. The third direction is the refinement of factors and methods now being used.

The final Part IV is a classified, annotated bibliography of the studies used in writing this book. A separate listing (H.) includes published bibliographies, reviews, and other compilations of the literature.

---

* The term "set to learn" refers to a readiness to learn related to motivation. The term is discussed more specifically in Chapter 10.

Part I

Practical Applications

This is a summary of information on the application of readability principles and formulas based on a survey and interpretation of research in the field.

1. Useful Information for Communicators

THIS CHAPTER discusses the application of readability principles and formulas. It is based upon the survey of the literature presented in succeeding chapters, and represents an interpretation of these data.

Readability for the Reader

Much of this report treats readability as an entity. This approach has the advantage of simplicity because it avoids the problem of repeatedly qualifying what is said. But it may leave the impression that readable writing is desirable and important for its own sake. The better point of view is that readable writing is desirable and important for the reader's sake. If it is not readable to an intended reader it is not readable, no matter how good a formula score it may receive. The reader must be the judge.

It is possible, of course, to consider readable writing only in terms of style. There were advocates of a plain style long before the technical study of readability began, and many of them had little immediate concern for readers. Some early writers have characterized an ornate style as somehow almost immoral; the same attitude can be seen in more recent criticisms which imply that those who write to "impress rather than express" are at least deceitful and certainly not democratic.

11

This kind of argument about the merit of various styles of writing is usually very personal. It cannot be supported in this book where the primary goal is the impersonal presentation of conclusions based on research. It is fair to say, however, that the *size* of a writer's audience depends to a large extent upon the readability of his writing. If he is interested only in a small, specialized, highly educated audience, the principles of readability presented here may not be of great concern. But if he is trying to reach a large, unselected, and less literate audience successfully, readability principles are of major importance.

Ideally, a writer should have a rather detailed picture of his audience. He should have information about reading, educational and intellectual levels, background or previous experience with the writer's topic, interests, level of motivation, and voluntary or involuntary attention to the material. In addition, the audience should be fairly homogeneous in these respects for greatest effectiveness in writing.

Few writers, though, can either impose conditions on their audiences or get to know audience characteristics fully. This is not the place to try to describe fully what is known about the characteristics of various groups of readers. Instead, the question considered here is the kind of information a writer *can* usually get. First, he can usually discover something about the reader's educational level, and, if he does, he can manage to get along without reading level and intellectual level, since the three are related (on the average). Educational level as used here refers to the last school grade completed, which is helpful because modern readability formulas provide ratings in these terms. Where detailed information on educational level of readers is not available from other sources, U.S. Census data may prove helpful, especially when the audience is small enough or homogeneous enough for a single value to be characteristic.

Here are some typical recent figures for the median number of years of schooling completed by adults, with projected values based on work done by the National Education Association: 1940, between 8 and 9; 1950, between 9 and 10; 1957, between 10 and 11; 1960, about 11; 1970, around 12; and 1980, slightly over 12.

A writer also frequently knows something about (or has some basis for an estimate of), his reader's previous experience with the topic (his amount of background). If this is known, a reader's interests become somewhat predictable because the amount of background a reader has is roughly correlated with his interest in a topic. Background determines also the degree of the naïveté or sophistication with special terminology a reader is likely to have. This is important because material difficult to a general reader might still be understandable to a reader with no greater educational level but with a specialized background.

A writer can sometimes infer a third characteristic, the reader's level of motivation, at least insofar as it may involve a strong or a weak "set to learn." Leisure reading, for example, will most likely involve weaker motivation than reading on a topic related to a person's occupation. Whether or not the reader is *required* to read is related to level of motivation, but not in a simple way. A person required to read will often have a strong set to learn, while a person reading voluntarily will usually have a weaker set to learn. But these relationships may be reversed. The problem of motivation is of greatest importance when the writer has a specific purpose in writing.

The Writer's Purpose

The writer's purpose may be viewed in several different ways, but attention here is limited to the writer's purpose in relation to the use of readability principles or formulas. If he wishes to know whether they can be effectively applied, he must consider whether reader understanding, or learning, or efficiency, or perhaps something else, is his main goal.

Reading Speed and Efficiency. If the writer's primary concern is for the reader's speed and efficiency in reading, more readable material consistently provides for an increase. This seems to hold true for most educational levels and amounts of background readers may have; even the most highly educated will read more readable materials with increased efficiency. This also seems to apply to both required and voluntary reading, and to either a stronger or weaker set to learn. There is some reason to believe, in fact, that readability is more important in voluntary reading, since the person who is not required to read may often stop altogether if he cannot proceed efficiently. He may choose some more effortless way of getting the desired information, or he may choose some other activity altogether. Perceptual habits in reading are rather mechanical, and more readable material provides greater efficiency than does less readable material, even with different levels and kinds of motivation. The use of the term "mechanical" should not imply "unimportant"; the tendency of humans to behave according to the "principle of least effort" shows this.

Reader Judgment. If the writer is interested chiefly in the reader's judgment of the readability of a piece of writing, and particularly its acceptability, more readable writing again provides for a consistent increase. Studies show that readers, as a group, rank materials in terms of readability in much the same order as the writer using a readability formula does. They consistently prefer a more readable version of the material to a less readable one; this holds remarkably well over the various educational levels of readers. Obviously an adult does not prefer the style of a first-grade reading text, but even a highly educated adult will generally find a ninth-grade level of style difficulty acceptable if the writing is expertly done. One qualification should be made here. If the reader has a large amount of background and experience with a topic, he may have some objection to a simple style, particularly if it seems to involve the avoidance of long and technical, but accurate, words. If, however, a topic falls outside the reader's speciality, studies show that even the more highly educated will prefer a simpler style. Once again, the level and type of motivation does not usually alter the reader's preference for more readable material. The reader may have a stronger or weaker set to learn, and may or may not be required to read, but still he will usually judge a more readable version more acceptable. And as before, this may well be most important for the reader who is not required to read; he may stop reading relatively unacceptable material because the effort does not seem justified.

Readership. If the writer is concerned chiefly with the probable number of his readers, more readable material again will provide for a rather consistent increase. Here, the level of readability often plays a rather direct role since a writer for the mass media must usually attract readers of a lower educational level if he wants wide readership. He cannot expect his readers as a group to have a high level of background or experience with his topic. Similarly, in most cases, he cannot expect them to have a very strong set to learn or to feel much compulsion to read. Therefore, level of readability becomes of major importance and the principle of least effort operates almost with a vengeance on the writer. There seems little question that highly readable, skilled writing will attract more readers than that which is less readable. Reader efficiency with more readable material, and preference for it, creates this predisposition.

Comprehension, Learning, and Retention. If the writer's chief aim is to increase the reader's comprehension, learning, and retention of his material, more readable writing may or may not provide them. Comprehension, learning, and retention are not necessarily the same thing, but they are considered together here because the few studies using learning or retention scores as criteria tend to agree with the bulk of studies using comprehension scores. The general conclusion to be drawn from this work is that the writer certainly cannot always count on improvements due simply to the use of more readable material. This is particularly unfortunate, because the first reason for the study of readability principles lay in the hope that their use would increase the reader's understanding, or at least predict what it would be.

Several reasons for negative results exist: *first* is the matter of educational level. The grade level at which a reader can read is not as precise as it sometimes sounds. A person who has finished no more than the ninth grade in school can — and sometimes must — read twelfth-grade material. But his motivation must be high, and even then it is *possible* to write beyond his level, as some legal writing demonstrates. This means that more readable writing probably will not be understood, learned, or retained better *unless* the less readable material with which it is compared is quite a bit harder and clearly beyond the reader's normal reading level.

Second, if the reader is not strictly limited in the time he may spend on a piece of writing or the number of times he may read it, an increase in readability may not produce a corresponding increase in comprehension. If, however, he must read material hurriedly, and may not re-read or puzzle over difficult passages, the readability level of the material clearly will have an effect.

Third, the greater the reader's background and experience with a given topic, and the greater the redundancy of the writing, the less effect an increase in readability will have. The expert probably will not understand an easy version of a piece of material in his field any better than a harder version, although he may read it faster. Once the topic is outside his field he may, in addition to reading it faster, understand it better and prefer it.

Fourth, the kind and level of the reader's motivation also will partially determine whether more readable material produces greater understanding, learning, and retention. Studies show particularly that the reader must have a strong set to learn before the advantages of a more readable over a less readable version become apparent. Without such motivation, the somewhat mechanical, least-effortful perceptual habits of reading play too dominant a role.

In summary, more readable written material is likely to produce greater comprehension, learning, and retention than less readable only when one or more of the following factors are present: the less readable is much harder than the more readable, and clearly beyond the reader's usual level; reading time is limited; the reader does not have a large amount of background or experience with the topic being covered; and, the reader has a relatively strong set to learn.

Listenability. If the writer's material is to be presented orally and he is concerned for its comprehension, more readable material again may or may not provide an increase. In fact, increased comprehension has been found in relatively few studies. The reasons for this are probably the same as those just stated for the comprehension, learning, and retention of written material, plus at least one factor peculiar to spoken material. This is the tendency for it to drop from memory rapidly without the possibility, as in written material, for the reader to go back to an earlier word, phrase, or section. Perhaps if there were some provision in speech for repetition when the listener desired it, or even at regular intervals, this limitation would disappear. At any rate, lack of possible repetition plus the qualifications applicable to written material are probably responsible for the finding of more negative than positive results in listenability studies.

Principles of Writing Readably

A most common criticism of readability formulas is that they make poor "formulas" for writing. They were not, however, intended for this purpose. Certain principles of readability, based on research done on and with formulas, *can* be used in writing. But this does not mean that a *formula* should be considered a dictator of good style by the writer or a basis for restricting individuality by the editor. Primarily, a formula is a means of rating a piece of writing *after* it has been written.

Writing is a complex bit of human behavior, and therefore a definition of good or satisfactory writing is hard to develop. There are rules for specific purposes, to be sure, but careful adherence to them does not guarantee good writing. In short, writing is an art and not a science. Certain principles can be taught and followed, however, and something is known of their effect. One of these, discussed earlier, concerns collection of adequate knowledge about the reader. The more important kinds of information are those related to educational level, motivation, and reader experience. A second principle concerns the writer's purpose; as mentioned previously, the writer should decide specifically what he wants to do. He may want to help the reader read more efficiently; judge whether the material is acceptable; read for comprehension, learning, and retention; understand orally presented material; or accomplish some combination of these and other purposes.

A third principle is concerned with the selection of words, particularly in terms of their high frequency of occurrence and consequent familiarity. In practice, the words to be used may be classified in many ways other than frequency or familiarity, including:

1. Words learned early in life
2. Short words (in terms of either syllable or letter length)
3. Words of Anglo-Saxon rather than of Norman, Greek, or Latin derivation
4. Nontechnical words (where possible)
5. Words familiar "in writing" (some spoken words, like "pshaw," are not as familiar in print as in speech)
6. Words used in a common meaning
7. Concrete or definite, rather than abstract, words.

It should be emphasized, of course, that not all the words used in a piece of writing can satisfy even one of these qualifications. The important thing is to keep the proportion of such words as high as the reader's and the writer's purposes demand.

A fourth principle relates to sentence construction. The basic factor involved is the length of sentences, but again other characterizations are possible. Two of the most notable ones are:

1. Sentences that contain few prepositional phrases

2. Sentences that have few compound, complex, or compound-complex constructions.

Emphasis should not be placed on making sentences as short as possible, or even on making all sentences short. The characteristics of the reader help to determine how short sentences should be, and style usually dictates a mixture of short and long sentences. The important thing here is to keep *average* sentence length as short as the needs of the moment demand.

A fifth principle concerns the use of a style that is high in "human interest," i.e., the inclusion of "personal" words and sentences. Rudolf Flesch (33) has described categories of words and sentences that increase the personal quality of writing, and has shown, for example, that fiction is high in this quality and scientific writing low. Certainly a writer at times may wish to use a very personal style, but evidence indicates it is not always the most readable. In itself it does not appear to contribute to the understanding of the material, or to the efficiency of the reader. And it may even make the material less acceptable; this seems to be the case when the reader is not expecting it, as in most technical writing. However, when it is expected, as in fiction or dramatic writing, the reader would probably find another style unacceptable.

How To Use a Readability Formula

The first draft of material should be made without regard to formulas, even though readability may be the writer's most important concern. The use of a formula as any kind of a specific guide can lead to mechanical writing and take away some of the individuality of style. The concern of the writer at this point should be not for readability, but for such basic problems as organization and emphasis.

Once the first draft is completed, the writer can use a formula to evaluate it for readability. Draft manuscript is good for such analysis, since it can be marked up as much as necessary to apply a formula efficiently. The results of the analysis can then be used to help the writer decide whether or not, with his given purpose in mind, he will reach his intended audience.

If the writer decides he may not reach his audience, revision is called for. During this revision, as during the original writing, formulas should be put aside. After all, they indicate only the general difficulty of the style, and revision involves more than just a change in level of difficulty. When to make changes and how to make them are up to the writer; merely chopping sentences in half, or substituting one word for another, will result in a better formula score but probably in poorer writing as well.

Once the material is revised, the next step may well be to run a second check to see whether the material is now at the desired level of difficulty. It is possible the writer may feel another revision and another check are necessary. Certainly the number of checks made can be reduced with some experience, because a writer soon gets a "feel" for the level of difficulty of a particular piece of writing. One or even no checks may be needed after a time.

In the process of checking material with a formula, it is best to use new samples for each analysis. Otherwise, only the selected samples may really be changed and therefore give unreliable results for the whole. While use of samples can give a good estimate of the difficulty of an entire piece of material, increasing the number of samples never hurts the accuracy of estimation. In all sampling, material for analysis should be taken from all parts of the piece of writing in about equal proportions. It is particularly important to sample from all authors' writings when several have contributed to the same publication.

This suggested method has been presented from the viewpoint of the writer's use of formulas. Editors using formulas for the purpose of checking readability have an additional responsibility — that of being certain that rewriting does not change intended meaning (unless slight changes are not important). In writing and revision, the emphasis is naturally on what might be called the structure of writing; the content of the material is decided by the author, and it should remain his concern.

Which Formula To Use

A writer, editor, or research worker who wants to use a formula must choose from among about 31 and their variations. How should the choice be made? Two major characteristics frequently are considered by users: the predictive accuracy of the formula and speed of application. These are not contradictory, and a user may want both; however, a research worker may be willing to use a somewhat more time-consuming method to gain a small amount of accuracy while a writer or editor may not mind sacrificing a small amount of accuracy for a significant gain in speed. Added to these considerations are others having to do with the special purpose the formula can serve. Examples here are range of applicability (specifically, usefulness with children's and/or adult materials); ability to measure level of abstraction and difficulty of ideas rather than mere style difficulty; and usefulness with materials not in contextual form, such as tests and questionnaires.

Such considerations as these indicate the impossibility of designating one formula as *the best*. Furthermore, insufficient research prohibits evaluating some formulas very completely. Speed of application, reliability, usefulness for a particular level of difficulty or kind of material, have not been measured for all formulas. Therefore, only general suggestions can be safely made; those below apply to formulas intended for adult materials.

    a. The most accurate formula: the Dale-Chall (23,24) is consistently more accurate than others in comparisons, though sometimes only slightly so. The user may wish to consider the recalculated version of the formula devised by Powers, Sumner, and Kearl (65), but the added predictive accuracy is probably not very great.

    b. The fastest formula to apply: the Farr-Jenkins-Paterson (30) simplification of the Flesch Reading Ease formula is probably the fastest, though formulas like Robert Gunning's (43) have not been thoroughly evaluated. The Farr-Jenkins-Paterson version is slightly less accurate than the Flesch Reading Ease formula, but the user who wants a "fast" formula that will give rough results may well choose it.

c. The most popular formula: the Flesch Reading Ease formula (33) is a compromise choice between the Dale-Chall and Farr-Jenkins-Paterson formulas, and has the advantage of being the one most often used and the one on which the most research data are available.

d. A formula for measuring abstraction level: The Flesch formula (34) uses a measure of abstraction to arrive at a readability score, but the method is cumbersome. Gillie (39) has proposed a shorter method.

e. A formula for noncontextual materials: the Forbes-Cottle formula (38) is useful for psychological tests and inventories.

No definite break exists between formulas intended for adult material and those intended for children's. Some formulas used primarily on adult writing actually reach down to a fairly low grade-level and can be used on children's material. The Flesch Reading Ease formula was developed on passages as low as fourth grade level, and the Dale-Chall formula as low as third grade level. Where only children's material is to be analyzed, however, an advantage is often gained by using a formula designed specifically for that general level. The following suggestions are made with that in mind.

a. Popular general children's formulas: the Washburne-Morphett formula (75) has been widely used and is among the most accurate formulas available; it is for the grade range of 1 to 9. The Lorge formula (56, 58), which reaches to grade 12, has been used for children's and some adult materials. Another widely used formula for about the same range is that of Yoakam (78).

  b. Formulas for lowest children's levels: both the formula by Spache (67) and Stone's version of it (70) are for grades 1 to 3; Wheeler and Smith's formula (76) is for primer level up to grade 4.

  c. A promising general children's formula: the recent formula of Tribe (72) for grades 2 to 8 has been carefully developed, and while it is too early to evaluate it fully, it appears to have good potential.

  d. A formula for measuring abstractness: the recent formula of Bloomer (21) is interesting both because it attacks the important problem of abstractness in children's material and because it approaches it from a new point of view, that of modifiers.

Limitations of Formulas

Something has already been said of what formulas cannot be expected to do — their limitations. Formulas have been criticized over the years, for example, because of the mistaken assumption that they were designed to measure all the important aspects of writing. On the other hand, some users have accepted formula scores uncritically even when there is evidence against their acceptance. So at least brief notice of the limitations of formulas seems called for.

First, formulas measure only one aspect of writing — style. Perhaps certain formulas, especially those concerned with abstractness of words or analysis of ideas, approach a measure of content, but they touch on this only indirectly. Yet work in readability constantly shows that unless content is interesting and relevant to the reader's need, it will not make much difference whether it is readable or not, since it will seldom be read. Nor is content the only concern. Formulas do not touch on organization, word order, format, or imagery in writing; they do not take into account the differing purposes, maturity, and intelligence of readers.

Second, formulas measure only one aspect of style — difficulty. Other aspects of style are important, as any literary critic can point out. Those that come to mind are the dramatic effectiveness of the writing, or its ability to create a mood; writing may sway opinions or satirize public life, but a formula will not measure its effectiveness in doing so.

Third, formulas do not even measure difficulty *perfectly.* Formulas appear to give scores accurate to, or even within, one grade-level. Yet actually they are seldom this accurate. The factors just mentioned frequently play a part in determining whether a piece of writing is at a particular level of difficulty in any given circumstance. And beyond these, a formula score may be inaccurate due to errors in sampling or in application.

Fourth, formulas are not measures of *good* style. Clearly, a poor piece of writing may sometimes be poor because it has a low readability score, but it would not necessarily be good if it had a good readability score. Therefore, the temptation simply to substitute an easy word for a hard one, to cut sentences in half, or to eliminate prepositional phrases even when they are needed may produce exactly the opposite of the desired result.

Thus style difficulty is shown to be only one characteristic of a piece of writing. It is often an important one, however, as shown by its relationship to reading speed, acceptability, understanding, and learning. If formulas are thought of as efficient predictors of difficulty, more accurate in prediction than individual writers most of the time, that is all that should be expected. At present, at least, content and all the other elements of writing, plus aspects of style other than difficulty, are not taken into account in formula scores. Formulas can be highly useful to the professional communicator if these limitations are kept in mind.

Part II

Measurements of Readability

This section documents methods of readability measurement, discussing historical precedents of formulas; the mechanics and developmental history of recognized readability formulas; other methods of measuring readability; major areas in which formulas have been applied; and the reliability and validity of formulas.

2. Historical Precedents of Formulas

MANY READERS these days automatically associate the word "formula" with the word "readability." Certainly, formulas are the best known of all the products and outcomes of research in this field. To discuss formulas only, however, does not provide full understanding of readability and its use; formulas are only one of several ways of judging the difficulty of reading material. Ruth Strang (13) lists as major methods the judgments of students, teachers, and various professional people; tests of difficulty in classroom and library; and the "clinical" approach; all in addition to the kind of quantitative analysis made with formulas. Furthermore, formulas have appeared only rather recently in the history of readability.

People have probably been concerned with readability (or its parallel, listenability) since symbols first were used and recorded. One of the favorite quotations of advocates of clear language, in fact, comes from I Corinthians 14:9, "Except ye utter by the tongue words easy to be understood, how shall it be known what is spoken? For ye shall speak into the air."

Not only was clarity considered early in history but its study had the inevitable moral overtones of the period. The first recorded attempt to examine specifically what we have come to call readability was, in fact, made by religious teachers. Irving Lorge (8) tells of word and idea counts made by the Talmudists in 900 A.D. so that they could use frequency of occurrence to distinguish usual from unusual senses (meanings). It is not surprising to find the first concern for readability among religious writers: they were the most, and almost the only, literate persons of their day.

Nor is it surprising to find the next evidence of serious interest among educators. W. S. Gray (5) points out that study of the elements of difficulty began centuries ago in connection with children's reading; evidence of this appeared about 1840, for example, when ease of understanding was considered in terms of vocabulary in the McGuffey Readers. The word count constructed in 1898 by F. W. Kaeding, a German, next provided a more scientific base for relating vocabulary to reading difficulty and establishing a basic vocabulary foundation (Lorge, 8). N. A. Rubakin, a Russian, compiled a list of 1500 familiar words in 1889, indicating something of the widespread interest in vocabulary lists by this time.

The work on word counts set the stage for what was easily the most important occurrence in the period just prior to the development of formulas, the publication in 1921 of *The Teacher's Word Book* by E. L. Thorndike (14). His tabulations of the frequency with which words occur in print not only influenced the teaching of vocabulary in the schools but also provided the basis for the work of Lively and Pressey in 1923 in developing the first method of measuring readability that can really be considered a formula. Many subsequent studies of reading and language generally have been based on one or another of Thorndike's books (14, 15, 16).

Apparently vocabulary was rather generally agreed upon as the important factor in reading difficulty, since so much of the early work focused on it. Attempts were made, however, to isolate other factors. Rubakin, for example, pointed to the excessive use of long sentences as a source of difficulty (Lorge, 8). But it was L. A. Sherman (12), a professor of

English literature, and his students, notably Gerwig (4), who apparently first studied sentence length quantitatively as an indicator of style. Sherman analyzed the average sentence lengths used by famous writers and discovered several interesting tendencies. He found that sentence lengths had been decreasing over the years, from around 50 words during the early period (down to Elizabethan times) to around 23 in his time. Related to this he found a corresponding "decrease of predication" or, conversely, an increase in the extent of simple sentences used in writing. Still another tendency among writers was remarkable consistency in the pattern of sentence lengths they used. Sherman showed that this made possible the analysis of samples instead of entire books, just as is done with readability formulas today. This also suggests the use of sentence-length analysis for literary detective work in the case of disputed authorship. G. U. Yule (19) has used the analysis of sentence lengths in just this way, showing quite convincingly that it must have been Thomas à Kempis, rather than Jean Charlier de Gerson, who wrote *De Imitatione Christi.* (See also C. B. Williams, 18.)

The developers of the first readability formulas did not, for some reason, draw upon the early work dealing with sentence length. Nor did they follow, apparently, the suggestions of H. D. Kitson (7), the pioneer applied psychologist. Though he did not say so in modern terms, he clearly recognized the importance of readability to the reader of advertising copy. To show the difference in "publics," he compared the "highbrow" Chicago *Evening Post* with the "lowbrow" Chicago *American,* and the *Century* magazine with the *American* magazine. He found that both word length, in terms of syllable count, and sentence length, in terms of number of words, were longer in the highbrow publications.

The use of syllable length as an index of word difficulty seems to have been independently arrived at by M. V. Bear

(1). She found that the percentage of monosyllabic words in a reading selection provided a fair index of reading difficulty. She also found a high correlation between the length of a word and the frequency of its use. Her work did not go unnoticed; G. R. Johnson (46) made use of it in developing his method of grading materials for difficulty. It is interesting to note, in passing, that the finding of a quantitative relationship between word length and frequency is generally credited to G. K. Zipf, whose work appeared eight years later.

Two more events in the middle Twenties deserve notice for their contribution to the development of readability. The first was the impetus given by librarians to the readability movement (Gray, 5). Whereas educators were primarily interested in readable materials for children, librarians campaigned for readable materials for adults. Scattered individual efforts to discover readable books were recognized by the formation in 1925 of the Sub-Committee on Readable Books of the Commission on the Library and Adult Education. There is evidence of similar Russian interest at about the same time, with primary concern for the literacy of the Red Army.

The second event, also in 1925, was the publication of W. A. McCall and Lelah Mae Crabbs' *Standard Test Lessons in Reading* (10). Though not used in early research, this set of graded reading passages later became the most used and most adequate of available criteria for the construction of readability formulas.

3. Methodology of Formula Development

A READABILITY FORMULA would seem to be clear-cut and easy to recognize. It should be possible, for example, to review the literature of readability, count the formulas developed, and report the number that has appeared up to any given date. It is not as simple as that, however, largely because the description of what, exactly, constitutes a formula has never been clearly stated. If the strict definition of a formula as a regression equation is adopted, several studies that deserve mention are excluded; if the looser notion of a formula as any method of measuring readability is accepted, it is difficult to set limits that are exclusive enough.

This situation has led, first of all, to the substitution of other terms for the word "formula." Klare (475, 476), for example, used the term "method" primarily; Dunlap (369) used "measure" or "technique"; Chall (469) used "quantitative associational study." This has, in turn, led to differences in the number of "formulas" reported: Chall counted 29 up to 1954, while Klare listed 39 and Dunlap 56.

As mentioned earlier, the term "readability formula" will be used in this book to refer to a method of measurement *intended as a predictive device*. The design of the method and the intention of the writer must have been to provide quantitative, objective estimates of difficulty for pieces of writing without requiring readers to take tests of any kind on them. Furthermore, the method must be general enough to provide estimates over a range of applicability and of difficulty, i.e., be more than a procedure set up to compare only a few specific books, especially those within a given school grade.

It is not possible, even with this restricted use of the term "readability formula," to describe a developmental procedure that will apply equally well to all formulas. However, since such a statement can help the reader evaluate the adequacy of particular formulas, a "general procedure" will be described briefly below. Illustrations helpful in understanding it have been drawn largely from Gray and Leary's *What Makes a Book Readable* (41).

As indicated, a readability formula is a method of estimating the probable success a reader will have in reading and understanding a piece of writing. It is predictive in the sense that it provides an estimate of difficulty for the writing without requiring the reader to read it and undergo tests on it. In other words, it provides the kind of information about readability that a writer or teacher would have to judge through experience, or measure through a reading test.

If a formula is to predict the difficulty of a piece of writing, there must be elements in the writing that are related to reader success. These elements could come from at least four general areas (according to a survey by Gray and Leary): content, style, format, and organization. Listed in order of importance, the first two are clearly of greatest importance. These authors found, however, that content, format, and organization could not be broken down into usable measuring factors. So they, like others who preceded and followed them, concentrated on style factors. They came up with 82 elements of style they felt were potentially useful, but only 64 of these could be counted reliably and only 44 occurred often enough in their samples to be useful for analysis. The next question was whether these elements were actually related to ease or difficulty of reading and, if so, how closely.

To answer this sort of question, it is necessary to have a criterion (basis) for relating the number of occurrences of an element to degree of reading success. In the case of Gray and Leary's study, the criterion was a set of reading test passages with comprehension questions on each. The passages were graded for difficulty on the basis of the number of questions that around 1,000 readers could answer correctly. Following this came the analysis of each passage to see if certain style elements occurred more or less frequently as the passages got harder. The extent of relationship for each element was expressed as a correlation coefficient, as is usually the case.* Gray and Leary's last step was then to combine the elements most highly predictive of difficulty into a formula. Their method was a regression equation, which weights the elements used in proportion to their contribution to the over-all score.

This procedure — survey and analysis of potential elements; counting and correlation of element occurrences with indices of difficulty in criterion passages; and combination into a regression equation formula — can be called the general pattern for the development of formulas. Approaches have varied considerably, but mostly in details. To begin with, a survey of expert opinion on potential elements has not always been attempted; frequently the elements are

---

* All positive correlations in this and the succeeding chapters have been reported, for convenience, without a preceding plus sign. Negative correlations bear a minus sign unless they represent a logically positive relationship. For example, high scores on some formulas represent easy material and on others hard material. Therefore, a correlation of formula scores may sometimes yield a negative coefficient that is confusing to the reader. For this reason this sort of correlation and any other that is negative for a similar reason will be reported as positive values.

selected on a logical or on a strictly empirical basis. Similarly, recent developers of formulas have seldom bothered with analysis of as wide a range of elements as Gray and Leary; this has not been necessary because of the accumulated knowledge in the field.

Perhaps the greatest variation has been in the criterion selected. The one thing common in each criterion has been the existence of a gradation of readability in the materials used. Beyond that, however, it has consisted of sets of judgments, reading speeds, comprehension tests, reading ability scores, and even readability scores derived from another formula or formulas. In relating the number of elements to the criterion, the early workers frequently used an inspection method; later workers have usually used the more refined technique of correlation. The later work also generally resulted in a regression equation formula, while in the earlier, an index number or normative table was common.

4. Developmental History of Formulas

Early Formulas, 1921–1934

IT IS DIFFICULT to know which study should be listed as *the first*. H. D. Kitson, as mentioned previously, used word length in syllables and sentence length in words as indices of the relative difficulty of two newspapers and two magazines as early as 1921. Despite the fact that his two elements and some of his terminology turned up in later readability research, they appear to have been adopted without awareness of his previous work. This has led Jeanne Chall (469) to award credit for the first quantitative study in readability to Bertha A. Lively and S. L. Pressey (55), whose paper on vocabulary burden was published in 1923. Whether one lists their work as the first or not, it is clear that certain later workers drew on it and also that it approached the modern concept of a readability formula somewhat more closely than Kitson's.

Lively and Pressey's method was designed to yield an estimate of vocabulary difficulty, based on a sample of 1000 words systematically selected throughout a book. Approximate analysis time per book was three hours. Their procedure was as follows:

Lively and Pressey

> Calculate *"vocabulary range"* — number of different words;

Assign an index of difficulty based upon the frequency of each word as given in Thorndike's *Teacher's Word Book* — e.g., a word in the most frequent 1000 was given a value of 10, one in the second most frequent 1000 a value of 9, etc., down to a value of 1 for those in the least frequent 1000;

Determine "zero-value words" — the number of words not in Thorndike's most common 10,000, which is an index of technical vocabulary;

Calculate "weighted median index number" — the median of the index numbers of the words with zero-value words counted twice. Thus, the higher the median index number, the easier the vocabulary.

As a criterion against which to compare their indices, Lively and Pressey used 16 different pieces of reading matter judged to be of different levels of readability. They found that the weighted median index numbers agreed fairly consistently with their difficulty ranking. For more reliable index values, where desired, they suggested taking further 1000-word samples and averaging the results; for wider applicability of the indices, they suggested the establishment of norms for various grades and types of books.

Lively and Pressey's work soon stimulated others to measure the reading difficulty of children's books. Carleton Washburne and Mabel Vogel (125) used Lively and Pressey's formula to analyze 700 books that had been named by at least 25 out of 37,000 children as being ones they had read during the school year and liked. Scores were available on the paragraph-meaning section of the Stanford Achievement Test for each child; the average (median) score for the children who read and liked a book could therefore be computed and used as a grade level. This grade rating was correlated with the "zero-value" factor scores in the Lively-Pressey formula and the surprisingly high coefficient of .80 was obtained.

The work of Washburne and Vogel was important not only in that it was the first validation study of a formula element using an outside criterion, but also because it provided a base upon which these authors could construct their own readability formula. Their technique, in turn, is of special interest because it represents the prototype of modern readability formulas.

Vogel and Washburne (74) first selected passages in 152 of the 700 books on their list so that the smaller sample would accurately represent the range of difficulty of books in grades 3–9. They next analyzed the passages for style elements potentially predictive of difficulty, examined 10 of these carefully, and finally used four in their formula. Their procedure was as follows:

Vogel and Washburne

> *Systematically sample* 1000 words of the book to be analyzed, noting prepositions;
> *Count* the number of different words in 1000 (x_2);
> *Count* the total number of prepositions (x_3);
> *Count* the total number of words not on the Thorndike list of 10,000 (x_4);
> *Count* the number of simple sentences in 75 sample sentences (x_5);
> *Apply* in the regression equation:
> $$X_1 \text{ (reading score)} = .085x_2 + .101x_3 + .604x_4$$
> $$- .411x_5 + 17.43$$

This formula is of particular importance because, in addition to its modern appearance, it yielded scores that correlated .845 with the reading test scores of the children who read and liked the criterion books.

Another study of readability appearing in 1928 was Edward Dolch's method of measuring "vocabulary burden" (26). Dolch analyzed textbook series ranging from primers to grade 5, using the following five indices of difficulty:

Dolch

Percentage of different words;
Percentage of difficult words (using his combined word study list);
Degree of difficulty of words;
Median frequency of difficult words;
Degree of difficulty for supplementary reading.

Dolch did not combine his indices statistically, but did suggest that more than one of them be used.

A. S. Lewerenz' first work was next to appear. Though he acknowledged the influence of Washburne and Vogel, his measure of readability (49) was one of the most unusual in the history of readability. His procedure was to:

Lewerenz — first technique

Take a systematically spaced sample of 1000 words and determine the number of different words;
Tabulate the number beginning with each letter of the alphabet, and get a total for the entire alphabet;
Determine the percentage of words beginning with "w," "h," and "b" — these are easy words; determine the percentage beginning with "i" and "e" — these are hard words;
Consult a table of norms to get a value corresponding to each percentage;
Average the five values; this provides a grade-placement score for vocabulary.

Lewerenz indicated that the grade-placement score should be interpreted in terms of the Stanford Achievement Test.

Eleven samples from it, ranging in grade placement from 2.5 to 12.5 were the criterion for his study; words beginning with "w," "h," and "b" showed high frequency in simple material, while those beginning with "i" and "e" showed low frequency.

Lewerenz' second technique (50, 51) was a complete departure from his first. Rather than tabulate words beginning with certain letters, he substituted the following:

Lewerenz — second technique

> *Vocabulary difficulty* — the ratio of simple Anglo-Saxon words to difficult technical and special meaning words of Greek and Roman derivation;
>
> *Vocabulary diversity* — the ratio between words appearing in "Clark's first 500" and the total number of different words used.

A count of each of these elements provided a separate vocabulary grade-placement score (details not specified); the scores for various kinds of newspaper content showed a considerable and expected variability.

In 1935 and again in 1938, Lewerenz (52, 53) added the element of vocabulary interest, which he described as an estimate of the image-bearing or sensory words used by an author. In 1939, he referred to the additional measures of polysyllabic words and vocabulary mass. Again, each separate measure provided a separate vocabulary grade-placement score, based on the graded material in standardized reading tests. Because Lewerenz has provided little information on the development, validation, and application of any but his first (49) formula, evaluation is difficult. For example, it appears that the several elements are used separately rather than in combination; yet at times reference is made to the "Los Angeles Vocabulary Grade Placement Formula" as though it were one formula. For the purposes of this book, the 1929 and 1930 techniques will be considered as basic and different formulas, and the others as minor variations. A second formula that appeared in 1930 and influenced Lewerenz' later work was that of George R. Johnson (46). He had been searching for a method of determining the difficulty of reading matter for children that was simple to administer as well as reliable and, following the work of Bear (1), used polysyllabic words. His method is as follows:

Johnson

> *Select* thirty 100-word samples systematically throughout the book to be analyzed;
> *Count* the number of polysyllabic words;
> *Determine* the percentage of polysyllabic words.

Though he does not give general norms for the relation of percentages to grade levels, it is possible to use in a normative manner data he collected on readers and on geography and language texts for various grades.

Johnson's method proved to be both "simple" and "reliable." As evidence for the convenience of the method, he says a book can be rated in 30 minutes. Evidence of the adequacy of a polysyllable count came from five sources: (1) better comprehension by students who read a story in monosyllabic words than by those who read it in polysyllabic words; (2) increase in percentage of polysyllabic words with a decrease in Thorndike frequency; (3) increase in percentage of polysyllabic words with increasing grade level of material used in books intended for higher grades; (4) increase in polysyllabic words in books written expressly for consecutive grades; and (5) close relationship between percentages of polysyllabic words and technical words used in seven books.

The next formula to appear in the early period of development of readability formulas was that of Patty and Painter

(63), designed as a measure of vocabulary burden. Their procedure contained the following steps:

Patty and Painter

> *List* all words located on third complete line of each fifth page;
>
> *Determine* Thorndike word value (index number) for each different word;
>
> *Determine* frequency of each different word as found in the above sample;
>
> *Obtain* a weighted value *(W. V.)* of each word by multiplying the Thorndike Index Number *(T. I. N.)* by the sample frequency *(F.)*;
>
> *Determine* average-word-weighted-value *(A. W. W. V.)* by dividing total weighted values *(T. W. V.)* by total words in the sample *(T. W. S.)*;
>
> *Calculate* the index number *(I. N.)* by dividing the average-word-weighted-value by the range *(R.)*, or number of different words per sample, and apply in any one of the following formulas:

$$I.N. = \frac{T.W.V.}{T.W.S.} \div R., \text{ or } I.N. = \frac{T.W.V.}{T.W.S.} \times \frac{1}{R.}, \text{ or } I.N. = \frac{T.W.V.}{(T.W.S.)R.}$$

If desired, it is possible to determine the vocabulary burden of an entire year of high school by getting an average index number (see Patty and Painter, 64).

In the case of both index number and average index number, a relatively low value indicates difficult vocabulary and a high value easy vocabulary.

Patty and Painter made no attempt to check their formula against a specified outside criterion, letting its validity rest indirectly upon that of Thorndike's word count. Thorndike himself, in the last formula of this early period (71), presented a similar method of getting an approximate rating for difficulty of reading. Thorndike's procedure was to:

Thorndike

Take a sample of at least 10,000 words from a book;

Count the number of words it contains that are in the various categories of the *Teacher's Word Book;*

Consult the norms for each grade given by Thorndike (e.g., grade 3B words are those from 2501 to 3000 in Thorndike's list).

It is appropriate to consider Thorndike's work as the last of the early period, because it is a typical study. This period can be characterized by the following: primary attention to vocabulary as a basis for predicting readability; (b) dependence upon Thorndike's *Teacher's Word Book* as the basis for measures of vocabulary difficulty; and (c) use of relatively crude criteria of reading difficulty.

Detailed Formulas, 1934–1938

Four new readability formulas appeared in 1934. One of these, Thorndike's, was mentioned in the last section because it was most like the earlier studies. Actually, the first study to be published in 1934 was that of Ralph Ojemann (62). He set out to investigate reading ability among adults; the factors most closely associated with reading difficulty; and the characteristics of materials at various levels of difficulty. To do this, he arranged sixteen 500-word passages in order of difficulty as determined by the test scores of subjects on them. He then set out to see how closely each of 17 quantitative and qualitative factors varied with the difficulty of the passages. The factors he studied were:

Ojemann

Sentence factors
   a. Number of simple sentences
   b. Number of complex sentences
   c. Number of compound sentences
   d. Number of dependent clauses
   e. Number of prepositions
   f. Number of prepositions plus infinitives
   g. Average length of dependent clauses
   h. Ratio of total words in independent clauses to the total words in a selection

Vocabulary factors
   a. Per cent of words in Thorndike's first 1000
   b. Per cent of words in Thorndike's first 2000
   c. Per cent of words known by 70% of sixth-grade pupils
   d. Per cent of words known by 90% of sixth-grade pupils
   e. Mean difficulty of different words
   f. Mean difficulty for each word

Qualitative factors
   a. Concreteness versus abstractness of relations
   b. Obscurity in expression
   c. Incoherence in expression

Of the sentence factors, three correlated .60 or better with the criterion (the numbers of simple sentences, prepositions, and prepositions plus infinitives); all vocabulary factors correlated .60 or better. Though he felt the qualitative factors were of considerable importance, he could not measure them quantitatively and therefore could not compute a correlation with the criterion. He did, however, arrange his sample passages so that they could be used for comparative judgments of readability on new passages. This method, he felt, brought the qualitative elements into the picture.

The next work to appear in 1934 bore a close resemblance to Ojemann's. It was Dale and Tyler's study (25) of the factors influencing reading difficulty for adults of limited reading ability. The authors followed these steps:

Dale and Tyler

> *Secure* a valid criterion of difficulty of a series of paragraphs;
>
> *Make* quantitative studies of factors influencing difficulty;
>
> *Run* a series of correlations between the factors and the index of difficulty.

The criterion used was a series of 74 selections on personal health; subjects were asked to choose the best and poorest conclusions from among five listed possibilities for each, thus providing an ordering of selections in terms of difficulty.

Dale and Tyler's next step was to correlate 25 factors with the criterion; they may be roughly grouped as follows:

1. Technical vocabulary — words known to readers;
2. Easy words — 769 words common to Thorndike's first 1000 and to the word list of the International Kindergarten Union;
3. Hard, nontechnical words — unfamiliarity rating based on use of Dale's list of 8000 words for pupils in grades 4, 6, and 8;
4. Type and length of sentences used — simple, complex, and compound;
5. Number of clauses and prepositional phrases;
6. Number of personal pronouns;
7. Number of monosyllabic words;
8. Other (miscellaneous) factors.

Ten of the factors correlated .30 or more with the criterion; the closest relationships were found for the number of different technical words in the selection, the number of hard, nontechnical words in the selection not known by 90% of sixth-grade pupils, and the number of different, hard, nontechnical words in the selection. The most efficient combination of factors for predictive purposes was: (a) the first of the above measures of technical words, labelled x_2; the second of the above, called hard, nontechnical words and labelled x_3; and the number of indeterminate clauses, labelled x_4. These yielded a multiple correlation of .51 with the criterion; they were used in the following regression equation:

$$X_1 = -9.4x_2 - 0.4x_3 + 2.2x_4 + 114.4 \ (\pm 9.0)$$

X_1 stands for the percentage of adults of third- to fifth-grade reading ability who can comprehend a passage.

The final study to appear in 1934 was that of McClusky (60). He selected one passage each from a book of fiction, political science, economics, sociology, psychology, and physics. He then constructed true-false questions on each and devised speed-of-reading tests (one of the few investigators to use speed rather than comprehension as an index of readability). Finally, he studied the following as possible contributors to difficulty:

McClusky

    Number of ideas per 100 words;

    Number of letters per word (average);

    Number of words per sentence;

    Number of various types of nouns used (technical versus nouns as names of common objects).

He found that difficulty varied for subject matter (fiction easiest, physics hardest), but also that easy material as such had short, concrete words and short, simple sentences. There was no difference, surprisingly enough, in the number of ideas per 100 words for easy and hard material.

The next study to appear, by W. S. Gray and Bernice Leary (40), emphasized not only the trend to detailed studies of readability but also its curious, near-simultaneous beginnings in 1934 among a number of research workers. Gray and Leary actually published their book, *What Makes a Book Readable*, in 1935, but their article by the same title reporting the completion of much of their preliminary work appeared in 1934. Had not their study been the most extensive in the history of readability, it might well have come out as soon as the other 1934 formulas. Like the other influential study of that year, Dale and Tyler's, it was intended as a study of what makes a book readable to adults of limited reading ability.

As indicated earlier, Gray and Leary first made a survey to uncover factors contributing to readability. A study of previous work, the opinions of approximately 100 experts, and the reactions of 170 library patrons, yielded 289 factors. These were classed in four major categories: content, style of expression and presentation, format, and general features of organization. Of these, the style category, containing 82 factors, was selected for intensive study.

In order to get some idea of how well adults read, as well as to develop a criterion for the intensive study of style factors, Gray and Leary built the "Adult Reading Test." This test, containing both fiction and nonfiction paragraphs, required that readers answer a summary question and a detail question covering what they had read. A series of correlations was then run to show how the 44 style factors found in the paragraphs were related to the criterion — the reading score. The other 38 factors either could not be counted reliably enough or did not occur often enough in the paragraphs to be used in the statistical analysis. Finally, 20 of the

44 factors were found to be significantly related to readability.

Gray and Leary's final step was to combine these elements in a regression equation to predict readability. Since the factors tended to correlate with each other, only five were necessary to give almost as high a multiple correlation with the criterion, .6435, as many more factors gave. The procedure in using the formula was to:

Gray and Leary

  Select a passage of 100 words from each chapter of a book to be analyzed;

  Analyze each passage to determine:

    a. Number of personal pronouns (x_5),

    b. Number of different hard words not common to the Dale list of 769 words (x_2),

    c. Average number of words per sentence (x_6),

    d. Percentage of different words (x_7), and

    e. Number of prepositional phrases (x_8);

  Calculate the average occurrence of each element for the book as a whole;

  Substitute the obtained values in the equation:

$$X_1 = -.01029x_2 + .009012x_5 - .02094x_6 - .03313x_7 - .01485x_8 + 3.774$$

  Solve the equation for X_1, which is the average comprehension score a group of adults of limited reading ability probably would make if tested on the content of the book.

In addition to the above regression equation, Gray and Leary presented an 8-factor equation containing these same factors plus the number of easy words found in a passage of 100 words, the percentage of polysyllables found in the passage, and the number of simple sentences used in the passage.

This longer, more cumbersome formula raised the multiple correlation with the criterion to .6450, an insignificant increase. Nine 4-factor equations were also presented, yielding correlations ranging from .634 to .640. Despite the very small gain in value with the 5-factor formula, it has usually been preferred to any of the 4-factor equations by most analysts using Gray and Leary's work.

It is difficult to date very accurately the appearance of the next device for measuring readability, the "Idea Analysis Technique" of Elizabeth Morriss and Dorothy Halverson (61). The mimeographed copy of the unpublished manuscript presenting the technique is simply dated 1938; Chall (469, p. 25), however, gives 1935 as the actual date of development.* Whatever the date, the study clearly fits, ideologically, with the period of interest in the development of detailed formulas.

The Morriss and Halverson technique is basically a method of word analysis, but it differs from the commoner methods in that words are analyzed only in context. The problem of easy versus hard meanings, a frequent criticism of the simpler word analysis methods, is thus overcome. And, by considering only "key" or "content" words, ideas rather than mere meanings are analyzed. The method involved is to identify words as members of one of four classifications:

Morriss and Halverson

> *Fundamental or elemental word labels* learned early in life by a member of a given culture ("father," "water," "eat," etc.);
> *Simple localisms* unconsciously learned by children, and all ordinary word labels usually learned by American

---

* Oddly enough, even some disagreement exists about the spelling of Miss Halverson's name. It is listed as "Holversen" by many writers referring to her work.

children before the end of the sixth grade or age 12 ("corn," "cattle," "tide," etc.);

Concrete word labels acquired through further education and social contacts with educated people ("Van Gogh," "Iraq," "filament," etc.);

Abstract word labels or concepts comprehended through education ("torrid," "intellectually," "delete," "culminate," etc.).

Morriss and Halverson clearly intended that their method serve to predict difficulty of reading matter, since they described how books should be analyzed, and they presented at least some minimal norms for interpretation of counts of words in the various classes. However, very little other information was given regarding development, validity, or applicability. Most of the evaluative work on the method has, in fact, been done by Irving Lorge (56); he found words in classes 3 and 4 to be related to difficulty, and in class 1 to be related to ease. He also found a multiple correlation of .74 using these three classes with a criterion of McCall-Crabbs passages.

The Morriss-Halverson technique was clearly different from most of the readability methods that preceded and followed it, except for some of the most recent. For this reason, as well as its relative inaccessibility and cumbersomeness, it has not achieved great popularity.

This period as a whole was characterized by the use of (a) more and different factors (compared to the preceding work), (b) less emphasis on Thorndike's word count, and (c) a generally increased concern for an adequate criterion.

Efficient Formulas, 1938 to 1953

From about 1938 on, formulas seemed to emphasize efficiency and simplicity of use. The first important formula of this new period was the revision by Carleton Washburne and Mabel Vogel Morphett (75) of their original (Vogel-Washburne, 74) formula. An earlier study by Bergman (20) appears to be simply a preliminary version of this revision; since the Bergman version differed only in the constant used, the two will be considered together.

Washburne and Morphett, in their revision, reduced the number of factors from four to three by dropping the count of prepositional phrases; in addition, they changed their count of the total number of words not on Thorndike's list of 10,000 to the number of different uncommon words not in Thorndike's 1500 commonest. This simplified the formula and made it easier to apply without materially changing its accuracy: the multiple correlation of the new 3-factor formula with its criterion was .86, while that of the old 4-factor formula was .845. The new formula, in addition, was intended to cover grades 1 and 2 (the criterion was expanded to include books for these grades), and to compensate for the skewing at the extremes of the grade distribution which was apparent with the original formula.

The new formula involved the following steps:

Washburne-Morphett

> *Systematically select* a sample of 1000 words;
> *Count* the number of different words (x_2);
> *Count* the number of different uncommon words (not in Thorndike's first 1500) (x_3);
> *Count* the number of simple sentences in 75 sample sentences (x_4);
> *Apply* in the formula:
> X_1 (grade placement) $= .00255x_2 + .0458x_3$
> $$- .0307x_4 + 1.294$$

The Bergman version of the formula was identical except that the final constant used was $+ 1.084$. This would make a

minor constant difference of .21 grade level lower in all ratings.

A formula which appeared in 1945 was considered by its
author, Ronald Edgerton, to be largely a short version of the
Washburne-Morphett formula (Edgerton, 28). It consisted
of the separate factors of number of different uncommon
words, which was borrowed from Washburne and Morphett,
and average sentence length in words, said to be borrowed
from Bernice Leary (used in the Gray-Leary formula).

The next significant work in readability was that of Irving Lorge (56) in 1939. Even though Washburne and Morphett's formula was revised with increased ease of application as one goal, it was Lorge who used efficiency as a major
basis for the retention or rejection of formula elements. He
was able to reduce his formula to three elements, yet retain
predictive accuracy, primarily because he used the McCall-
Crabbs *Standard Test Lessons in Reading* (10) as a criterion.
This extensive set of passages has been more often used since
Lorge's time than any other single criterion. And Lorge's
formula, probably at least partly due to its efficiency of application, was the first to be used rather generally in fields other
than education.

Lorge began his search for an efficient formula by computing a series of multiple correlations between various combinations of Gray-Leary factors and McCall-Crabbs test
scores. He achieved a maximum value of .7722 using all five
Gray-Leary factors and a weighted index for words based on
the Thorndike count. He was then able to raise even this
value slightly, to .7821, by using certain of these elements
plus Morriss and Halverson's word classifications 1, 3, and 4.

Lorge felt that the slight increase in prediction achieved
with the complex formulas did not justify the great increase
in labor they entailed. Consequently, he developed a three-
factor formula with a correlation of .7669 with McCall-
Crabbs test scores. Subsequent recomputations in 1944 with

still other elements (Lorge, 57) did not increase this value, so the three-factor formula was retained. His procedure was to:

Lorge

Compute average sentence length in words (x_2);

Compute number of prepositional phrases per 100 words (x_3);

Count number of different hard words per 100 words not on the Dale 769 word list (x_4);

Substitute in the formula:

$$X_1 \text{ (grade placement)} = .07x_2 + .1301x_3 + .1073x_4 + 1.6126$$

In this formula, the grade-placement value refers to the average reading ability required to answer three-fourths of the questions on a test passage correctly.

This formula has remained unchanged in general appearance, but an error in the original computations found later necessitated a slight change in certain values (58). The corrected Lorge formula was then published as:

$$X_1 \text{ (grade placement)} = .06x_2 + .10x_3 + .10x_4 + 1.99$$

Here, X_1 stands for the average reading ability required to answer correctly one-half of the test questions on a passage, rather than three-fourths as before. If the reading grade at which three-fourths of the questions are answered correctly is desired, an additional 1.866 should be added to the score.

Another formula that made its first appearance in 1939 was that of G. A. Yoakam (78). Only mimeographed instructions were available at that time, and again when it was revised in 1948. It was published later, in 1955, in the Appendix of Yoakam's *Basal Reading Instruction* (79). The procedure for applying the 1948 version is as follows:

Yoakam

> *Systematically select* 10 pages of a book as the sample to be analyzed;
>
> *Assign index numbers* to all words which are beyond the third thousand in Thorndike frequency — a rating of 4 — up to the twentieth thousand — a rating of 20. All words beyond this are also valued at 20;
>
> *Compute* the "page index number" by adding the index numbers of all words with a rating of 4 or above on the sample page;
>
> *Add* the page index numbers and divide by 10 (to get the average);
>
> *Determine* grade placement by consulting the Reading Difficulty Scale.

Adjustments are made for page size (number of running words) and for the lower grade levels of 2 to 4 so that the formula covers the range of grades 2 to 14.

The work of Gray and Leary has served as the base for a number of studies of readability, among them several formulas. One such formula was that of Edward Kessler (47), who developed a shortened version of Gray and Leary's formula by using only two of their factors. His procedure was to:

Kessler

> *Select* 10 paragraphs of approximately 100 words;
>
> *Count* the number of words, sentences, and different hard words in the passages;
>
> *Determine* average sentence-length in words and average number of different hard words per 100 words; and
>
> *Compare* the obtained averages with the standards suggested by Gray and Leary (41).

Kessler did not combine these elements, nor did he provide a criterion against which to check them singly. He did, however, find that his difficulty ratings for 35 books coincided with those given by Lewerenz (181) and with the recommendations given by the *Standard Catalog for High School Libraries*.

Following Kessler's work came a formula that was destined to become one of the best-known in the history of readability — the first formula of Rudolf Flesch (32). Its popularity was due to several things. It was a relatively simple formula of three factors, yet it had satisfactory predictive power, yielding scores that correlated .74 with McCall-Crabbs test scores. It carried a special claim to being a new departure among formulas by measuring something other than vocabulary (this claim has been disputed, however). But most important of all, the formula became widely known because of Flesch's skillful popularization. In a series of articles and books he brought his formula, his views on readable writing, and the whole notion of readability to the attention of many writers in journalism, business, government, etc. Prior to Flesch's time, readability was a little-used word except in educational circles, but he made it an important concept in most areas of mass communication.

Since Flesch's formula became so widely known and used, it deserves a careful appraisal. Flesch, in connection with his position in the Readability Laboratory at Teachers College, Columbia University, had occasion to try a number of existing readability formulas. He found several deficiencies in them which he hoped his formula would overcome. First, he felt most formulas were not very suitable for adult materials because they emphasized vocabulary at the expense of other factors. Second, he felt too little attention was being paid to the part abstract words played in determining difficulty. Third, he felt sentence length *was* a satisfactory measure.

With this in mind, Flesch set up, to test his hypotheses, a criterion of magazine articles at five increasing levels of difficulty. He found that a count of abstract words and a count of affixed morphemes (his new factors designed to measure abstractness), were more closely related to the magazine levels than the factors used by Lorge (Flesch, 31). Building on this, he developed a three-factor formula using the McCall-Crabbs *Standard Test Lessons* as a criterion (32). His procedure was to:

Flesch

> *Systematically select* samples of 100 words throughout the material to be rated;
> *Compute* average sentence length in words (x_s);
> *Count* the number of affixes (x_m);
> *Count* the number of personal references (x_h);
> *Average* the results and insert in the formula:
> $$.1338x_s + .0645x_m - .0659x_h - .7502$$

The resulting figure placed most material somewhere between classes 1 (easiest) and 7 (most difficult). Adding a constant of 4.2498 instead of .7502 gave the reading grade placement at which 75% comprehension resulted. A further correction, based on the study of magazines mentioned earlier, gave a more accurate grade-level score for difficult adult materials. Finally, since Flesch's work was based partially on some of Lorge's computations, a later correction was necessary to take care of the error in Lorge's data that was mentioned earlier (58). The corrected formula then became:

$$.07x_m + .07x_s - .05x_h + 3.27$$

This correction was made in his revised Reading Ease formula (33) before it was published. In the new formula, Flesch also corrected certain shortcomings in the old one. These concerned chiefly the count of affixes, which was difficult and time-consuming; the count of personal references, which was misleading; and the scoring system of 1 to 7, which was hard to get used to. Flesch did not dispense with his count of personal references entirely; instead, he incorporated it into a new "human interest" formula. The reason for this was an interesting series of incidents. S. S. Stevens and Geraldine Stone (68) tried Flesch's formula on psychology textbooks used in graduate and undergraduate courses at Harvard University, and found the difficulty of William James' *Psychology* to be overestimated and Koffka's *Principles of Gestalt Psychology* to be underestimated, according to student judgment (see Stevens and Stone, 68; Rosenzweig, 66; Hebb and Bindra, 44). The questionable contribution of personal references to the measurement of readability was emphasized by Koffka's use of personal words for impersonal (editorial) purposes, which inappropriately raised the readability score; Flesch subsequently suggested the use of nondeclarative (personal) sentences as a way of showing James' superiority over Koffka (Stevens and Stone, 69).

As an outcome, partly at least, of this series of comments, Flesch developed two new formulas, one for "Reading Ease" and one for "Human Interest." The steps in the two formulas follow:

Flesch

A. Reading Ease

   Systematically select 100-word samples from the material to be rated;

   Determine the number of syllables per 100 words (wl);

   Determine the average number of words per sentence (sl);

Apply in the following reading ease equation:
$$R.E. = 206.835 - .846wl - 1.015sl$$

B. Human Interest

Systematically select 100-word samples (as above);

Count number of personal words per 100 words *(pw)*;

Count number of personal sentences per 100 sentences *(ps)*;

Apply in the following human interest equation:
$$H.I. = 3.635pw + .314ps$$

Formula A correlated .7047 with the McCall-Crabbs criterion, and B correlated .4306. Flesch maintained that (1) the new count of syllables was still a measure of abstraction because it correlated .87 with the old count of affixes, and (2) the new formula was simpler and quicker to use. The use of a syllable count was clearly responsible for the increased efficiency of application; whether or not it measured abstractness is not as clear, since studies show it to be measuring virtually the same thing as most vocabulary counts. But the increased ease of applying the new formula, as well as the adult grade-levels it provided (continued from the original formula), proved valuable to persons in many fields. It was destined to continue the wide popularity accorded the original, and, in fact, it has become the most frequently used of all readability formulas.

Another formula that appeared in 1948 can safely be called the second most frequently used. It was developed by Edgar Dale and Jeanne Chall (23, 24), and was designed, as Flesch's revision had been, to correct certain shortcomings in the original Flesch formula. These authors based their work on the hypotheses that (1) a larger word list would predict better than the Dale 769-word list used by Lorge, particularly at the upper levels of difficulty, (2) the count of personal references as used by Flesch was unnecessary, and (3) a shorter, more efficient formula could be developed using only a word factor and a sentence factor. The procedure for using the new formula was:

Dale and Chall

> *Select* 100-word samples throughout the material to be rated;
>
> *Compute* the average sentence length in words (x_2);
>
> *Compute* the percentage of words outside the Dale list of 3000 $(x_1,$ or Dale score);
>
> *Apply* in the formula:
>
> $$X_{c_{50}} = .1579x_1 + .0496x_2 + 3.6365$$

$X_{c_{50}}$ refers to the reading grade score of a pupil who could answer one-half the test questions on a passage correctly. Subsequent experimentation with the formula then led to the development of a table for correcting the grade levels to correspond more closely to difficulty, particularly for harder materials.

Dale-Chall formula scores correlated .70 with McCall-Crabbs criterion scores. In addition, the Dale score (the vocabulary factor) alone correlated higher with the criterion scores than either the entire Lorge or orginal Flesch formulas when the errors in these two were considered. There is further evidence (Klare, 475; Powers, Sumner, and Kearl, 65) that the Dale-Chall formula is somewhat more highly predictive than any of the other popular formulas available today.

In addition to the Flesch and Dale-Chall formulas, which were intended for adult materials primarily, two formulas for children's materials appeared in 1948. The first of these, by Dolch (27), was a method of determining the "graded reading difficulty" of textbooks. He first examined three major ways in which books differ from each other: physical factors, content factors, and manner of presentation. Since, however, the first two are not readily controlled by writers and editors of school reading material, Dolch decided to concentrate on the third. He developed a formula for it, the procedural steps for which are:

Dolch

> *Take a sentence* from each page of a book as a sample (taking two sentences yields greater reliability);
> *Count* the number of words in each sentence, then get the average number to find the "middle" sentence;
> *Determine* the upper 10% point in sentence length, called the "long" sentence;
> *Count* all words in the sentence sample which do not appear in Dolch's "The First Thousand Words for Children's Reading" and convert to a percentage;
> *Compare* the values for the middle sentence, long sentence, and percentage of hard words with the standards provided;
> *If desired, count* again for the number of polysyllabic words, compute the percentages, and compare with the standards given.

As evidence of the validity of his formula factors, Dolch noted the steady progression in the counts mentioned above as he went from grade to grade in the sets of school readers he was analyzing. These data from the readers also provided the standards for each grade against which to evaluate scores.

The second technique for children's material was Lester and Viola Wheeler's "University of Miami" method (77). The three steps in applying the technique are to:

Wheeler and Wheeler

> *Tabulate* around 1000 words from page samples taken at 5- to 10-page intervals;

Determine the grade placement of the tabulated words
   by using Thorndike ratings;
Count the number of words in each grade level and tabulate the results as percentages.

This technique permits the analyst to make several evaluations of a single book; e.g., it can be given an average difficulty grade level, an instructional grade level, and an independent reading grade level. This leads Wheeler and
Wheeler to say that it is not a "single grade-placement formula," and for this reason to prefer it. It does, however, re-
semble the earliest formulas in its dependence upon Thorndike's word counts, even to the extent that no criterion other
than this is used to establish the validity of the technique.

In 1950, Flesch's "Level of Abstraction" formula appeared
(34). With this technique, Flesch estimated level of abstraction by computing the ratio of certain parts of speech to
others. Since level of abstraction is a basic element in readability, Flesch suggested that it also be used as a measure of
readability either by itself or in combination with other elements. The criterion for evaluation of factors was again the
McCall-Crabbs Test Lessons, so the new formula gave much
the same sort of scores as previous formulas. The procedure
for using the formula is too detailed to be presented fully
here — there are, for example, 16 categories of definite words
— but in brief the steps necessary to measure the level of
abstraction are:

Flesch, Level of Abstraction

Systematically select 100-word samples from the piece of
   writing to be analyzed;
Count the number, and determine the percentage of definite words (*dw*);
Consult a table to determine the relation between the

percentage of definite words and the level of abstraction.

If a measure of readability is desired, the following additional steps are necessary:

Count the syllables in the 100-word samples and determine the number per 100 words (wl);

Insert the values in the following formula:

R (readability) $= 168.095 + .532dw - .811wl$

If separate measures of abstraction and of reading ease are desired, Flesch recommends the use of his revised Reading Ease formula (33). The multiple correlation of the new Level of Abstraction readability formula with the criterion passages was .72, which is slightly higher than the .7047 of his Reading Ease readability formula.

The new formula was immediately criticized by James Jenkins and Robert Jones (45) as offering very little as a measure of readability. They felt that existing readability formulas were as good or better and certainly easier to apply. Flesch (35) agreed that the new count of definite words was rather complex, but felt that it offered new possibilities as a "diagnostic and clinical tool" in readability measurement.

It is clear that the Level of Abstraction formula was more the forerunner of a new trend to specialized formulas (to be described in the following pages) than an example of the existing emphasis on efficient formulas. However, it has been adapted for efficiency. Gillie published a version (39) with the frank purpose of making it easier to apply.

The steps for the revised formula follow:

Gillie

Count the number of finite verbs per 200 words;

Count the number of definite articles and their nouns per 200 words;

Count the number of nouns of abstraction per 200 words;
Apply in the following formula:
Abstraction level = 36 + (number of definite articles) +
(number of finite verbs) — (2 × nouns of abstraction)

Gillie states there are no precise and objective criteria for validating a measure of abstraction. He says one can only presume that since his measure is based on Flesch's total score, it cannot be any more valid than the total score itself, and that the only reason for its use lies in ease of application.

Another Flesch formula that was simplified was his Reading Ease formula. The authors of the new version were James Farr, James Jenkins, and Donald Paterson (30). These authors proposed that the syllable count then used be replaced by a count of one-syllable words to reduce analysis time and remove the need for a knowledge of syllabication on the part of the analyst. To apply the formula, these steps are necessary:

Farr-Jenkins-Paterson

Systematically select 100-word samples from the material to be analyzed;
Determine the number of one-syllable words per 100 words *(nosw)*;
Determine the average sentence length in words *(sl)*;
Apply in the formula:
New Reading Ease Index = 1.599*nosw* — 1.015*sl* — 31.517

The new formula was validated by comparison of scores on 360 passages with Flesch formula scores for the same passages. A correlation coefficient of .93 was found. A subsequent study of larger samples yielded a correlation of .95.

Another formula closely related to Flesch's Reading Ease formula is that of Robert Gunning (43). In it, the syllable count is replaced by a count of words having three or more syllables. The steps required in using this formula are:

Gunning

> *Take* systematic samples of 100 words;
>
> *Divide* number of words by number of sentences to get sentence length;
>
> *Count* the number of words of three or more syllables (with certain exceptions) to get percentage of hard words;
>
> *To get the Fog Index, total* the two factors above and multiply by .4.

The Fog Index is the reading grade level required for understanding the material. Evidence of the adequacy of the Fog Index was based on increasing values for hard words and sentence length found by Gunning in the various classes of American magazines ("pulps" to "class") and in McCall-Crabbs passages (grades 6 to 12).

Still another formula that appears to bear some resemblance to Flesch's Reading Ease formula, and perhaps even more to Gunning's Fog Index, is McElroy's Fog Count (42). McElroy started with the basic premise that difficulty arises when the number of ideas to be understood increases and the difficulty of the ideas themselves increases. He then was able to derive an index of readability by assuming that each word in a piece of writing represents an idea, and each separate sound needed to pronounce a word represents a counted element. It might appear thereby that his work is based on a count of phonetic sounds, or perhaps phonemes; actually, it is in practice simply a count of syllables. The procedure for using his formula is:

McElroy

> *Select* a number of sentences at random for analysis;
>
> *Assign* a value of 1 to each easy element in each sentence,

> i.e., each word that can be pronounced in one or two
> sounds;
> *Assign* a value of 3 to each remaining word, called a poly-
> syllable, or hard idea;
> *Add* the 1's and 3's to get the Fog Count for each sen-
> tence;
> *To get* a reading grade level from a Fog Count, divide
> the total count for all analyzed sentences by the num-
> ber of sentences — if the average is over 20, divide by 2,
> and if under 20, substract 2 and then divide by 2.

McElroy gives no statistical information on the development
or adequacy of his formula.

An indication of the prevailing notion of efficiency during this period was the publication of several sets of tables designed to make formula application quicker and easier by
eliminating some of the computation necessary to get formula
scores. James Farr and James Jenkins (29) prepared tables for
the Flesch "Reading Ease" and "Human Interest" formulas.
Dik Twedt (73) provided such a table for Flesch's Level of
Abstraction readability formula, and George Klare (48) developed a similar table for the Dale-Chall formula. Farr,
Jenkins, and Paterson (30) took the ultimate step by providing a table for their formula in the article in which the
formula itself was published.

Specialized Formulas, 1953-1959

An example of the new trend to specialization was the
formula for determining the readability of standardized tests
developed by Fritz Forbes and William Cottle (38). These
authors point out that existing formulas were not designed
to measure tests even though they had sometimes been used
for that purpose. As a criterion to use in the development
of their new formula, they computed the mean score of the

Dale-Chall, Flesch, Lorge, Lewerenz, and Yoakam formulas as applied to each of 27 standardized tests. Scores from the new formula were found to correlate .95 with the means of the five. The formula (usually referred to as the Forbes formula) is applied in the following way:

Forbes

> *Select* three samples of 100 words each from the beginning, middle, and end of a test;
> *Assign* a weight, based on the *1942 Thorndike Junior Century Dictionary,* to each word above the most common 4000;
> *Determine* the index of vocabulary difficulty by totaling the weights and dividing by the number of words;
> *Consult* a table to get the grade level corresponding to the formula score.

This formula was designed for use with the instructions for a test as well as the test itself, and was suggested for measuring the readability of public opinion poll questions and of headlines and slogans in advertising copy.

Two formulas for primary-grade reading materials also appeared about this time. The first of these was developed by George Spache (67). The procedure of applying his formula is as follows:

Spache

> *Select* 100-word samples for analysis;
> *Determine* average sentence length in words (x_1);
> *Count* number of words outside the Dale "Easy Word List" of 769 words (x_2);
> *Use* the following formula:
> $$Grade\ level = .141x_1 + .086x_2 + .839$$

The multiple correlation coefficient for formula scores and level of classroom use of 152 books used in grades 1 to 3 was .818. Clarence Stone (70), however, felt that the accuracy of Spache's formula could be increased by revising the Dale list. He proposed that 173 of the 769 words be deleted and replaced by a similar number taken from L. L. Krantz's "The Authors Word List" and his own *A Graded Vocabulary for Primary Reading*. This revised list, he states, yields a lower rating than the original Dale list.

The other primary-grade readability formula was developed by Lester Wheeler and Edwin Smith (76). It bore a resemblance to Spache's formula in the sense that the criterion used was determined by publishers' grade designations for books, in this case, the combined means for nine basic reading series. It was also similar to Gunning's formula, since it used much the same factors. The procedure for use of the formula follows:

Wheeler-Smith

Take a random sample of 10 to 20 pages of the book to be analyzed;

Count the number of words in the sample and the number of units in the sample (units are similar to sentences, but may end with punctuation other than the common terminal marks);

Count the number of polysyllabic words in the sample;

Determine average unit length and percentage of polysyllabic words, multiply these two figures together, and then multiply this score by 10;

Consult the table given for the grade placement of the material.

In 1954, Rudolf Flesch published a new "experimental" readability formula (36). The new technique first appeared in a book for writers called *How To Make Sense,* and like the earlier Level of Abstraction formula is relatively complex.

The technique has two parts, one designed to measure realism, specificity, and concreteness (the "*r*" count); and the other to measure energy, forceful delivery, and vividness (the "*e*" count). Both are determined on the basis of 100-word samples; the procedure for applying them is briefly given below:

Flesch — "experimental"

  A. The "*r*" count:
    1. Count all references to one or more specific human beings, their attributes and possessions, all named or numbered things, locations, dates, times, and colors;
    2. Consult the table provided to interpret the "*r*" score.
  B. The "*e*" score:
    1. Count all directions for oral delivery, including indications of pauses, variations of pitch and stress, assumed voices of quoted speakers, etc.;
    2. Consult the table provided to interpret the "*e*" score.

Flesch did not, as he had in the past, use the McCall-Crabbs Test Lessons as a criterion against which to check formula scores. In this technique, evidence of validity was found in the "*r*" and "*e*" score differences (in the expected direction of high to low) in the writing of fiction and drama, journalistic writing, and academic and professional writing.

Edward B. Tribe (72) developed a formula designed for elementary school materials based upon Rinsland's *A Basic Vocabulary of Elementary School Children.* As a criterion,

Tribe used the 1950 revision of the McCall-Crabbs *Standard Test Lessons in Reading,* but in a unique way: he actually administered 10 of the passages to each of 406 children rather than simply using available test data as other formula makers had. He found a multiple correlation of .761 between formula scores and test scores.

The procedure for applying the formula is:

Tribe

> *Choose* a sample of approximately 100 words from about every tenth page in a book to be analyzed;
>
> *Count* the total number of words in each sample;
>
> *Count* the number of different words not on the Rinsland list and get the basic list score by dividing by the total number of words, then multiplying this by 100 (x_5);
>
> *Count* the number of sentences in the sample;
>
> *Determine* the average sentence length score (x_1);
>
> *Use* the following formula:
> $$C_{50} = .0719x_1 + .1043x_5 + 2.9347$$

In this equation C_{50} is the uncorrected grade level score for subjects who could answer one-half the reading test questions correctly; the Dale-Chall correction table (24) is then used to get a corrected grade level.

Earlier in the history of readability formulas the McCall-Crabbs Test Lessons were described as being very important because they were one of the best, if not *the* best, criteria on which to build formulas. In 1950 a revised edition of the *Lessons* was published. R. B. Powers, W. A. Sumner, and B. E. Kearl (65) used the 383 prose passages as a criterion for the recalculation of four well-known adult formulas — Flesch's Reading Ease, Dale-Chall, Farr-Jenkins-Paterson, and Gunning. The computations yielded the following formulas:

Flesch Reading Ease: $-2.2029 + .0778$ (sentence length) $+ .0455$ (syllables per 100 words)
Dale-Chall: $3.2672 + .0596$ (sentence length) $+ .1155$ (per cent of non-Dale words)
Farr-Jenkins-Paterson: $8.4335 + .0923$ (sentence length) $- .0648$ (per cent of monosyllables)
Gunning: $3.0680 + .0877$ (sentence length) $+ .0984$ (per cent of polysyllables)

The coefficients of multiple determination for the four formulas (with the new criterion) were .5092 for the Dale-Chall, .4034 for the Flesch, .3440 for the Gunning, and .3407 for the Farr-Jenkins-Paterson. These would be comparable to multiple correlation coefficients of .71 for the Dale-Chall, .64 for the Flesch, .59 for the Gunning and .58 for the Farr-Jenkins-Paterson formulas. The values presented originally in the development of the formulas were .70 for the Dale-Chall and .70 for the Flesch; similar values were not reported for the other two. They indicate that the Dale-Chall formula is " . . . the much more powerful tool for predicting reading difficulty" (65, p. 101), and that the Flesch formula is the best one of those not using a word-list.

All four recalculated formulas were used on a sample of 113 passages from 15 magazines. New norms for the magazines were determined, and the formulas themselves were compared. It was found that all four formulas agreed with each other more closely than the original Dale-Chall and Flesch formulas did.

Flesch (37) published yet another formula in the year that the article by Powers, Sumner, and Kearl appeared. The new formula was a measure of the dimension of "formality" to "popularity" in style of writing; it was designed to yield scores which followed a logical ranking of magazines from the formal academic and scientific journals, e.g., the *Columbia University Forum,* to very popular mass circulation fiction, e.g., *Ellery Queen's Mystery Magazine.* The steps in using the formula include:

Flesch — *"formality"* – *"popularity"*

> *Count off* approximately five 100-word samples randomly from each 3000 words of text;
> *Count* one point for each of the following:
>> a. Any word with a capital letter in it;
>> b. Any word that is underlined or italicized;
>> c. All numbers (unless spelled out);
>> d. All punctuation marks except commas, hyphens, and periods following abbreviations;
>> e. All other symbols, such as #, $, ¢, %, &;
>> f. One extra point each for the beginning and ending of a paragraph;
> *Total* the points and find the interpretation on a scale ranging from 1 to 35 ("formal" to "very popular").

The new formula, just as his previous "r" and "e" formulas of 1954, was intended for use by writers primarily.

The last formula to be published during the period covered in this report was Richard Bloomer's technique (21) for measuring the level of abstraction as a function of the modifiers in a piece of writing. He found that modifiers make reading more specific and thus more difficult, and that he could therefore predict the readability of material with a count of modifiers. The procedure for doing so follows:

Bloomer

> *Select* three samples long enough to include 10 modifiers
> each and the words between;
> *Determine* the number of words per modifier* (words
> used as adjectives and adverbs);
> *Determine* the sound complexity of the modifiers;
> *Predict* grade level of material using these two variables.

Bloomer used 23 commercial readers from primer to sixth grade level as his criterion, assuming that they progressed normally in difficulty. The multiple correlation of his two variables with grade level was found to be .78.

This most recent period in the history of readability formulas was marked more by an interest in developing specialized formulas than by any other. There had been specialized formulas before, but the primary emphasis lay in something else — achieving maximum prediction with detailed formulas, or developing efficient formulas, or presenting general formulas of wide applicability. During the years from about 1953 on, either special aspects of readability such as level of abstraction or special audience levels such as primary grade, were the object of prediction. It seems likely that the immediate future will continue to be characterized by specialized formulas for particular purposes.

---

* In the article by Bloomer this phrase reads ". . . numbers of modifiers . . . ." It seems quite clear, however, that this is an error and should have read ". . . number of words per modifier . . ." or something equivalent. Otherwise, with a sample always containing 10 modifiers, there would be no differentiation of samples. Furthermore, a table in the article shows that number of words per modifier has the highest correlation with the criterion except for sound complexity, the other variable he used in the formula; and yet it also has the lowest correlation with sound complexity itself. Therefore, the error is almost certain on both semantic and statistical bases.

The various formulas and formula versions developed over the years are summarized in Table 1.* To make possible a concise presentation, only the following, in this order, are given: (1) name of author or authors; (2) reference number; (3) date of publication; (4) approximate range of difficulty of the reading material used in the development of the formula; (5) the formula itself, as best it can be presented in a condensed fashion; and (6) a comment on the formula where something deserves special notice. The order of presentation is chronological, except that variations of existing formulas (indicated by the letter "A" after the serial number) follow immediately the formulas they were based on, regardless of date of publication. The reader who wishes further details can consult the text at the appropriate places.

---

* Only English language formulas have been discussed here and listed in Table 1. Several foreign language formulas are available; these are discussed briefly in Chapter 6.

TABLE 1

Summary Presentation of Readability Formulas

Author(s)	Bibliography Number	Publication Date	Range of Difficulty	Formula	Comment
1. Lively and Pressey	(55)	1923	Grade 2–College	Weighted median index number = median of Thorndike index numbers, with zero-value words counted twice.	This probably can be called most accurately the first true readability formula.
2. Vogel and Washburne	(74)	1928	Grades 3–9	$X_1 = .085x_2 + .101x_3 + .604x_4 - .411x_5 + 17.43.$ (X_1 = reading score; x_2 = number of different words in 1000; x_3 = total number of prepositions; x_4 = total number of words not on the Thorndike list of 10,000; x_5 = number of simple sentences in 75 sample sentences.)	The prototype of modern readability formulas.
3. Dolch	(26)	1928	Primer–Grade 4	More than one of the following measures should be used: (1) percentage of different words; (2) percentage of difficult words (using the Dolch Combined Word Study List; (3) degree of difficulty of words; (4) median frequency of difficult words; and (5) degree of difficulty for supplementary reading.	
4. Lewerenz	(49)	1929	Grade 2–College	Determine percentages of words beginning with "w," "h," "b," "i," and "e" (first three considered easy, last two hard); consult table for each, and average the values to get a grade-placement score.	
5. Lewerenz	(50, 52, 54)	1930, 1935, 1939	Presumably Grade 2–College	Any of the following (each yielding a separate grade-placement score) may be used: (1) vocabulary difficulty–ratio of Anglo-Saxon words to Greek and Roman words; (2) vocabulary diversity—ratio of words appearing in "Clark's first 500" to total of different words; (3) vocabulary interest—estimate of image bearing or sensory words; (4) polysyllabic word count; and (5) vocabulary mass.	First two factors referred to in 1930, the third factor included in 1935, and the fourth and fifth in 1939.
6. Johnson	(46)	1930	Primer–Grade 8	Percentage of polysyllables; use tabled norms for grade placement.	

TABLE 1 (cont.)

SUMMARY PRESENTATION OF READABILITY FORMULAS

Author(s)	Bibliography Number	Publication Date	Range of Difficulty	Formula	Comment
7. Patty and Painter	(63)	1931	Grades 4–12	Index Number $= \dfrac{T.W.V.}{T.W.S.(R.)}$ or $\dfrac{A.W.W.V.}{R.}$ ($T.W.V.$ = total weighted [Thorndike] values for words; $T.W.S.$ = total words in sample; $R.$ = range [number of different words]; $A.W.W.V.$ = average-word-weighted-value.)	
8. Ojemann	(62)	1934	Primarily Grade 8–College	Readability scale provided by use of 16 passages ranked in order of tested difficulty; relation of sentence and vocabulary factors, and three qualitative factors, to above criterion provides further scale.	
9. Dale and Tyler	(25)	1934	Primarily below Grade 8	$X_1 = -9.4x_2 - 0.4x_3 + 2.2x_4 + 114.4$ (± 9.0). (X_1 = percentage of adults of third to fifth grade reading ability who can comprehend a passage; x_2 = number of difficult technical words; x_3 = number of different, hard, non-technical words; x_4 = number of indeterminate clauses.)	Interesting in that it is one of the first true formulas for adults, even though actually for low-ability readers.
10. McClusky	(60)	1934	Primarily above Grade 8	Three factors used independently: (1) number of letters per word, (2) number of words per sentence, and (3) number of various types of nouns used; compare materials on these bases.	
11. Gray and Leary	(41)	1935	Grade 2–College	$X_1 = -.01029x_2 + .009012x_5 - .02094x_6 - .03313x_7 - .01485x_8 + 3.774.$ (X_1 = average comprehension score for adults of limited reading ability; x_2 = number of different hard words [not common to Dale List of 769 words]; x_5 = number of personal pronouns; x_6 = average number of words per sentence; x_7 = percentage of different words; x_8 = number of prepositional phrases.)	Because of the detailed analysis made, Gray and Leary's work has been a landmark in the study of readability.

11A. Kessler	(47)	1941	Presumably Grade 2–College	Two factors used independently: (1) average sentence length in words, and (2) average number of different hard words per 100 words. The values obtained are compared to Gray and Leary's standards.	The only formula to analyze words in context.
12. Morriss and Halverson	(61)	1938	Presumably Adult Level	The larger the proportion of words in Classifications III and IV and the smaller the proportion in I, the harder a book is. Classification I = simplest word labels; Classification II = localisms; Classification III = concrete ideas; Classification IV = abstract ideas.	
13. Washburne and Morphett	(75)	1938	Grades 1–9	X_1 (grade placement) = $.00255x_2 + .0458x_3 - .0307x_4 + 1.294.$ (x_2 = number of different words; x_3 = number of different uncommon words [not in Thorndike's first 1500]; x_4 = number of simple sentences in 75 sample sentences.)	One of the most used children's formulas.
13A. Bergman	(20)	1936	Presumably Grades 1–9	X_1 (grade placement) = $.00255x_2 + .0458x_3 - .0307x_4 + 1.084.$	This formula is an early version of the Washburne-Morphett, identical except for the final constant.
13B. Edgerton	(28)	1945	Presumably Children's Level	Two factors used independently: (1) number of different uncommon words, and (2) average sentence length.	This formula was considered to be mainly a short version of the Washburne-Morphett formula by its author, though it also depended on Gray and Leary's work.
14. Lorge	(56)	1939	Grades 3–12	X_1 (grade placement) = $.07x_2 + .1301x_3 + .1073x_4 + 1.6126.$ (x_2 = average sentence length in words; x_3 = number of prepositional phrases per 100 words; x_4 = number of different hard words per 100 words not on Dale 769-word list.)	This is really the first of the modern efficient formulas.
14A. Lorge	(58)	1948	Grades 3–12	X_1 (grade placement) = $.06x_2 + .10x_3 + .10x_4 + 1.99.$	This version differs from the above (1939) version only in slightly changed numerical constants.

TABLE 1 (cont.)

SUMMARY PRESENTATION OF READABILITY FORMULAS

Author(s)	Bibliography Number	Publication Date	Range of Difficulty	Formula	Comment
15. Yoakam	(78)	1939	Grades 4 to High School	Vocabulary given Thorndike index numbers, with page indexes formed by adding word indexes; grade placement of book then based on average of page indexes.	An unusual formula in that only one factor—vocabulary—is used.
16. Flesch	(32)	1943	Grades 3–12	Grade placement $= .1338x_s + .0645x_m - .0659x_h + 4.2498.$ (x_s = average sentence length in words; x_m = number of affixes; x_h = number of personal references.)	The first Flesch formula, and the formula that attracted widespread popular interest to readability.
17. Flesch	(33)	1948	Grades 3–12	$R.E.$ (Reading Ease) $= 206.835 - .846wl - 1.015sl.$ (wl = number of syllables per 100 words; sl = average number of words per sentence.) $H.I.$ (Human Interest) $= 3.635pw + .314ps.$ (pw = number of personal words per 100 words; ps = number of personal sentences per 100 sentences.)	
17A. Powers, Sumner, and Kearl	(65)	1958	Approximately Grades 3–8	$X_{c_{50}} = -2.2029 + .0778sl + .0455wl.$ ($X_{c_{50}}$ = reading grade score of pupil who can answer correctly one-half the McCall-Crabbs test questions on a passage.)	Flesch's formula, as recently recalculated for greater accuracy.
18. Dale and Chall	(23, 24)	1948	Grades 3–12	$X_{c_{50}} = .1579x_1 + .0496x_2 + 3.6365.$ ($X_{c_{50}}$ = reading grade score of pupil who can answer correctly one-half the McCall-Crabbs test questions on a passage; x_1 = percentage of words outside the Dale list of 3000 [Dale score]; x_2 = average sentence length in words.)	
18A. Powers, Sumner, and Kearl	(65)	1958	Approximately Grades 3–8	$X_{50} = 3.2672 + .0596x_2 + .1155x_1.$	The Dale-Chall formula, as recently recalculated for greater accuracy.
19. Dolch	(27)	1948	Grades 1–6	Three or four factors used independently: (1) "average sentence" length; (2) "long sentence" length (upper decile of sentence lengths); (3) percentage of words not in Dolch's list; (4) number of polysyllabic words. Compare the values with the standards given.	

20. Wheeler and Wheeler	(77)	1948	Presumably Children's Level	Select 1000 words and obtain grade placements by using the Thorndike list; compare the number of words at each grade level (as percentages).	
21. Flesch	(34)	1950	Grades 3–12	R (readability) $= 168.095 + .532dw - .811wl.$ (dw = percentage of definite words; wl = number of syllables per 100 words.)	This formula uses a measure of abstraction to get at readability; another formula —simply percentage of definite words —measures level of abstraction by reference to a table of levels.
21A. Gillie	(39)	1957	Presumably Grades 3–12	Abstraction level $= 36 +$ (number of definite words) $+$ (number of finite verbs) $+$ (2 times number of nouns of abstraction).	A shortened version of Flesch's level of abstraction formula.
22. Farr, Jenkins, and Paterson	(30)	1951	Presumably Adult Level	New Reading Ease Index $= 1.599nosw - 1.015sl - 31.517.$ ($nosw$ = number of one syllable words per 100 words; sl = average sentence length.)	This is a simplification of the Flesch "Reading Ease" formula.
22A. Powers, Sumner, and Kearl	(65)	1958	Approximately Grades 3–8	$X_{c50} = 8.4335 + .0923sl + .0648$ (per cent of monosyllables).	The Farr-Jenkins-Paterson formula, as recently recalculated for greater accuracy.
23. Gunning	(43)	1952	Presumably Grades 6–12	Reading grade level $= .4$ (average sentence length $+$ percentage of words of 3 or more syllables, or polysyllables).	
23A. Powers, Sumner, and Kearl	(65)	1958	Approximately Grades 3–8	$X_{c50} = 3.0680 + .0877$ (average sentence length) $+ .0984$ (percentage of polysyllables).	The Gunning formula, as recently recalculated for greater accuracy.
24. McElroy	(42)	1953	Presumably Adult Level	Fog Count = Sum of ones (easy elements in sentence) and threes (polysyllables or hard ideas).	To get reading grade level, divide total count for all analyzed sentences by number of sentences; if the average is over 20, divide by 2; if under 20, subtract 2, then divide by 2.

TABLE 1 (*cont.*)

SUMMARY PRESENTATION OF READABILITY FORMULAS

Author(s)	Bibli-ography Number	Publi-cation Date	Range of Difficulty	Formula	Comment
25. Forbes and Cottle	(38)	1953	Grade 5–College	Index of vocabulary difficulty = sum of Thorndike weights of words above most common 4000.	A table yields corresponding grade levels. Note also that this formula was designed for use with psychological tests and inventories.
26. Spache	(67)	1953	Grades 1–3	Grade level = $.141x_1 + .086x_2 + .839$. (x_1 = average sentence length; x_2 = number of words outside Dale list of 769 words.)	
26A. Stone	(70)	1957	Presumably Grades 1–3	Grade level = $.141x_1 + .086x_2 + .839$. (x_1 = average sentence length; x_2 = number of words outside a list composed of words from Dale List of 769, Krantz's "Authors Word List," and Stone's *A Graded Vocabulary for Primary Reading*.)	The revised list is said to yield lower ratings than the original Dale list, and therefore lower grade-level scores.
27. Wheeler and Smith	(76)	1954	Primer–Grade 4	Index number = 10 (average unit [sentence] length × percentage of polysyllables).	To get a grade-placement score, consult formula tables.
28. Flesch	(36)	1954	Presumably Adult Level	"r" count = sum of references of a realistic, specific, or concrete nature; "e" score = sum of references of an energetic, forceful, or vivid nature.	For both equations, consult formula tables for interpretation of values.
29. Tribe	(72)	1956	Grade 2–8	$C_{50} = .0719x_1 + .1043x_5 + 2.9347$. ($x_1$ = average sentence length; x_5 = number of different words not on Rinsland list, with basic list score determined by dividing by number of words and multiplying this by 100.)	The Dale-Chall tables are suggested as a basis for corrected grade levels.
30. Flesch	(37)	1958	Presumably Adult Level	Score ("formality" to "popularity") = sum of occurrences of a "formal" to "popular" nature.	A table is provided to interpret scores.
31. Bloomer	(21)	1959	Primer–Grade 6	Grade level predicted on the basis of two variables, number of words per modifier, and sound complexity of modifiers.	This formula was designed to measure level of abstraction as a function of modifier load.

5. Other Methods of Measuring Readability

MENTION WAS MADE EARLIER (Strang, 13) of the tendency to consider readability only in terms of readability formulas, or at least to consider readability measurement only in such terms. Other methods of measuring readability do exist, however, and they are used frequently. The "clinical" or individual approach, such as that used by Clarence Dewey (91), probably is not often used because of the expense of individual attention. Note, however, the frequent use of combined judgments of students or of teachers and other experts as indicators of readability. An early large-scale use of student ratings was Carleton Washburne and Mabel Vogel's *What Children Like to Read* (124, 125, 220); John Hayes (98) used and compared author and teacher ratings, and H. E. Smith (114) compared teacher ratings for difficulty of items with tested difficulty. Although such studies are not reviewed in this book, it should be noted that judgments, especially in informal studies, are recognized as subject to considerable error. For this reason, those who have used judgments have frequently done so in conjunction with readability formula ratings (see, for example: Rue, 205; Carpenter, 142; Morphett and Washburne, 195; Strang, *et al.,* 213; Fihe, Wallace, and Schulz, 155).

Another method of measuring readability is to use a test. Usually this takes the form of a test of comprehension, speed, or some other such index. Again, no attempt has been made to review here all of the published studies, but the work of George Kyte (103), C. O. Matthews (109), and Cutright, Halvorson, and Brueckner (85) are worth noting because they provide examples of the kinds of grade placements that later were estimated more easily by using formulas. The chief difficulty in measuring readability directly by testing is that building and administering a test is a difficult, time-taking process. This time problem is unfortunate, since certain special kinds of testing devices like Ralph Staiger's (116) "Word Error Quotient" (the proportion of errors made to total possible errors in reading a selection orally) may be useful, empirical methods for determining reading difficulty.

Another way of checking readability is to use a paired comparison technique where every passage to be judged is compared with every other. Ray Hackman and Alan Kershner (97) used such a technique on 37 passages differing in readability. The greatest difficulty with this approach is that using it, like tests, is a very lengthy, laborious process. In the process of their research, however, the authors found that the quick, simple measure of reading-time put 29 of the 37 passages in almost the same rank order as the more cumbersome judgments.

Working from this finding, Hackman and Kershner selected the 11 hardest and 11 easiest of the passages to serve as criterion groups for the study of the relationship of reading-time to 11 variables commonly used in readability studies. The passages were analyzed on the basis of standard units of 2000 type spaces since it was felt that the length units commonly used varied with length of words. Their counts were of: x_1 — different hard (non-Dale) words; x_2 — prefixes; x_3 — average sentence length; x_4 — personal words; x_5 — sentences; x_6 — affixes; x_7 — personal sentences; x_8 — words; x_9 — prepositional phrases; x_{10} — definite words; and x_{11} — average word length.

A discriminant function was then calculated using the first nine variables on the hard and easy passages. This treatment resulted in the following prediction equation:

$$x_t = .010361x_1 + .005159x_2 + .007646x_3 + .002113x_4$$
$$+ .000280x_5 + .001767x_6 - .004487x_7 - .008809x_8$$
$$- .00032191x_9$$

Use of this equation differentiated the hard and easy passages to the extent of a highly significant t-value of 5.191 ($P <$ .001). The biserial correlation coefficient based on the predicted values was .95.

This equation is not a readability formula as the term is used here since it was not intended for use with new passages. However, the study does confirm the importance of vocabulary variables, since the count of words not on Dale's 3000-word-list was the best single factor. In addition, the way was opened for the use of reading-time as a criterion of reading difficulty in place of the more time-consuming and difficult comprehension testing method.

Two other recent techniques also have been used to increase or measure readability without the time and effort that most tests require. The first of these is the so-called "peak-stress" method of W. F. Dearborn, P. W. Johnston, and L. Carmichael (88). The method involves the stressing, by capitalization or some other device, of the one word in each sentence of a manuscript to which its author would give maximum or peak stress. The method was originally intended as a device for increasing reader comprehension by emphasizing meaning. The authors found it would accomplish this purpose: the comprehension gain in five experiments using college students ranged from 10 to 30%, with a median of 18%. The subjects in the first of these experiments also showed a very marked preference for the stressed material (preference was not measured in the four subsequent experiments).

In addition to its use in increasing comprehension, the method was suggested as a measure of readability (89). The procedure was to have two undergraduate psychology majors read twenty 100-word passages from each of five psychology textbooks and indicate which word in each sentence they would stress if reading that sentence aloud. The percentage of agreement in stressed words was then used as an index of readability. It was found that this method ranked books in a very different order from that of Flesch's original readability formula. The authors suggest that this method provides the better index of readability because it shows a high relationship with reading test scores. Flesch (96) has criticized this interpretation, feeling that it might work for straight expository material, but would probably not for an informal, popular style. The work of G. R. Klare, J. E. Mabry, and L. M. Gustafson (386, 100) and of G. R. Klare, E. H. Shuford, and W. H. Nichols (unpublished) suggests another interpretation. These authors compared an unstressed version with four different kinds of stressed versions: peak stress, stress of "important" (usually technical) words, stress of words to appear in comprehension test answers later, and random stress (one randomly selected word stressed in each sentence). They found no over-all increase in comprehension, but did find a tendency for more able airmen subjects to profit from stress and less able subjects to be "confused" by it. Since Dearborn, Johnston, and Carmichael used college students in all of their studies, it seems likely that they would correspond in ability to the more able airmen. Perhaps, therefore, either or both ability of subjects and style of writing interact with stress in producing results.

In their earliest report of the peak stress method (88) its authors describe an experiment in which, as a test of comprehensibility, subjects were asked to fill blanks representing words that had been deleted from written material. This technique has since been called "cloze" procedure by Wilson Taylor and used by him in a series of studies (119, 120, 121). Taylor considers it primarily a measure of readability, and gives the following steps for comparing the readability of two or more passages:

1. *Delete* an equal number of words from each passage by some essentially random means;
2. *Replace* each word with a blank of standard size;
3. *Ask* subjects to fill in the missing blanks;
4. *Count up* the correct insertions and compare passages.

This method was found to yield results highly related to both Flesch and Dale-Chall readability scores (Taylor, 119, 121) and to be more sensitive than either to difficulties such as are found in the works of James Joyce and Gertrude Stein. It was found useful also in measuring the "listenability" of spoken messages (Taylor, 120).

It is worth noting that the deletion method apparently does not measure the same thing as a readability formula when the materials deleted are letters and spaces rather than words. Chapanis (430) found no relationship between measures of correctly supplied letter and space deletions and readability as measured by the Flesch formula.

Just as the equation of Hackman and Kershner was not a readability formula because it did not predict the readability of new, untested passages, so "cloze" procedure is not a formula (even though it might "predict" difficulty for a large group of readers based on results from a small sample). It is, however, a quick, easy, and versatile testing technique that may well be used for developing criteria in the construction and validation of readability formulas.

Other published methods of measurement are available that do not satisfy the definition of a readability formula used here. As indicated, the design of the measure and the intention of the writer must be to provide quantitative, objective predictions of difficulty without requiring any kind of test of readers or writing. But also, the method must be general enough to provide estimates over a range of applicability and of difficulty. The following kinds of studies (others will be described later) were therefore not included among the formulas:

(1) Measurements of the readability of one or of a few books, not intended for application to other books — for example, see Jesse Ward and P. R. Stevenson's study of a history text (123), or Robert Brown's analysis of the vocabularies of history and reading textbooks (82);

(2) Checks for the readability or variability of books within only one grade — examples are F. D. Keboch's investigation of word difficulty in five American history texts (99), and Clarence Stone's study of twelve series of readers (117);

(3) Pure vocabulary counts not intended for formula use — such as Paul Witty and Lou LaBrant's study of classic and popular novels (127), or Elizabeth Stadtlander's detailed scale for various kinds of reading matter (115). The reader who wishes to check other such peripheral measures may do so in Carolyn C. Dunlap's dissertation, "Readability Measurements: A Review and Comparison" (369).

Many of the early studies in which methods other than formulas were used to measure readability involved the use of vocabulary counts. Thorndike's first word-list was used as a basis for analysis in most of these. Examples are the Ward and Stevenson, Keboch, Brown, Witty and LaBrant, and

Stadtlander studies already mentioned. Among the common procedures in such studies were (1) classification of words by thousands according to Thorndike frequencies, or simply Thorndike index numbers; (2) weighting of words according to Thorndike frequency; (3) examination of words outside the Thorndike list, etc. Studies have sometimes involved other counts. For example, E. V. O'Rourke and C. D. Mead (111) used the Gates list in a study of third grade arithmetic textbooks, and V. R. DeLong (90) used vocabulary levels set up by Stone in developing reading levels. Sometimes several vocabulary factors and several lists are used in one study. For example, Elizabeth Becker (80) used four difficulty factors and four word-lists in evaluating 31 pre-primers, and Clarence Stone (118) used five word-lists to set up his own graded vocabulary list. On the other hand, vocabulary counts have been combined with testing methods; a thorough investigation of this sort is that of Francis Curtis (84).

No attempt has been made here to review completely the use of word counts and vocabulary counts (see Dale and Reichert, 87, for a compilation of vocabulary studies). Such counts have been used so frequently in readability measurement, however, that some attention to criticisms is in order. Paul McKee (107) pointed out that word-lists may (1) give an indication of visual recognition (or of sight vocabulary) rather than conceptual meaning (or meaning vocabulary); (2) be defective in the sense that frequency of occurrence is not an infallible guide to vocabulary difficulty; (3) provide no indication of the many possible meanings of words; and (4) encourage the questionable practice of removing all unfamiliarity from content reading. E. W. Dolch (94) suggested a number of similar considerations in the use of vocabulary lists for predicting readability and some additional ones: (1) the size of the list used should vary with the user's needs; (2) the words "not on the list" should be studied; (3) the source of the list should be examined; (4) special subject matter lists should not be overlooked. Herman Bongers (81) has also raised criticisms of some word counts and vocabulary controls. He presents a history of word counts before describing his own lists.

Attempts have been made to avoid one of the most serious criticisms — the problem of the different meanings a word may have. Marie Mehl (110) proposed a count of concepts using an occurrence of each different meaning as a different concept rather than using an added frequency of one for the word. Dixie Marcum (108) used a somewhat more general definition of a concept, but it was based at least partly on the notion of meanings in context. Edward Dolch (93) used a still different, but related, definition for "fact." In his analysis a fact is an item a teacher might examine for mastery of, but a word analysis is used to get a count of facts. In view of the continuing interest in counts of word meanings, it is surprising that Lorge's *The Semantic Count of the 570 Commonest English Words* (104) or Lorge and Thorndike's *A Semantic Count of English Words* (105) have not been given much attention. One of the authors' findings was that the commonest (most frequent) words had the greatest variety of meanings.

Another kind of readability study, in addition to vocabulary, is not included in the section on formulas. It is that in which the analysis was either not quantitative or not objective in nature. A major category of studies here involves variations in style of writing other than style difficulty, the common variable in readability. One of the first studies of the above sort was that of Finis Engleman (95). The author compared the relative merits of two forms of discourse, conversational and narrative expository, with material given to fourth- and seventh-grade pupils. The study showed that the subjects preferred factual content written in conversational style and read it faster than narrative expository; there was no significant difference in comprehension. Cassie Burk (83) made a similar study in which fourth-grade children were tested for interest, rate of reading, and comprehension. In her study, the story variations were combinations of narrative vs. play style, direct vs. indirect conversation, short simple vs. long complex sentences, and compound vs. mixed sentences; in all, nine combination versions were used. The subjects were not consistently more or less interested in a single type of sentence or form of story. There was, however, some tendency for them to prefer a direct conversational style and to comprehend it better and read it faster.

Francis DiVesta (92) made a study similar to both Engleman's and Burk's, but with correspondence course material. He compared three styles of writing, popular and personal, formal expository (as in textbooks), and study-guide (training material divided into several different study units). It was found that style of writing had no effect upon either achievement test scores or retention test scores.

Another study of language style was Francis Robinson's (113) comparison of ordinary legal writing with a revision in which familiar synonyms replaced unfamiliar words. His results showed that language structure, as well as vocabulary, is important to comprehension; the complex, unfamiliar structure of legal writing could not be satisfactorily clarified for ordinary readers simply by substitution of familiar for unfamiliar words.

A somewhat different approach was used by Mary C. Wilson (126), who amplified material and compared the comprehension of an original 300-word version with expanded 600- and 1200-word versions. No special attempt was made to simplify vocabulary or sentence structure, but all versions, according to Gray-Leary formula analyses, were below the reading level of the sixth- and seventh-grade pupils who served as subjects. Several results of her study are particularly interesting: (1) In general, amplification increased comprehension, once even when the amplified material was more difficult according to a readability formula; (2) Concepts caused more difficulty than structure, and those concepts which were more difficult in the short versions were also more difficult in the longer.

As indicated earlier, studies of other factors that affect ease of understanding have not been included here because of the limits set in this report. Typography, for example, has not been included, though it is sometimes called one aspect of readability (see Paterson and Tinker, 11, or Burtt, 3) and even though typographic arrangement has been shown to affect comprehension and efficiency of reading (see Klare, Nichols and Shuford, 101, for a review of such studies). Similarly, interest-value in content has been excluded, even though it has been shown to influence comprehension directly (see Bernstein, 2). Interest of the noncontent sort used by Eleanor Peterson (112) in her study of history material has also been excluded, at least partly because her definition of interest appears too subjective for others to duplicate her work. The only exceptions to the exclusion of interest are the human interest studies based on Flesch's method of analysis, because they involve objective style changes usually associated with readability. In fact, personal style is actually a better term for this factor than human interest. Finally, the organization factor has been excluded because it is either difficult to define objectively (see Peterson, 112) or because it essentially involves format changes (see Klare, Shuford, and Nichols, 102, for a review of such studies).

Most published studies of readability in recent years involve formulas rather than other possible measures. Because of this and the lack of published information on other measures, Chapters 7 and 8, concerned with evaluative studies of readability measures, will be almost solely concerned with the adequacy of formulas.

6. Applications of Readability Measures

ONE READABILITY FORMULA or another can be applied to almost any contextual material; some formulas can even be applied to noncontextual material in which words are not strung together in sentence form. For this reason, the number of potential applications of formulas seems almost limitless. Certainly if there were some basis for estimating the number of unpublished studies to add to those that have been published, the total number of applications would be large indeed. In the published work alone, the number of studies is much greater than all other kinds of readability studies taken together.

The number of applications can, by itself, make for confusion, since most studies present rather detailed results. Furthermore, the results are often specific to the materials analyzed and not of general interest; they may even involve rather out-of-date materials. For these reasons, this chapter will be brief. Each of the major areas in which formulas have been used will be introduced briefly, and specific fields of application indicated within each area. Little discussion of specific references has been provided; the reader who wishes to examine the references in any major area can consult the classified and annotated Bibliography.

Education

Within the larger area of published applications, by far the greater number of studies has been in the various subdivisions of the education field. Similarly, the earlier studies are found here. This reflects the origin and original purpose of readability measurement. Teachers for all ages, grades, and intellectual levels have some concern for the readability of the written materials they assign, and must make a judgment of suitability on the best bases available (see, for example, Leary, 177). One of the earlier graded book lists, that of Washburne and Vogel (220), presented a grade placement for 700 books, but the time and effort involved were almost prohibitive. It is interesting, in this connection, to note the authors' early use of a readability formula (220) and development of one themselves (Vogel and Washburne, 74). In their own later work on book lists (195) and in that of others (Lewerenz, 179, 180, 181; Broening, 137; Rue, 205; Carpenter, 142; Strang, *et al.*, 213; Fihe, Wallace and Schulz, 155), formulas were used increasingly for grade placement, or at least as an aid to it.

Along with the early use of formulas went questions about the advisability of their use. Broening (137), in one of the first discussions, decided that the Winnetka (Washburne-Vogel) formula need not level down the creative reading and creative expression of boys and girls so long as it was used intelligently. And she felt that it need not result in a decrease of the literary merit of children's books. However, DeBoer felt that formulas could unduly regiment reading (150). Much of the argument on this topic was never published, of course. And the argument is hardly settled; Larrick (176), as recently as 1951, discussed and answered misunderstandings and objections concerning the use of formulas in reading to children, controlling vocabulary and sentence length, and determining grade level. Hildreth and Wagner (164) felt it necessary to emphasize that formulas can help teachers provide books easy enough to master but difficult enough to challenge.

The influence of readability formulas upon educational practices is not limited to teachers' and administrators' use. The small number of published reports masks the fact that publishers have come to make extensive use of formulas. Beust (135), for example, says formulas are invariably applied to reading texts; Chall's statement (469) that measurement has been used almost as a secret tool by publishers suggests one of the reasons that this widespread use is not reflected by a large volume of literature.

All in all, applications in the general area of education have been as widespread as they have been numerous. The specific fields of application are listed below.

1. Elementary education. The chief emphasis has been on reading textbooks, but studies have also been made in history, geography, and general social studies; health, science, and arithmetic; and English, spelling, poetry and general literature. Many studies were concerned primarily with vocabulary, and readability formulas as such were not used in these.

2. Secondary education. Science materials have been most thoroughly studied; special attention has been given also to mathematics, biology and health, history and other social studies, literature, and even occupational materials and business-law textbooks.

3. Collegiate education. Psychology texts have been analyzed more often than any others, but some applications have been made in the fields of biology, botany, chemistry, physics, and natural and physical sciences generally. It appears that writers, editors, and publishers have all used readability formulas at one time or another in the preparation of introductory texts.

4. Adult education. Materials for adults, particularly those with limited reading ability, have long been a focus of

attention. Of note here has been the work done by members of the Readability Laboratory at Columbia University (see especially Bryson, 138 and 139).

Business and Industry

Applications of readability formulas and research findings to industrial and business materials have begun only recently in the history of readability. Generally the approach has taken the form of alerting management to the idea that readability, and communication generally, should be a matter for concern. This has been accomplished, primarily, by the work of private consultants like Robert Gunning and John McElroy, and by the reports of Donald G. Paterson, his associates, and other university research workers. Little has been published by the private consultants, probably because they are engaged in a competitive enterprise; research workers have, however, built up a rather considerable body of literature. This has been done largely in the following fields:

Labor-management communication. This work has concerned information sheets, rejection letters, and union-management agreements and contracts.

Industrial publications. House organs have been given the most attention, but employee handbooks and corporate reports have been analyzed also.

Journalism and Mass Communications

One of the "natural" areas of application of readability formulas and research would seem to be newspapers and other organs of mass communication. Certainly here, if anywhere, readability poses a direct communication problem since the need for readability increases with the size and variability of the intended audience. Scattered studies were made early

(Kitson, 7; Lewerenz, 179; Gray and Leary, 41), but large-
scale application did not begin until the publication of
Flesch's 1943 formula. At that point, journalists themselves
began to study the problem of readability. Their analyses
led to the two general conclusions that newspapers and other
media frequently contained too hard reading for their intended publics and that readability and readership were related (see the chapter on validity of formulas for more complete information on the latter). The analyses have covered
the following fields:

Newspapers. The work here has been done by readability
consultants, teachers, writers, and editors, and has extended from individual newspapers to the large news-
gathering organizations.

Other media. Applications have included the Bible, other
best sellers, and magazines; special attention has been
given to advertising copy.

Legal and Governmental Writing

A favorite target of advocates of plain talk is the awkward,
often incomprehensible writing found in legal documents
of one sort or another. The severest critics have been lawyers
themselves. And government publications have been among
the most vulnerable. Their style of writing was colorfully
termed "gobbledygook" by Maury Maverick, the former
Congressman from Texas.

The work done in this area actually covers a wide range;
a few specific fields have been included here for convenience
to the reader.

Legal writing. Much of the work here has been concerned
with readability in a general sense rather than the specific
sense of formulas.

Governmental writing. The writings coming from a number of government bureaus have been analyzed; publications of the armed forces and the U. S. Department of Agriculture have been given particular attention. Miscellaneous documents, such as the speeches or writings of famous Americans, have been studied also.

Psychological Tests and Questionnaires

Psychological tests drew the first attention of readability formula users, along with textbooks and other educational materials. This despite the fact that application is more difficult for tests (and questionnaires) than for most writing. Many formulas require contextual material for satisfactory analysis and many test items are not in sentence form; other problems, such as small sample size and incomplete sentences, also arise. Apparently, the persistent attempts to use formulas here have stemmed from concern that a test cannot give a good estimate of what it is intended to measure unless the subject can understand the directions and the items. Some of the work in this area is indicated below:

Tests. Analyses have been made largely to indicate probable difficulty of existing tests, but tests have actually been built with readability scores in mind and test analyses have even been the basis for one readability formula (Forbes and Cottle, 38).

Questionnaires. Work here has centered on the difficulty of personal opinion questions asked of probable respondents.

Writing

Readability techniques are primarily designed to measure the readability of material that has already *been* written. That is, formulas are intended for *rating*, not for *writing*.

Critics were quick to point out that writers could easily forget this, with dire consequences; formula developers were equally quick to say that if the writers forgot, it was not the developers' fault. But about applying the *principles* of readability to writing there was less controversy.

It is difficult to separate clearly this category of readability application from the other categories used in this section. Some of the references cited in another connection have been basically concerned with increasing the readability of writing. Those cited here appear in this, rather than another category, because they refer to *writing in general* and do not report formula application itself except perhaps incidentally. Also, the work in this area can be grouped better around the *names* of writers than around the *principles* they advocated.

The most famous name here, of course, is that of Rudolf Flesch, whose writings popularized readability and readability formulas. Edgar Dale's work, both in readability and in other areas of communication, has been less popularly directed than Flesch's; his writing (frequently with Jeanne Chall) has had its chief impact on other academic research in the field. Other writers whose names should be mentioned are Irving Lorge and Robert Gunning of America, and Sir Ernest Gowers of England.

Speech

The extent of the similarity of reading and listening as educational media has long been of interest to research workers. Therefore it seemed natural to investigate the applicability of readability formulas to spoken material. Studies of formula validity using listenability criteria (presented more fully in the chapter on formula validity) indicated that such application was, at least, possible. This, in turn, provided some justification for the applications which began to appear, as did the available studies on reading and listening comprehension. Conclusions from the work in these fields is presented briefly below:

Reading and listening comprehension. The results indicate generally that easy material is somewhat easier, and hard material somewhat harder, when heard than when read.

Listenability. Applications of formulas have been made to newscasts, public opinion questions, and even election speeches.

Foreign Languages

Except for certain preliminary work reported in the chapter "Historical Precedents of Formulas," very little readability research and formula development have taken place in other countries. This has made it rather natural for American research workers to apply American formulas to foreign language material or to devise specific formulas in the language of the materials being analyzed. The work in this area is summarized below.

Foreign Language Formulas. Apparently the first person to attempt to devise a foreign language formula was James B. Tharp (336), who worked with French language materials. He proposed an *Index of Difficulty* for French texts, based upon the factors of *Density* and *Frequency*. *Frequency* figures for words came from the *Basic French Vocabulary* in much the same way they came from Thorndike's lists of English words. *Density* values came from dividing the number of running words in a selection by the number of "burden" words. The proposed *Index of Difficulty* was then the *Frequency Index* divided by the *Density*. In his application of this formula to stories and to elementary readers, Tharp concluded that some of the readers have too high a vocabulary level to remain "elementary."

In 1951 Seth Spaulding published two formulas for estimating the relative reading difficulty of Spanish passages for persons who know Spanish as a second language (333). Twenty selections of approximately 200 words each, ranked for reading difficulty by 46 judges, served as the criterion for formula construction. The two formulas are:

(1) *Difficulty* $= 4.115\ (FI) + 0.154\ (ASL) - 2.383$
(2) *Difficulty* $= .1609\ (ASL) + 33.18\ (D) + 2.20$

In these equations, *FI* stands for frequency index, based on Buchanan's list, *ASL* for average sentence length, and *D* for density, based on a Density Word List. The reason for the two formulas is that the first is slightly more accurate, but the second is much easier to compute. The two give such similar results that the second has come to be preferred, as indicated in a more recent article by Spaulding (335). In it he presented a formula identical to the second except for a change in decimal places. The new formula is:

Difficulty $= 1.609\ (ASL) + 331.8\ (D) + 22.0$

In addition to the formula, a readability graph to facilitate computations was included.

Formula Applications. Formulas have been used both in the preparation of foreign language materials, especially for new literates, and in the analysis of existing materials, including translations. An interesting variation was Sukeyori Shiba's use of the "cloze" (word-deletion) method on Japanese texts (332).

Summary

This chapter presents a picture of the range of materials to which measures of readability have been applied. A glance at the Bibliography shows the large number of studies that has been published. Unpublished studies are undoubtedly much more numerous still. In all the areas of application, formulas show that much of the analyzed material is too difficult for an intended audience. This conclusion, however, has been based all too often on a rather uncritical acceptance of formula scores as being almost perfectly accurate and final pronouncements on readability. Formulas are not perfect measuring devices; the following two chapters should provide some notions of how effective they can be in particular circumstances.

7. Sampling Adequacy and Analyst Reliability

THE MAJOR CONCERN WITH ANY MEASURING DEVICE is the achievement of satisfactory measurement. If the measurement is to serve also as a predictor, as readability formula counts do, the need for valid measurement becomes even more acute.

No formula is a perfectly accurate measuring device, but it must be constructed so that: (1) the sample measured will represent, with maximum accuracy, the entire piece of writing from which it was taken; (2) two or more analyses of the same material, whether made by the same or different analysts, will agree as closely as possible; and (3) formula scores will, as nearly as they can, predict actual readability. The first two of these will be considered in this chapter; the third — validity — in Chapter 8.

Sampling

Sampling is not necessary in the use of readability formulas, since they can be applied to an entire piece of writing. In fact, developers of formulas usually suggest that this be done when the piece is short. The function of sampling is to save time and money, and it has been used for such purposes throughout the history of readability formulas. Bertha Lively and S. L. Pressey used a sampling method with their pioneer formula (55), and raised at that time the question that is still being raised: how large a sample is necessary to get a reliable indication of difficulty? They used the technique most often followed since — selecting samples at intervals throughout the book being analyzed.

In turn, the first study of sampling adequacy, made by Jesse Ward (348), concerned the Lively-Pressey formula. Ward compared counts he made by using their method, analysis of 1000 words at intervals throughout a book, with a count of *all* the words in the first 100 pages. He found the number of different words in two 1000-word samples to be 473 and 492, while it was only 121 in the 100 pages themselves. He also found similar discrepancies in zero-value words — 26 and 32 versus 13 — and in weighted median index numbers — 40 and 42 versus 20. The discrepancies he found led him to conclude that a 1000-word sample, far from saving time, was itself a " . . . waste of time, money and energy" (348, p. 98).

Edward Dolch (338) felt that a sampling of the difficult words in a book could not represent the whole book because the words in some books are repeated much more than in others. To demonstrate the inadequacy of sampling, he compared the percentages of difficult words in each of three entire school readers with three different samplings of every tenth page. His results showed that the samples consistently gave larger values than the whole books.

It is clear that Dolch's results must hold for any formula which contains a count of the number of different words or of percentages of words outside certain frequency categories. The reason for this is that the smaller the sample, the smaller the number of repeated words. For example, one sentence seldom will have more than one or two repeated words in it, while 10 sentences may have many words in common and 100 may have very few *different* words. This also applies to sample sizes and books as a whole. To the suggestion that an allowance be made for sample size, Dolch replies that repetition is not uniform enough for this to work.

W. L. Chase (337) felt, just as Ward and Dolch had, that readability scores for books would vary with the analysis. He demonstrated this with a comparison of three samplings, using the Vogel-Washburne formula:

(1) Third full line on each page chosen;
(2) Fifth full line on the pages following those used in (1);
(3) Fifth full line on the pages used in (1).

Chase found a variation of one-half to one grade for the three and concluded that variation of a grade between two books analyzed with the Vogel-Washburne formula would not be sufficient evidence to say that one was more difficult than the other.

W. S. Gray and Bernice Leary (41) made a similar kind of sampling study. They compared two different sets of samples of the same size, 100 words, taking one sample from each chapter of a book. Since they found no significant differences between the two samplings in the means of the five factors they used in their formula, they felt that their sampling method was adequate.

Catherine Elliott (340) also compared different samples to see if there would be inconsistency in formula ratings. She used two separate samples for each of five formulas, Lively-Pressey, Patty-Pointer, Yoakam, Washburne-Vogel, and Gray-Leary, and analyzed 28 books ranging from primers to sixth-grade books. She then ranked each book within one given grade level from easiest to hardest by the five formulas, calling a formula consistent if both samples gave the same relative rank within the grade level. From such data for all books she computed a percentage of consistency. The values for the formulas follow: (1) Winnetka (Washburne-Morphett), 39; (2) Gray-Leary, 43; (3) Lively-Pressey, 50; (4) Patty-Painter, 60; and (5) Yoakam, 60. The Yoakam formula was used with only 20 instead of 28 books, primers and first readers being excluded. This was done presumably because the formula was not standardized on books at this level. However, this is equally true of the other formulas, and it seems possible either that they would have yielded increased consistency figures if similarly handled, or the Yoakam yielded a decreased value on the entire list of 28 books.

Another question about her procedure concerns the very restricted range of one grade level she used in making her comparisons; this seems to require greater accuracy than can be expected of a formula. All in all, Elliott's study affords little satisfactory evidence for her statement that formulas using only a vocabulary factor are more consistent than those which use an added sentence or prepositional phrase factor.

The sampling study of Bertha Leifeste (346) was similar to Dolch's in that she compared sample scores for entire books, but she used only the Yoakam formula in this case. She compared (for 12 textbooks) various kinds of sampling to the "true measure" (based on an entire book), and found: (1) the usual sample of 100 words was least accurate of all methods attempted; (2) a 200-word sample was an improvement; (3) the sampling of every tenth full page was the most accurate of all, but the most time-consuming; (4) the sampling of 15 selected pages per book was almost as accurate as every tenth page but took only about one-third as long; and (5) in general, size of sampling and degree of reliability were related.

Several things should be kept in mind in evaluating Leifeste's results. First, the size of the books in pages, and the size of the pages themselves, are not given; yet this would seem to be important in interpretation. Second, the significance of the observed differences is not given. Third, the Yoakam formula uses only a vocabulary factor, so that the results may well be different for most other formulas.

George Klare (475, 385) compared three sizes of sampling on 52 books with a formula that uses a vocabulary factor, the Dale-Chall, and one that does not, the Flesch "Reading Ease." Mean values obtained on the basis of 28 samples for each book were compared to means based on one-half of the samples, 14, and one-fourth of the samples, 7. It was found that although the larger number of samples gave slightly "harder" ratings with both, the differences due to sample size were not significant for either formula, or for books with a large, versus a small, number of pages. It is interesting that this tendency is opposite to that found by Dolch. It should be recalled, however, that his study was made of a vocabulary factor involving a count of the number of *different* words whereas the Dale-Chall vocabulary factor includes repeated words and the Flesch formula does not use a word-list factor at all. Apparently, sampling problems due to use of counts of different words are not significant in formulas where repeated words are counted. It must be remembered, however, that Klare's results hold only for the means of a number of books taken together; undoubtedly, individual books would have shown greater variation due to number of samples.

Richard Powers (347) made an empirical study of sampling as it is generally used in formulas. He compared counts of a number of variables on samples chosen one word at a time versus cluster samples, which involved sampling by sentences. He found no significant difference in the incidence of parts of speech (nouns, verbs, etc.), whether the

1000 sampled words were chosen individually or by cluster. He did, however, find that a cluster sample significantly over-estimated the percentages of "short," "structural," and "easy" words. Powers felt that these differences were due to the tendency for the sentence to impose an orderliness on the use of words that biases the clustered sample when readability factors are being counted. This is not a serious problem in readability studies since only relative values are necessary; if, however, absolute values of short or easy or structural words are ever needed, Powers' results will have to be considered.

Thus it is quite apparent from the sampling studies that no single sample size can be considered best for all situations. In general, the size of the sample should be increased when: (1) a count of the number of different words, or percentage of words within a given frequency category, is made; (2) a high degree of accuracy of measurement is desired; and (3) application time is not a matter of great concern. With the newer, popular formulas, where only a rough indication of readability is usually demanded, and when time for application is limited, even a decrease in the number of samples suggested by the formula developers appears permissible. While no user of formulas would want to add deliberate error to formula scores, it should also be pointed out that increased and more precise sampling alone can never entirely eliminate inaccuracy in formula predictions. No formula, even under the most favorable of sampling conditions, is a perfect predictor of readability.

Analyst Reliability

Just as formulas are not perfect predictors, humans are not perfect analysts. Obviously, any error they make adds potentially to prediction error. Yet, a certain amount of human error is probably unavoidable, since mood, physical condition, and amount of experience, among other things, may contribute to variations in accuracy from time to time. On the other hand, the complexity of the formula may itself be a primary cause of analyst error. Therefore, it is important that the formula be sufficiently easy to apply so that error is held to a minimum.

Two major aspects of the problem of analyst reliability are: Can an analyst, analyzing the same sample at different times, agree with himself in his counts? Can two different analysts, analyzing the same sample, agree with each other's counts?

The only formulas that have been thoroughly studied are the Flesch Reading Ease and Human Interest formulas and the Farr-Jenkins-Paterson formula. Patricia Hayes, James Jenkins and Bradley Walker (344) tested analyst-to-analyst reliability on the Flesch formulas with two experienced and two inexperienced analysts. Counts were made of number of syllables, sentence length, personal words and personal sentences — the factors in the formulas — and these were then analyzed again as total formula scores. The written materials used consisted of two 100-word samples from each of 40 prize-winning letters in a national contest; the letters were felt to differ widely in difficulty, style, structure, and content.

The results of a first study follow:

1. Tests of significance of differences on the four variables and the two formula scores: differences between analysts not significant at the 5% level.
2. Rank difference correlations of scores on the four variables and the two formula scores: all positive and significant. The agreement was very close on word length and sentence

length, 10 out of 12 correlations being in the .90's; all 6
Reading Ease score correlations were in the .90's. The
reliability on personal words was high, all 6 correlations
being in the .90's; on personal sentences reliability was
lower than desirable, with correlations ranging from .60
to .89. Three of the correlations on Human Interest
scores were in the .90's and 3 were not.

3. Differences in score points between analysts on identical
samples: very close agreement; 75% of Reading Ease score
comparisons were within 2 points of each other; and
75% of Human Interest score comparisons were within 5
points of each other.

4. Comparisons between analysts in terms of descriptive
categories: of the total of 240 comparisons, in only about
6% was there a difference between analysts in the category assigned to Reading Ease, and in less than 1% was
the difference greater than one category; in the case of
Human Interest, in only about 12% was there a difference in category, and in less than 2% was the category
difference greater than one.

5. Comparisons between experienced and inexperienced
analysts: no significant differences.

In a second study published at the same time, 18 students
analyzed samples of 500 words from 63 industrial house
organs (magazines published by companies for their staffs
and customers). Correlations were computed between counts
of two independent analysts on each sample. The results
were essentially the same as in the first study.

The remaining studies of reliability grew out of a controversy regarding the Farr-Jenkins-Paterson simplification of
the Flesch Reading Ease formula. Flesch (343) and Klare
(345) questioned whether the new formula would be as
precise as the Reading Ease formula, and whether it would
be any quicker and easier to use.

Farr, Jenkins, Paterson, and England (342) recomputed data on 11 samples previously used, and analyzed 7 new samples, as a check on the reliability of the counting procedure used in their formula. A comparison of the figures shows close correspondence in the counts of the several analysts.

A more thorough study of the relative reliabilities of the Flesch and Farr-Jenkins-Paterson formulas was made by George England, Margaret Thomas, and Donald Paterson (341). Thirteen pairs of inexperienced analysts first computed scores by both formulas for each of 196 hundred-word samples drawn from 49 house publications. Correlations between pairs of analysts on the separate factors in the formulas (sentence length, syllables per word, and number of one-syllable words) and the total formula scores ranged from .90 to .97. In a second part of the study one analyst computed reading ease scores by both formulas for each of 196 hundred-word samples drawn from 28 books. Then this analyst recomputed the data for 77 of the samples (11 books) at a later date. Test-retest reliability coefficients for the separate factors and the total formula scores ranged from .95 to .99.

This study confirmed the high reliability found for the Flesch Reading Ease formula by Hayes, Jenkins, and Walker, and demonstrated high reliability for the Farr-Jenkins-Paterson formula. It also showed, as had the previous study, that the sentence-length count is relatively less reliable than either a count of syllables or one-syllable words.

A third study, by Marvin Dunnette and Paul Maloney (339), also bears on the reliability of both the Flesch Reading Ease and Farr-Jenkins-Paterson formulas. Using 72 male and 72 female college freshmen as untrained analysts, and materials of a wide range of difficulty, counts were made of syllables and one-syllable words. It was found that: (1) one-syllable words could be counted in about three-fourths the time required for syllables; (2) boys counted one-syllable words significantly more accurately than number of syllables (the difference for girls was in the same direction but not significant); and (3) the syllable count was performed more accurately for easy material and the one-syllable word count for difficult material.

Thus it is clear that the Flesch Reading Ease and Farr-Jenkins-Paterson formulas have high analyst reliability. No published studies of other formulas permit any similar conclusions. One might suppose that reliability would be dependent upon at least three major factors: the complexity of the formula, the motivation of the analyst, and the experience of the analyst. But such speculation is dangerous, as can be seen from the lack of a significant difference between experienced and inexperienced analysts in the studies cited. It is clear that further studies of analyst reliability are needed. The few available studies, in the meantime, are encouraging.

8. Validity

THE REQUIREMENT that a measuring device actually measure what it is intended to measure, commonly called validity, is the most critical of the three characteristics a readability formula must have. The sampling procedure and analyst reliability of most recent formulas need further investigation, but are probably not seriously inadequate. If they were, something could be done about them by a change in the sample used or instructions to the analyst. But if a formula does not measure — in this case, predict — readability adequately, little can be done about it. It is not as easy to add a factor or two to a formula as it is to add samples to measure. Even if it were, adding presently known factors would probably not materially increase predictive power.

The validity of formulas therefore needs careful evaluation. In this section, three kinds of validity data will be considered. The first is the extent to which formula scores are related to, or predict, the original criterion scores used in developing the formula. This is important, but it is not sufficient. After all, the particular factors used in a formula are usually selected because they *are* the most highly related to the criterion. This is almost analogous to pulling oneself up by the bootstraps.

The second kind of validity data might be called comparative. It is the extent to which scores derived from two or more formulas agree with each other. This again is useful, but is still not enough. It is conceivable that all formulas might in some particular instance agree with each other — and all be wrong in their predictions. This is a kind of consistency check more than anything else.

The third kind of validity data concerns the ability of formula scores to predict an "outside criterion" of readability. This usually means, in practice, the degree of relationship between formula scores and estimates of readability arrived at in some other way — comprehension scores, judgments, readership, etc. Sometimes, however, materials are prepared in such a way that they will differ in terms of formula score, and the versions are then tested experimentally to see if this difference is borne out. The former, usually called cross-validation, is important to one who wishes to measure the readability of prepared materials. The latter, called experimental validity, is important not only for measuring the readability of prepared materials, but for preparing readable materials. Since a major goal of many writers on readability is to encourage readable writing, it is very important that experimental validity be demonstrated. It is clearly the hardest kind to demonstrate.

Original Criterion Prediction

It is desirable to have a refined criterion in developing a readability formula because the criterion serves as a basis for selecting or rejecting potential factors. The more refined the criterion, the better such decisions can be made. In the case of most recent formulas the criterion has been a set of graded test passages, with the number of occurrences of a given style factor in the passages being related to the grades.

The method of relationship most often used has been that of correlation. The resulting coefficient can be used to indicate the accuracy of the formula in accounting for the readability (reading difficulty) of the criterion passages. No formula is perfect in the sense that it accounts for all of the variation, or variance, in the passages. The correlation coefficient for recent formulas has hovered around .70, as the earlier descriptions of the formulas showed. This, in turn, means that roughly one-half of the variance in readability of criterion passages is accounted for by such popular formulas as those of Lorge, Flesch (both his 1948 and 1950 formulas), Dale and Chall, and the recent formula of Tribe.

This approximate level of validity is somewhat higher, for example, than the relationship usually found between psychological test scores and college course grades. Thus these readability formulas can be considered of relatively high validity, in a general sense. The recalculated Dale-Chall and Flesch formulas presented by Powers, Sumner, and Kearl (65) were found to have validity coefficients surprisingly close to the originals, the Dale-Chall showing a slight increase in coefficient from .70 to .71, and the Flesch a slight decrease, from .70 to .64. Such a study is an important, if indirect, justification of the original values, since it shows at least that they were not "flukes" arising from peculiarities in sampling or counting in the original investigations. The recalculated Gunning and Farr-Jenkins-Paterson formulas yielded coefficients of .59 and .58; no similar values were available for the original formulas.

The lack of validity data based on a comparable criterion for all formulas makes interpretation difficult. The highest correlations, for example, are found for the original Farr-Jenkins-Paterson and Forbes-Cottle formulas, but they were validated against criterion passages scored with other formulas. Their coefficients of .93 and .95 must be scaled down for comparison, as the value for the recalculated Farr-Jenkins-Paterson formula shows. The recent formulas of Spache and Bloomer have a correlation of .82 and .76 with their criteria, in both cases, textbook grade levels. But this may be due, as Chall (469) suggests, to the tendency of present-day authors to control vocabulary and sentence structure, particularly in beginning books. In other words, these formulas are validated against materials prepared by the use of formulas, and this naturally raises the correlation above normal expectations. Still another high correlation, that for the Washburne-Morphett formula, was between formula scores and grade levels of books children had read and liked. Whether this criterion is easier to predict than a comprehension test criterion is not definitely known, but this seems probable at least.

Several recent formulas have not been validated by correlation of scores with a criterion. Examples are the Dolch, Wheeler and Wheeler, Gunning, McElroy, and 1954 and 1958 Flesch formulas. In such cases, the usual procedure has been merely to make a rough comparison of formula scores with some criterion or to use some "logical" basis for the assumption of validity.

In summary, recent formulas probably have a maximum correlation of around .70 with a criterion of readability. This means that around 50% of the criterion variance in readability has been accounted for, or predicted by, the formula. To put formula accuracy another way, Washburne and Morphett (75) give a probable error of + .8 grade for their formula. This would mean about 50% of the grade ratings for books based on their formula would fall within .8 grade of a "true" rating. Chall (469) has estimated, further, that the readability indexes of individual books and passages based on recent formulas can be expected to be within about one grade of empirically determined difficulty. The work of Powers, Sumner, and Kearl in recalculating several recent formulas, as mentioned above, yielded the following standard errors, in grades: Dale-Chall, .77; Flesch Reading Ease, .85; and Gunning and Farr-Jenkins-Paterson, .90. This means about 68% of the grade ratings using these formulas would fall within these limits away from an empirically determined value. And this, in turn, suggests that Chall's estimated error value of around one grade level is probably fairly reasonable.

Comparative Validity Data

The existence of so many readability formulas makes it seem that the various formulas certainly must measure something different in order to be justified. A glance at the many factors that have been used in the various formulas appears to bear this out. Yet, on the other hand, if all of them pretend to measure readability accurately they must be measuring much the same thing. The obvious question is which of the two assumptions is relatively more correct.

The early studies of Alice Beal (350) and Catherine Elliott (340) were concerned with the evaluation of a number of formulas, but only general conclusions were reached regarding *lack of agreement* among formulas. Alfred Lewerenz made a more specific comparison, but only of scores from his formula and from that of Washburne and Vogel; he found that his formula placed books approximately two grades lower.

Many studies have made formula comparisons; in the following pages, brief reference will be made to the studies but the discussion will emphasize conclusions that can be drawn. The data will be organized around the individual formulas compared, with the formulas considered generally in terms of historical order.

1. *Lewerenz Formula*

Klare (475), Russell and Fea (412),* and Forbes and

---

* Wherever reference is made to the work of Russell and Fea (412), the reader may also wish to consult Russell and Merrill (411) on the same study.

Cottle (38) compared scores derived from Lewerenz' formulas with those of other formulas. Generally, the highest inter-correlations (.60 to .70) were with the Lorge, Dale-Chall, and Flesch Reading Ease formulas. There was, naturally, some disagreement in the values from the various studies, but only in the case of correlation with the Washburne-Morphett formula was this very great (from high to very low), probably due to the samples of books used in the comparison studies. The Lewerenz formula gave among the lowest (easiest) grade ratings of all the formulas compared; on the average, they were usually a grade or more lower than the Dale-Chall and Flesch ratings.

2. *Gray-Leary Formula*

The Gray-Leary formula was compared with other formulas by Walther (418), Swanson (414), Klare (475), and Dunlap (369). High intercorrelations (.70 to .80) were found with Dale-Chall and Washburne-Morphett scores, with those for Flesch scores lower in some cases. Gray-Leary grade ratings were consistently found to be several grades lower than those from other formulas, in some cases even as much as eight grades lower.

3. *Washburne-Morphett Formula*

A number of studies have involved the comparison of Washburne-Morphett scores with those of other formulas. Among these are the work of Walther (418), Miller (402), Klare (475), Russell and Fea (412), and Larrick (353). The highest intercorrelations of the Washburne-Morphett scores (around .60 to .80) have been with Dale-Chall and Yoakam scores; those with Lewerenz scores, as previously noted, have been high as well as very low. The Washburne-Morphett formula rather consistently places books at somewhat higher grade levels than do the other formulas, except possibly the Yoakam.

4. *Lorge Formula*

The Lorge formula has been compared with others by Yoakam (359), Lostutter (354), Latimer (392), Swanson (414), Kerr (351), Russell and Fea (412), Smith (356), Forbes and Cottle (38), Larrick (353), and Dunlap (369). With as large a number of comparisons as this, the differences and contradictions in the results make general statements difficult. However, consistently high intercorrelations are found with Dale-Chall scores (.54 up to .90); values for Lewerenz and Washburne-Morphett scores are also in this range, while those for Flesch scores are sometimes reported as high and other times as very low. In terms of grade-level ratings, the Lorge formula tends to place primary-level material at very nearly the same grades as other formulas (particularly the Dale-Chall); as adult levels are reached, however, the Lorge formula placements become relatively lower (easier) until a difference of as much as eight grades is sometimes found between them and Flesch or Dale-Chall scores.

5. *Yoakam Formula*

The Yoakam formula has been examined in some of the same studies as the Lorge; those including it were Yoakam (359), Latimer (392), Russell and Fea (412), Smith (356), Forbes and Cottle (38), Aber (349), Larrick (353), and Swarts (357). Yoakam scores consistently intercorrelated highly with Dale-Chall scores (.68 and over); values with scores from other formulas have not been consistent. The several studies of grade placement are not in agreement either, one comparison showing Yoakam grade levels as much as a grade or more lower than those from another formula and others showing them as much as two grades higher.

6. *Flesch Formulas*

The Flesch formulas have been involved in published comparative studies more often than any others. These include the work of Miller (402), Lostutter (354), Latimer (392), Chall and Dial (367), Swanson (414), Kerr (351), Terris (358), Klare (385, 475), Tubbs (see Vernon, 417), Young (421), Kinzer and Cohan (352), Russell and Fea (412), Selikson (355), Forbes and Cottle (38), Aber (349), Larrick (353), Dunlap (369), Swarts (357), and Powers, Sumner, and Kearl (65). Since Flesch's 1948 revision virtually replaced his 1943 formula, the generalizations to follow apply primarily to it. By far the highest intercorrelations have been with Dale-Chall scores, in one case being as high as .98. Some low values have been reported, but the majority have been high. Similarly, the estimated grade placements derived from the Flesch formula have been the most comparable to those from the Dale-Chall formula. They are usually somewhere between the high grades provided by the Washburne-Morphett formula and the low grades provided by the Lewerenz formula.

7. *Dale-Chall Formula*

Since its publication in 1948, the Dale-Chall formula has been involved in many of the same published comparative studies as those mentioned for the Flesch formula: Chall and Dial (367), Swanson (414), Kerr (351), Terris (358), Klare (385, 475), Tubbs (see Vernon, 417), Young (421), Kinzer and Cohan (352), Russell and Fea (412), Selikson (355), Forbes and Cottle (38), Aber (349), Larrick (353), Dunlap (369), Swarts (357), and Powers, Sumner, and Kearl (65). As already mentioned, the Dale-Chall and revised Flesch formulas yield the most nearly similar values of any two formulas, both in terms of intercorrelation coefficient and grade levels. The one possible exception to the above statement would be the intercorrelation of Dale-Chall formula scores to those from the formula developed by Forbes and Cottle. However, the correlations of Forbes scores with others have not been given special consideration since the formula itself was developed on the basis of its relationship with mean scores from five other formulas. On the other hand, the grade levels assigned to tests by the various formulas in the Forbes-Cottle study show a great deal of disagreement, sometimes as high as eight or more grades. These, again, are difficult to interpret because some formulas, particularly those using a measure of sentence length, are not readily applied to test materials.

No comparative studies exist based on Powers, Sumner, and Kearl's revisions of the Dale-Chall, Flesch, Gunning, and Farr-Jenkins-Paterson formulas. The authors do report, however, that the average difference in grade levels assigned by the recalculated Dale-Chall and Flesch formulas to 113 hundred-word passages is only .54 grade, whereas it was .78 grade using the original formulas. Comparisons among the other formulas are roughly similar, and all four recalculated formulas were found to agree more closely with each other than the originals did.

The comparative studies made to date are difficult to interpret because of several problems. First, different sets of material have been analyzed, and different formulas used by the various investigators making their comparative studies. Second, some formulas yield grade-level scores directly while others require corrections designed to provide more accurate values, particularly at higher levels of difficulty. Third, the various formulas predict different criteria; for example, some predict a C_{50} criterion, the level at which 50% of the questions on a given passage can be answered, while others predict a C_{75} criterion, and still others an entirely different criterion. Fourth, some investigators have used the rank-order correlation method while others have used product-moment correlations. The result is that numerous disagreements exist in the data. However, the following conclusions justifiably can be drawn:

1. In the available studies, the Dale-Chall and Flesch Reading Ease formulas provide the most consistently comparable results in terms of both correlational and grade-placement data.

2. The Washburne-Morphett formula tends to yield higher grade levels, and the Lewerenz formula lower grade levels, than the Dale-Chall or Flesch formulas. The Lorge formula yields similar grade levels for easy materials but lower grade levels for hard materials, compared to these two formulas; scores based on the Yoakam formula have shown no very consistent relationship to other formulas.

3. More of the high intercorrelations have involved Dale-Chall scores than those of any other formula, relative to the number of comparisons made.

4. The various formulas do not necessarily give comparable grade-level results even though they frequently show high intercorrelations. This indicates that attempting to place materials *within* a grade level by means of formula score is certainly questionable.

5. Some agreement should be reached on the most appropriate criterion for grade levels, that of 50% correct (C_{50}) or that of 75% correct (C_{75}). Or, lacking this, formulas should be presented for both criteria so that the user may choose the one he wishes.

6. It is useful to have corrected grade levels for the various formula scores, but they are also responsible for much of the disagreement in grade placement. Further work on the accuracy of these corrections is badly needed, especially in view of the fact that they are, in most cases, merely estimates.

A final word to the user of grade-level ratings is in order.

When two formulas disagree in the ratings they provide, a decision must be made as to the grade in which a book can most appropriately be used. A formula which yields *lower* (easier) grade ratings may cause the user to put the book in the hands of students who are too young and who may therefore find it *hard;* a formula which gives *higher* (harder) grade ratings may cause the user to give it to students who are older and may therefore find it too *easy*. This reverse implication of "easier" versus "harder" ratings, based on two different formulas, should be kept in mind when actually using grade-level ratings.

Validation Against Outside Criteria

When a readability formula has been validated simply on the basis of prediction of the original criterion, or in terms of high intercorrelations with other formulas, several critical questions still remain. Will it be able to predict the readability of a new sample of materials? What measures or indices of readability can be predicted? Is specially prepared material that is more readable in terms of formula scores actually more readable by empirical test?

The studies considered next have in common the use of an outside (external, or independent) criterion of readability against which formula scores are compared. Since a number of different criteria have been used, many of the studies could be grouped either in these terms or in terms of the formulas used. Grouping by criteria has been used here both because some studies were not attempts to validate particular formulas as much as the notion of readability itself, and because formulas do not seem to differ as much among themselves in predictive power as in the relative extent of the relationship of formulas per se with outside criteria of readability. The criterion groupings which have been used are: (1) reading comprehension, (2) reading speed, (3) judgments, (4) readership, (5) listenability, and (6) writer characteristics.

Reading Comprehension Criteria. One of the first kinds of criteria used, and the kind used frequently in later validity studies, has been comprehension (or learning, or retention). This is not surprising, since the notion of readability is more closely associated with comprehensibility or understandability than with any other characteristic. The studies themselves make use of this criterion in two ways. One type of study uses an existing outside criterion, such as graded passages other than those used in developing the formula. The other compares materials constructed according to principles of readability in order to observe the effect upon comprehension.

Some of the first studies did not involve readability formulas directly, but rather only factors common to formulas. An early study of this kind was that of Bernice Orndorff (407) on the effect of sentence length upon comprehension. In three separate investigations with elementary pupils, she found no significant differences in comprehension with short versus long sentences. A secondary effect on reading speed was ambiguous. Helen Gibbons (375), using a different approach, found a tendency for the ability to see relationships between the parts of a sentence to be a factor in both understanding the sentence and in measuring reading ability. She used disarranged phrases from sentences as her test, and third-grade pupils as subjects. Unfortunately, her sample was too small for adequate statistical treatment of the data. Perhaps the chief conclusion to be drawn is that mere changing of sentence length, a major factor in formulas, does not produce an automatic increase in comprehension.

A similar conclusion must be drawn from the early studies of the effect of vocabulary changes upon comprehension. Three early studies of a similar nature were made by Charlotte Foster (374), Huberteen Kueneman (391), and Lois Clarke (368). Foster used history selections, Kueneman geography, and Clarke social science; all rewrote the material in the vocabulary of a preschool child, using the *International Kindergarten Union List.* They administered the original and revised versions, and then gave multiple-choice and true-false comprehension tests. Slight differences appeared in the results of the studies, but all might be described as showing primarily that simplification of vocabulary produced little change, and certainly no automatic increase in comprehension.

Karl Nolte (406) made a thorough study of the effect of simplifying vocabulary upon comprehension, and came to much the same conclusion. He used three versions of three selections: an original; a version rewritten using the 2500 most frequent words in Thorndike's *A Teacher's Word Book of 20,000 Words*; and a version using Ogden's *Basic English List* of 850 words. Judges determined that meaning was not changed. No significant differences in comprehension were found between the various versions, using 1112 sixth-grade pupils as subjects. Additional testing using pictorial devices showed that both vocabulary and concepts were misunderstood. Nolte's analysis suggested that simplification of vocabulary alone, with other elements constant, does not materially help understanding.

In contrast to those conclusions, Francis Robinson (410) found that comprehension could be increased in simplified versions compared to original versions. He used selections from the Bible, the *Kellogg-Briand Peace Pact,* and Gibbon's *Decline and Fall of the Roman Empire,* and had the simplifications written by qualified writers in order to insure equivalence of meaning and smooth style. He found, using paired comparisons, that the inspirational value of the original and simplified versions was no different for his high school and college student subjects. On the comprehension check, however, there was a significant difference favoring the simplified (Goodspeed) version of the Bible as compared to the original (King James) version. It appears, however, that the difference may have been due as much to changes in organization as to simplification of vocabulary, so that results of the previous studies are not necessarily contradicted (Chall, 469).

The first study dealing with formulas was that by Elizabeth Stadtlander (115). She constructed a scale of 21 passages for evaluating the difficulty of reading materials for the intermediate grades. The passages were within five-point intervals on the Yoakam index; comprehension checks were made by giving multiple-choice questions on each passage to over 2000 children in grades 4, 5, and 6 who had taken the Stanford Reading Test. A positive relationship was found between comprehension scores and the index of difficulty of the Yoakam formula. Stadtlander's work was later used by Yoakam for grade-level standards for his formula.

Leo Miller's study (402) was not designed to validate formulas as such, but rather to determine the proper grade-level placement for books that had been given the John Newbery Prize. In the process, however, he determined Vogel-Washburne grade levels for some of the books, Washburne-Morphett levels for all but three, and 1943 Flesch formula levels for all of the books. These were compared to grade levels based on comprehension tests he built covering samples of the books. He found the books too difficult for their intended elementary audience, having an average grade placement of 8.4; in addition, he found the Washburne-Morphett formula gave an average grade placement of 7.4 and the Flesch formula an average of 7.5 to the books. These results are very close, especially considering the unrefined nature of Miller's tests.

Edward Latimer (392) compared the Yoakam, the 1943 Flesch, and the Lorge formulas. He used religious textbooks, comparing formula grade placements to publishers' placements and to comprehension test results on selected passages. He concluded that the Yoakam formula not only assigned the values closest to the publishers', but also to those from the comprehension tests. Latimer's conclusion that the Yoakam formula was more valid and reliable than the Lorge or 1943 Flesch must, however, be interpreted in the light of his using the Yoakam formula to select, and in some cases to rewrite, the test passages. Chall (469) points out that re-analysis of the data shows the Lorge formula to be equally, if not more highly, valid.

Philip Griffin (377) published a study of reader comprehension of news stories which Rudolf Flesch (373) subsequently explained in terms of readability. Griffin had compared two versions of a story, the original, A, as it appeared in a newspaper and a rewrite, B, by a competent reporter. The difference between them, according to Griffin (377, 378), was primarily in the development of a different lead, rearranged structure, and tighter organization in B. Flesch (373), however, attributed the superiority of B to greater reading ease and human interest, as measured by his 1948 formulas. Griffin's final comment (378) indicated the important thing was that his methods of analysis and Flesch's, while different, were able to agree. Flesch himself took special interest in Griffin's use of a recall test, and in what he considered the only study up to that time of the important relationship of readability and recall.

Interest in comprehension tests as a basis for validity studies began to increase greatly in the Fifties. The first work during this period was Robert Hites' proposal of a theory of the relationship of readability and format to retention in communication (382). He wrote three versions of a passage on map reading; each contained the same content, but one was at approximately the 7–8 grade level, another at 11–12 grade, and the third at college level by Dale-Chall and

1948 Flesch ratings. He also prepared three additional treatments, one paragraphed as to subject matter, one unparagraphed, and one with subject headings. A retention test was developed to test both retention of facts and ability to use the facts; Air Force R.O.T.C. freshmen were used as subjects. He drew the following major conclusions from his study:

1. The paragraphed material resulted in significantly higher scores than the unparagraphed, but the headed material did not result in higher scores than the paragraphed.

2. Material with short sentences resulted in no increase in score over that with longer; material with fewer difficult words produced no higher scores than that with more difficult words.

3. Subjects with above the median intelligence-test scores made significantly higher retention scores than those below.

Klare (475) also studied the relationship between readability and comprehension scores, but in a somewhat different way. He applied the Gray-Leary, 1948 Flesch, and Dale-Chall formulas to adult reading tests for which score data already existed. He found the following correlations between formula scores and scores on the 16 passages in Ojemann's adult reading test (62):

1. Dale-Chall formula, .87 ± .06;

2. Gray-Leary formula, .82 ± .09;

3. Flesch formula, .82 ± .08.

None of the differences between these correlations was significant. He found the following correlations using the Gray-Leary Adult Reading Test, with the 48 passages from Forms 1 and 2 combined:

1. Gray-Leary formula, reported by Gray and Leary (40), .64 ± .09;

2. Dale-Chall formula, .61 ± .09;

3. Flesch formula, .55 ± .10.

Again, none of the differences was significant.

Note that the highest correlation was for the Gray-Leary formula on the Gray-Leary test. This is not surprising, since the statistical procedure involved in developing a regression equation would tend to make it so; it does not mean that the higher correlation represents that degree of superiority over the other formulas. Other considerations in interpretation of these correlations are the small number of passages (16) in Ojemann's test and the use of adults with limited reading ability in Gray and Leary's work.

James Brown (364) reported on another use of readability formulas with reading tests. He compared Parts I and II of Test A of the Harvard University Reading Course; both were of the same length and covered the same subject matter. He found the difference between them of 24 points on Flesch's 1948 formula was paralleled by a difference of 8 points in comprehension. He concluded that readability formulas can help both student and teacher in using and in selecting reading materials.

Charles Swanson and Harland Fox (415) made a thorough experimental test of the validity of formulas using a monthly paper sent to employees of a company. They prepared easier and harder versions of 12 articles with judges agreeing that content was not changed. The easier versions had average scores of 73 and 7–8 grade on the 1948 Flesch and Dale-Chall formulas; the harder, 59 and 11–12 grade. The versions were then randomly sent to employees, who later took a 43-item retention test if they had read a particular article, and a 10-item comprehension test before and after re-reading the articles. No difference was found in retention scores or readership, but the difference in comprehension favoring those who read the easy version was significant.

Swanson and Fox comment that the relatively high interest in the articles (60% readership) may have prevented differences in readership of the easier and harder versions from showing up. They also feel that the lack of differences in retention may be due to motivational factors inherent in content when free choice of reading is permitted. They feel that readability may be more critical where reading is required.

Robert Pitcher (409) also made an experimental validity test on adult materials, using the 1948 Flesch formula. He used a total of nine passages, with three levels of difficulty: 30 to 40, 50 to 60, and 70 to 80, in formula score; and three kinds of content: familiar, abstract, and technical. Subjects first read a practice passage, then three test passages with a 10-item comprehension test following each. Only "good readers" who scored 70% or above on each of the three tests were used in the final tabulation. The following results were found:

(1) No significant differences appeared in percentage of comprehension scores. This, he felt, was due to the use of good readers only.

(2) A change in subject matter (familiar, abstract, or technical) resulted in differences more significant than a change in formula score. All the familiar passages were significantly more readable than the technical and abstract passages.

Carolyn Dunlap (369) also conducted an experimental study of the relationship of readability measures to comprehension, but with eighth-grade pupils rather than adults as subjects. She used 24 hundred-word samples from the book *Davy Crockett,* with 10 questions on each passage serving as a "Direct Comprehension Check," or D.C.C. She also applied the measures of Beal and Boder (not actually readability measures); Dale and Chall; Flesch 1943, 1948, and 1950; Gray and Leary Long and Short formulas; Johnson; Kessler; and Lorge 1939 and 1948. She reached the following conclusions regarding validity on the basis of her study:

(1) The book, *Davy Crockett,* was found to be too difficult for eighth-grade pupils by the D.C.C.

(2) Formula ratings for the total book ranged through easy, fairly easy, average, sixth grade, seventh grade, to 8.6 by 1943 Flesch formula and 10.1 by Dale-Chall formula.

(3) The Dale-Chall formula was the only one which gave a rating for the book comparable to the D.C.C. The 1948 Flesch formula was one of the easiest to apply and also ranked samples adequately in comparison with the D.C.C. ranking.

(4) The 1943 and 1948 Flesch, 1939 Lorge, Dale-Chall, and Kessler measures gave higher correlations than the other techniques when ranking of passages was compared to D.C.C. ranking.

(5) These findings, plus the writer's evaluation based on application of the measures, indicated that the Dale-Chall, 1948 Flesch, 1939 Lorge, and Kessler techniques were the most practical and reliable for the materials used in the study.

Klare, Mabry, and Gustafson (386 or 388) reported another experimental study of the effect of style difficulty (readability) upon immediate retention (comprehension) and delayed retention. An Air Force "study guide," or technical training lesson, in aircraft mechanics was prepared in two versions, "easy" and "hard." These were then tested along with the standard version. Three formulas were used to measure the differences in the versions, the Dale-Chall, 1948 Flesch Reading Ease, and 1950 Flesch Level of Abstraction.

The easy version was rated at 7–8 grade level, the standard at about 11–12 grade level, and the hard at about 16 + grade level. All versions had the same number of words, the same technical terms, and were judged by technical experts to be the same in content. Subjects were airmen in aircraft mechanic training and airmen who had just been inducted into the Air Force. Both groups were given a 50-item test for immediate retention, and the inductees were given the same test two weeks later as a measure of delayed retention.

For the trainee subjects, no immediate retention test-score differences appeared between the versions. But there *were* differences for the inductees on immediate retention, the easy version producing significantly higher scores than the standard, and the standard producing significantly higher scores than the hard. Differences in delayed retention were in the same direction, but the over-all difference was significant in only one of several analyses. The authors attributed the lack of difference with the trainees to their high level of background information. The material had been chosen to avoid overlap with previous material, but trial administration of the test with several groups *before* the study guide was read yielded, on an average, one-half to two-thirds correct items. With inductees, where background information was low, consistently significant differences in retention were found for several different analyses. The authors gave several possible reasons for the lack of greater differences in delayed retention scores, including the difficulty of the test, the motivation of the subjects, and particularly, the long interval between tests.

Klare, Shuford, and Nichols (389) studied how style difficulty (or readability), practice, and ability of subjects were related to immediate retention scores. The passage used was again taken from the technical training study guide mentioned above, with easy and hard versions prepared at

7–8 and 16 + grade levels (no standard version was used in this study). An eye-movement camera was used to present experimental materials to subjects, who were airmen in aircraft mechanic training. Modified recall (fill-in, or completion) and recognition tests were used to measure retention.

All of the mean values were in the expected direction; that is, use of an easy style, or three readings, or high ability produced higher recall and recognition scores than use of a hard style, or one reading, or low ability. The easy style produced significant differences only on the recall test; the other effects were significant on both tests. The authors point out that the recall tests were closer to a "comprehension" measure than the recognition tests, where the subject was asked merely to pick out technical terms he had read and where the correct words were common to both versions. The authors also point out that it was necessary to induce a strong "set to learn" in subjects before test scores were high enough and reliable enough for measurement. This increased motivation was provided by a preliminary reading and a difficult test in which few answers could be correctly given; mere exhortation to "work hard" did not produce such a set.

A related study by Klare, Mabry, and Gustafson (386 or 387) concerned the effect of human interest upon immediate retention of technical material. The same study guide mentioned previously was used, but was presented in a high human interest version — "interesting" as measured by Flesch's human interest formula — as well as the standard version, which had low human interest — "dull" by Flesch's formula. No significant difference appeared in immediate retention test scores for the two versions as measured by a 50-item test.

Margaret Peterson (408) compared 1948 Flesch readability

formula scores with a test of reading comprehension based on "popular" material. She condensed and rewrote *Reader's Digest* anecdotes to yield five 100-word passages each at 10 equidistant readability score levels from 5 to 95. Ten passages judged approximately equal in interest (one at each level) were then selected for use. High school students first took the *General Reading and Comprehension* subtests of the *Survey Section: Upper Level of the Diagnostic Reading Tests* (DRT); then they read the 10 passages, after each of which six multiple-choice questions were given. A significant correlation of .69 was found between the comprehension test score over the passages and DRT scores. Six out of nine *t*-tests of score differences at adjacent levels of the comprehension test were significant. Peterson concluded that the Flesch formula adequately estimates the comparative difficulty of "popular" adult reading materials.

James Marshall (401) used the 1948 Flesch formula to determine the readability of seven physics textbooks approved for use in New York State high schools. He used a standard passage, score 47, and rewrote it in an easier version, score 65. Two groups of high school physics students were used in the study; one read the original version and one the easier version, and both took the same comprehension test over the passages. No significant difference in comprehension was found between the original and rewritten passages. The author concludes that the Flesch formula is not useful for measuring the readability of science materials.

The validity studies using reading comprehension (or retention) criteria have been summarized in Table 2. The results of the studies have been characterized as "positive" (meaning the presence of a reasonably high relationship between readability indices and comprehension scores); "indeterminate"; or "negative" (lack of a reasonably high relationship). The assignments to one of these categories are, of

TABLE 2

VALIDITY STUDIES USING READING COMPREHENSION CRITERIA

Author(s)	Bibliography Number	Publication Date	Nature of Study	Results*
1. Orndorff	407	1925	Effect of short vs. long sentences	Negative
2. Gibbons	375	1941	Disarranged sentences	Indeterminate
3. Foster	374	1931	Simplified vocabulary versions	Negative
4. Kueneman	391	1931	Simplified vocabulary versions	Negative
5. Clarke	368	1933	Simplified vocabulary versions	Negative
6. Nolte	406	1937	Simplified vocabulary versions	Negative
7. Robinson	410	1940	Simplified vocabulary versions	Positive
8. Stadtlander	115	1940	Passages differing in readability	Positive
9. Miller	402	1946	Formula prediction of test results	Positive
10. Latimer	392	1948	Formula prediction of publishers' grade placements	Positive
11. Griffin	377	1949	Version with better readability scores	Positive
			Version with better human interest scores	
12. Hites	382	1950	Version with shorter sentences	Negative
			Version with fewer difficult words	Negative
13. Klare	475	1950	Correlations of formula scores and test scores	r's from .55 to .87 (Positive)
14. Brown	364	1952	Version with better readability scores	Positive
15. Swanson and Fox	415	1953	Version with better readability scores	Positive
16. Pitcher	409	1953	Version with better readability scores	Indeterminate
17. Dunlap	369	1954	Version with better readability scores	Positive
18. Klare, Mabry and Gustafson	386	1954	Version with better readability scores	Positive
19. Klare, Shuford and Nichols	389	1957	Version with better readability scores	Positive
20. Klare, Mabry and Gustafson	386	1954	Version with better human interest scores	Negative
21. Peterson	408	1956	Correlations between comprehension scores and passages of differing readability	.69 (Positive)
22. Marshall	401	1957	Version with better readability scores	Negative

* The results of each study have been labeled "positive," "negative," or "indeterminate," depending primarily upon the author's interpretation of whether or not a high, low, or uncertain relationship was found between readability indices and comprehension scores. Where correlation coefficients (r) are concerned, those above .50 have arbitrarily been considered positive, those at or below .50 negative.

course, judgments, and qualifying details have had to be omitted from the table. However, the author's interpretation of the results has generally been followed. In addition, correlations greater than .50 have arbitrarily been called positive; those equal to or less than .50, negative. The reader should recognize that interpretations of the results other than those of the author are possible, and that in experimental work on so complex a subject as writing, these interpretations may be equally plausible. For example, versions which differ in readability may also inadvertently differ in such characteristics as organization and emphasis, and the results found may have been due to these changes. Nevertheless, adhering to the author's interpretation unless negative evidence was available seemed the best procedure. It was felt, furthermore, that the over-all picture presented here, however crude, would be helpful.

The basic results of this analysis show 12 studies judged positive, 9 negative, and 2 indeterminate (note that Hites' study has two parts, making the total here 23 rather than 22). Two studies, those of Griffin (377) and Klare, Mabry, and Gustafson (386 or 387) involved "human interest," which is not strictly comparable with readability. Removing them from consideration makes the figures 11, 8, and 2. Note also that in many studies only one readability factor, vocabulary or sentences, was varied, and of these 1 was positive, 7 negative, and 1 indeterminate. All work except that of Hites, incidentally, was published in 1941 or earlier. In the later studies in which readability as a whole (both words and sentences, presumably) was varied or measured, the figures were positive 10, negative 1, and indeterminate 1. All of these studies except that of Stadtlander appeared in 1946 or later.

One might conclude from these results that variation of one factor was not sufficient to provide increased comprehension, but that a combination of the two was. A conservative interpretation would be that readability formula scores are related to, and can be used to predict, comprehension and retention under proper conditions, but that automatic gains should not be expected.

Reading Speed Criteria. Reading speed (or reading efficiency more generally) has been used only rather recently as a criterion in validity studies. It is, perhaps, not so readily associated with the notion of readability as comprehension is. Yet, on the other hand, reading difficulty is logically related to speed of reading, so that the connection seems reasonable and makes it seem surprising that reading speed was not used earlier or more often as a criterion. At any rate, tests of the relationship of reading speed to readability have been made more often recently, especially in conjunction with tests of comprehension. Many of the studies to be reported here are therefore simply the appropriate aspects of those described in the foregoing section.

Apparently the first suggestion that readability was related to reading speed came from Rudolf Flesch (372). He used data from a study in which Carmichael and Dearborn found a higher average reading rate, in terms of lower blink rate and smaller number of fixations and regressions, for a selection from a popular novel than from a classic. He applied his 1948 formula to the two selections, and found that the one from the popular novel gave a higher readability score. This indicated to him that his formula could predict reading speed.

Hackman and Kershner (97), in the study described earlier, showed experimentally that the elements commonly used in readability formulas were related to reading speed. They suggested the increased use of reading speed as a criterion because of its greater convenience over the use of comprehension measures.

The study of James Brown (364) indicated that a difference of 24 points on the 1948 Flesch scale could result in an increase of 70 words per minute in rate, as well as an increase in comprehension score. Robert Pitcher (409) also discovered that speed of reading was related to level of readability. He found significant differences in speed between passages at Flesch scores of 70–80 versus 50–60 and 30–40 versus 50–60. Another interesting finding of Pitcher is that when reading rate is computed in terms of "ems" per minute the results are different from using words per minute. Differences due to readability that were clear in words per minute either disappeared or became unpredictable when measured in ems per minute.

The studies of Klare and associates also showed reading speed to be a function of readability when measured in regular ways. When easy, standard, and hard versions were used, number of words read paralleled these differences (386 or 388). When shorter easy and hard passages were read before an eye-movement camera (389) the easy version produced significantly more words read per second and per fixation. Higher ability of subjects and three readings also produced increases as compared to lower ability and one reading. It is rather interesting to note that the strong "set to learn" described earlier, while producing increased retention, also resulted in a *decrease* in number of words read per second and per fixation compared to a weak "set to learn." An unpublished study indicated, furthermore, that when rate is measured as inches (of text) read per fixation, rather than words, the differences due to readability tend to disappear; differences in inches read per second, as well as words, tend to remain. Comparison of a version high in human interest with one that was low (386 or 387) yielded results that were equivocal but favored the high version very slightly.

TABLE 3

VALIDITY STUDIES USING READING SPEED CRITERIA

Author(s)	Bibliography Number	Publication Date	Nature of Study	Results*
1. Flesch	372	1949	Version with better readability scores	Positive
2. Hackman and Kershner	97	1951	Version with better readability scores (on various formula factors)	Positive
3. Brown	364	1952	Version with better readability scores	Positive
4. Pitcher	409	1953	Version with better readability scores	Positive
5. Klare, Mabry, and Gustafson	386	1954	Version with better readability scores	Positive
6. Klare, Shuford, and Nichols	389	1957	Version with better readability scores	Positive (both words/sec. and words/fixation)
7. Klare, Mabry, and Gustafson	386	1954	Version with better human interest scores	Indeterminate

* See TABLE 2 footnote, page 133.

The validity studies using reading speed (or efficiency) criteria are summarized in Table 3. As before, they are presented in as concise fashion as possible and under the same conditions. The results indicate that six studies gave positive results, no studies gave negative results, and one study was indeterminate; this last study, based upon analysis of the effect of human interest (Klare, Mabry, and Gustafson, (386 or 387), might well be eliminated from consideration. The general results indicate clearly that readability and reading speed are related. This measure appears to be both a sensitive and consistent criterion.

Judgment Criteria. Among the earliest bases used for checking the validity of readability formulas was expert judgment. Subsequently the judgment of readers came to be used also. And, as the use of judgments of all kinds increased, the complexity of the statistical treatments and the range of measures employed also increased, so that it seems fair to say that some of the most adequate studies of formula validity involved judgments.

Bergman (20), in the first published study known to the writer, analyzed the grade placements of 70 supplementary reading books and story books using his early version of the Washburne-Morphett formula. He then correlated these values with teachers' judgments, and found a correlation between the two of .69.

Three studies that followed using judgment criteria can be considered only tangential checks on formula validity. James Wert (419) reported a correlation of only .40 between Gray-Leary scores and the quality of magazines based on an analysis of readers. Mabel Jackman (383) found an even lower and negative correlation, − .129, between judgments of maturity of books of fiction and Gray-Leary readability scores. She felt there was little, if any, relationship between maturity of content and her measures of structural difficulty. Cyrilla Walther (418), on the other hand, found that the ranking of magazines in difficulty according to Gray-Leary and Washburne-Morphett scores agreed fairly closely with the cultural rankings of Morgan and Leahy. She found also a high correlation of .80 between the readability scores of the September and January issues of the magazines she rated.

J. Allen Figurel (371) also made an indirect check on formula validity by the use of judgments. He analyzed seven classic books with the Yoakam formula, then compared the grade placements with the preferences of ninth-grade pupils who were poor readers. He found a "high correlation" between the difficulty level of a classic and its preference rating, indicating a relationship between readability and popularity.

Sig Guckenheimer (379) made a more direct check on the

relationship of readability and judgments, using pamphlets on international affairs that he analyzed with the soon-to-appear Dale-Chall formula. He found them too hard for the average high school student, and by implication for the average adult. He also found a correlation of .86 between Dale-Chall ratings and the difficulty judgments of seven experts (four teachers and three readability analysts) on 36 paragraphs. Dale and Chall themselves, in their original presentation of their formula (23), report a correlation of .90 between teachers' judgments of difficulty of 75 foreign affairs passages and Dale-Chall grade levels. Also, they report that Dale-Chall grade levels on 55 passages from a health education text correlated .92 with teachers' and readability experts' judgments of difficulty. These latter grade levels also correlated .90 with the reading grades of children and adults who could answer three-fourths of the questions on 30 health passages.

As mentioned earlier, Stevens and Stone (68) found Flesch 1943 formula scores on undergraduate and graduate psychology textbooks generally agreed with classroom experience and judgment of teachers and students. The exceptions they reported became, as previously indicated, one of the reasons for Flesch's formula revision presented in 1948. Alberta Gilinsky (376) also made a study of Flesch formula validity using psychological materials in part of her work. She first used prose samples from such varied sources as pulp fiction and technical treatises to build a Thurstone scale as a criterion of validity. Subsequently, to rule out the interaction effect of subject matter with readability, she used a second series of prose passages on rod and cone vision. Correlations between readability judgments and Flesch counts, by 1943 and 1948 formulas, ranged from .61 to .84.

A. E. Tubbs (see Vernon, 417) applied both the 1948 Flesch and the Dale-Chall formula to 30 secondary school geography textbooks. He found "general concordance," for most of the books, with gradings for difficulty given by teachers. Russell and Fea (412) evaluated six readability formulas against the grade-placement judgments of 63 children's librarians on 12 juvenile books. Actually, the converse also appeared to be emphasized, the judgments being validated against the formulas (see Russell and Merrill, 411). At any rate, it was found that the mean formula ratings based on the Dale-Chall, 1948 Flesch, Lewerenz, 1948 Lorge, Washburne-Morphett, and Yoakam formulas were very similar to the librarians' average ratings. The Dale-Chall, Flesch, and Lorge formulas were considered about equally good measures of difficulty, though the Flesch formula did not give the same comparative ratings as the other two. The Washburne-Morphett formula yielded ratings about two grades harder than the Dale-Chall.

Another study using judgmental criteria of readability was that of Hackman and Kershner (97), mentioned earlier. These authors used reader judgments, paired-comparison method, to study a number of factors commonly used in formulas. They found a high relationship between these factors and judgments, suggesting that a set of reader judgments might profitably serve as a readability criterion.

Pitcher (409), in addition to his checks on comprehension and rate of reading of passages of three different levels of readability and three different contents, also obtained subjects' personal reactions to the interest and the difficulty of the passages. He found a correlation of .42 between judged difficulty and performance, .31 between interest and performance, and .59 between interest and difficulty. Of special note here is the use of an interest judgment.

Klare and associates used a judgment criterion similar to Pitcher's. In the study (386 or 388) of passages at three levels of style difficulty (readability), they presented split versions in which one-half of the passage was presented at one of the levels and the other half at another of the levels. Subjects were asked which half they thought easier to read and which half more pleasant to read; this was done only if they had previously indicated they noticed a difference. It was found that content played a much larger part in pre-ferences than style, but the use of split versions permitted equating for content in order to study the effect of style. Style had the predicted effect, the number of judgments of easier and more pleasant being significantly greater for levels of style from "easy" to "hard." Tetrachoric correlation co-efficients of judgments of "easier" and "more pleasant" ranged from .86 to .97. The judgment of the easy style as more pleasant was made approximately as often by high as by low ability subjects.

In the subsequent study of human interest (386 or 387), it was found that subjects consistently preferred the *low* level of human interest, or impersonal style, to the high level, or personal style. As before, content played a larger part than human interest in the preferences, but this was equated by the use of split versions. The authors commented that the subjects may have disliked the personal style because technical material is usually written in an impersonal style.

Raymond Bernberg (362) made a somewhat different use of judgment criteria by studying the effect of differences in written material, socio-economic status, and sex upon judg-ments of reading ease and human interest of magazine arti-cles. He then also compared these judgments to 1948 Flesch formula scores. He found that the lower the socio-economic status, the harder and less interesting the material was judged; type of material and sex had no significant effects. The Flesch formulas were found to yield lower (more severe) values than the judges; the author also concluded that they were not sensitive to differences in the important cognitive and motivational areas of reading.

Certainly one of the more interesting uses of judgment

criteria was that of Roy Carter (365) in applying Flesch's 1948 Reading Ease and Human Interest formulas and his newer "r" (Realism) and "e" (Energy) formulas to cross-cultural materials. The study was designed to evaluate eight pamphlets distributed by the U. S. Information Agency to Filipinos who read English as a second language. It was found that judgments of difficulty correlated .79 with Reading Ease scores, and judgments of interestingness correlated .90 with Human Interest scores and .77 with Realism scores.

Robert Lockman (393) also made a somewhat unusual use of judgment criteria. He constructed a rating scale to measure the understandability of prose. He felt it should supplement readability measures for highly selected groups where readability scores were not accurate or relevant. To make a comparison he correlated Flesch scores with understandability ratings of Naval Aviation cadets on nine sets of directions for standard psychological tests. He found a rank-order correlation of − .65 and a product-moment correlation of − .52, the former significantly different from zero but the latter not. He concluded that his understandability ratings and Flesch scores were not measuring the same thing; it might perhaps also be said that his correlations showed a fairly high relationship.

Textbooks were used as the subject matter in a study using judgments as readability criteria. R. L. Herrington and G. G. Mallinson (381) compared the estimates of 92 reading experts with scores from the Flesch, Lorge, and Dale-Chall formulas. The materials used were 199 samples from 39 science texts used in grades 4–8. It was found that the formulas judged the grade level of texts much more consistently than the experts, leading the authors to conclude that both experts and teachers should use formulas in conjunction with their own judgment.

The validity studies using judgment criteria are presented

in a summary fashion in Table 4 under the same conditions as for Tables 2 and 3. They have been judged to yield positive results in 13 cases, negative results in 3, and indeterminate results in 3. Once again removing the studies involving human interest (Klare, Mabry, and Gustafson, 387; Carter, 365) reduces the figures to 12, 2, and 3. Most of the studies using judgment criteria seem to provide evidence for the validity of readability formulas as predictors of readability. They also provide evidence that more readable material, in the sense of easier style, is clearly preferred to less readable.

Readership Criteria. When readability formulas were first developed, most research workers felt that their chief use would be in predicting the comprehensibility of written material. Therefore, most of the early validity studies involved a criterion of either comprehension or judged difficulty. The use of reading speed, though not begun until relatively recently, was certainly reasonable on a logical basis and therefore the positive results found were not too surprising. The use of readership as a validity criterion was not as predictable, and therefore when the first studies appeared showing readability and readership to be related, they caused a considerable stir.

The credit for the first work belongs to Donald R. Murphy, then editor of the magazine *Wallaces Farmer*. In his first study (404), he used a split-run of one article. One-half the issues carried a version that rated 3.66 on Flesch's 1943 formula, which is approximately *Reader's Digest* level, or around eighth to ninth grade; the other half carried a 1.5 version, which is around sixth-grade level. He found that readership of the easy copy was 18% greater than that of the hard, the added readers appearing to be new readers rather than just previous part-readers. Since changes from Flesch scores of 5.03 to 3.92, 3.32, and 2.47 were also tried but with-

TABLE 4

Validity Studies Using Judgment Criteria

Author(s)	Bibliography Number	Publication Date	Nature of Study	Results*
1. Bergman	20	1936	Correlation of formula scores and teacher judgments of readability	$r = .69$ (Positive)
2. Wert	419	1937	Correlation of readability scores and quality judgments	$r = .40$ (Negative)
3. Jackman	383	1941	Correlation of readability scores and maturity judgments	$r = -.13$ (Negative)
4. Walther	418	1943	Ranks based on readability scores and ranks based on cultural rankings	Positive
5. Figurel	371	1942	Comparison of readability scores and pupil preferences	Positive
6. Guckenheimer	379	1947	Correlation of readability scores and expert judgments	$r = .85$ (Positive)
7. Dale and Chall	23	1948	Correlation of readability scores and teacher and expert judgments	$r = .90$ to $.92$ (Positive)
8. Stevens and Stone	68	1947	Comparison of readability ranks and student and teacher judgments	Indeterminate
9. Gilinsky	376	1948	Correlation of readability scores and student judgments	$r = .61$ to $.84$ (Positive)
10. Tubbs (Vernon)	417	1950	Comparison of readability scores and teacher judgments	Positive
11. Russell and Fea	412	1951	Comparison of readability scores and librarian judgments	Positive
Russell and Merrill	411	1951		
12. Hackman and Kershner	97	1951	Comparison of readability factor scores and reader judgments	Positive
13. Pitcher	409	1953	Comparison of various reader judgments	Indeterminate
14. Klare, Mabry, and Gustafson	386	1954	Comparison of readability scores and preferences	Positive
15. Klare, Mabry, and Gustafson	386	1954	Comparison of human interest scores and preferences	Negative
16. Bernberg	362	1954	Comparison of readability scores and reader characteristics	Indeterminate
17. Carter	365	1955	Comparison of readability and human interest scores and reader judgments	$r = .77$ to $.90$ (Positive)
18. Lockman	393	1956	Comparison of readability scores and understandability ratings	$r = -.52$ to $-.65$ (Positive)
19. Herrington and Mallinson	381	1958	Comparison of readability scores and expert judgments	Positive

* See TABLE 2 footnote, page 133.

out gain in readership, he concluded that a simplification to Flesch scores of 1 to 2 was necessary.

In a subsequent article (405), Murphy described further results of his split-run test, using four articles in both 3.5 and 1.5 versions. He took great care not to change anything except readability, keeping headlines, illustrations, subject-matter, and position the same. He found increases of 45% for a nylon article and 66% for a corn article. Most of the new readers appeared to be under 35 years old, and age was found more important than education.

Murphy was sufficiently impressed with these results that he decreased the usual readability level of *Wallaces Farmer* from 3 to 6 down to 1 to 2.5. Not all writers have been impressed, however; Lorge (448) and Chall (469) have pointed out that the gains in readership might well have been due to differences in organization, or to a personal, concrete, anecdotal approach, rather than readability. Whatever the reason for the gains, the effect was immediate. New articles on readability and readership appeared very quickly, and a report of Murphy's research was even rewritten later for another journal (Lyman, 397).

The first studies following Murphy's were not directly concerned with readership as related to readability. In the first, Wilbur Schramm (413) found that greater stylistic readability, as measured by Flesch's formula, seemed to encourage greater depth of reading. In the second (see Macfadden Publications, 398), analysis of more than 1000 advertisements of one-third page or larger was made over a period of three years. It was found that the three read most had a 1943 Flesch rating of 1.12 — comfortable reading for about 80% of the population — while the three read least had a rating of 3.36 — comfortable reading for less than 35% (see also Flesch, 257, for similar data on advertising).

The first of a number of studies more directly concerned

with readability and newspaper readership is that of Bernard
Feld (370). He grouped 101 stories from the *Birmingham
News* into those with high Flesch scores, requiring ninth-
grade education or more, and those with low scores, requiring eighth-grade education or less. He then compared them
for readership and found differences of from 20 to 75%
favoring the low score versions. Various categories of stories
were compared, i.e., local news, local features, short news
stories from the wire services, etc. A number of rules were
followed to neutralize the effects of all factors except those
measured by the Flesch formula. It should be noted that
the *actual percentage* of readership of both high and low
versions was quite small, so that the percentages of change
appeared unusually large. On the other hand, the gains in
all categories of stories were consistent; and furthermore,
as the author points out, on a large-circulation newspaper
only a small actual percentage gain can mean a greatly increased number of readers.

Charles Swanson (414), in a controlled split-run experiment, found increased readership to be related to increased
readability. He developed an easy version of a story with 131
syllables per 100 words and a hard one with 173 syllables,
then distributed each randomly to 125 families. To test
whether formula differences could be used to predict readership, he applied the original and revised Flesch, Dale-Chall,
Gray-Leary, and Lorge formulas to each version.

A survey of readers taken 30 hours after distribution
showed a gain for the easier over the harder version of 93%
in total paragraphs read, 83% in mean number of paragraphs
read, and 82% in number of respondents reading every paragraph. The difference in median number of paragraphs
read was found to be highly significant.

In a similar study, Merritt Ludwig (396) compared readability and readership in a split-run in *Wallaces Farmer;*
word difficulty was changed in two versions and human

interest in two other versions. The hard version had a score of 60 on Flesch's 1948 formula and the easy version a score of 82; the change in syllables per 100 words was from 158 to 132. The easy version produced a change in readership over the hard that was significant at the 10% level. The low interest version, in turn, had a Flesch formula human interest score of 30 and the high version a score of 72; this difference appeared to have little, if any, effect upon readership.

Ludwig concluded that when interest in content is high, "hard" words and "human interest" may have less effect on readership than content. This, he felt, may have happened in his study, since his topics were of the highest reader interest. He considered the relationship between readability and readership to be secure, whereas certain levels of human interest might repel rather than attract readers.

John Harvey (380) made an unusual use of the readership criterion in studying the content characteristics of best-selling novels. He compared pairs of novels that were the same in theme, approximate date of publication, marketing factors employed, wordage, order of publication, and favorability of reviews, but in which one member of the pair sold at least four times as many copies as the other. Sixteen variables emerged as important in distinguishing the best sellers from the poor sellers, and one of the most critical of these was readability, as measured by Flesch's formula.

E. B. Knauft (390) reported a study in which the results of content and readability analyses made six months apart were related to several aspects of readability of a house organ. Between the two dates there was a change in the amount of space devoted to various kinds of articles and also a reportedly "marked" increase in Flesch Reading Ease and Human Interest scores in some of them. It was found that, while frequency of readership did not increase, the percentage of respondents taking the publication home regularly increased significantly. Also, the percentage of people re-ing it as "excellent" increased significantly, and the number regarding it as "fair" correspondingly decreased.

It is difficult to determine whether the increased acceptance found was due to the change in allocation of space or to increased reading ease and human interest. The change in these latter variables seems too small to be responsible, ranging only from about 3 to 6 points in Reading Ease score and 4 to 19 points in Human Interest score. However, the author reports that the figures may be to some extent "misleading."

In an analysis of seven leading employee publications made by the Association of National Advertisers (361), readability measurements were one of many kinds of analysis made. It was concluded that in the publications studied there was little, if any, relationship between readability and readership. The average grade level of all publications was "some high school," as measured by Flesch's 1948 formula.

A summary of the validity studies involving readership criteria is presented in Table 5. Five of the studies were judged to yield positive results, 2 to give negative results, and 3 to have indeterminate results. The basis for these judgments is the same as for the preceding analyses reported in Tables 2, 3, and 4 — the author's interpretation of the results. No independent judgment based upon percentage increase in readership is implied. The total is greater than the number of studies listed because one study, that of Ludwig (396), had two parts; if that part involving human interest is removed as before, the results became 5, 1, and 3. Some of these studies provide conflicting data regarding the relation between readership and readability. Most of the studies report positive results, but the nature of some of them make readability only one of several possible causes of the results.

Listenability Criteria. The specific criteria used for predicting listenability are basically the same, largely comprehension and judgment, as those used in some of the studies described previously.

TABLE 5

VALIDITY STUDIES USING READERSHIP CRITERIA

Author(s)	Bibli- ography Number	Publi- cation Date	Nature of Study	Results*
1. Murphy	404 405	1947 1947	Newspaper versions differing in readability	18–66 % increase (Positive)
2. Schramm	413	1947	Newspaper versions differing in readability	Indeterminate
3. Macfadden Publications	398	1947	Advertisements differing in readability	35 % increase (Positive)
4. Feld	370	1948	Newspaper versions differing in readability	20–75 % increase (Positive)
5. Swanson	414	1948	Newspaper versions differing in readability	82–93 % increase (Positive)
6. Ludwig	396	1949	Newspaper versions differing in readability Newspaper versions differing in human interest	Indeterminate Negative
7. Harvey	380	1949	Readability and sales of novels	Positive
8. Knauft	390	1951	House organ versions differing in readability and human interest	Indeterminate
9. Assn. of National Advertisers	361	1953	Advertisements differing in readability	Negative

* See TABLE 2 footnote, page 133.

Jeanne Chall and Harold Dial (367) used both listener understanding and interest as criteria. The 1943 Flesch formula and the Dale-Chall formula were applied to 18 newscasts heard by college freshmen. The following correlations were found between readability scores and (1) comprehension scores — Dale-Chall, .74, and Flesch, .72; (2) listeners' judgments of understanding — Dale-Chall, .76, and Flesch, .63; and (3) listeners' judgments of interest — Dale-Chall, .77, and Flesch, .63. It is also rather interesting to note that judgments of interest and of difficulty correlated .93.

Robert Nuckols (300) applied the 1943 Flesch formula to 315 questions used by the major polling organizations in English-speaking countries. In the process, he correlated scores for Flesch's sentence-length and affix factors plus total formula scores with the percentage of "Don't Know" answers to 183 questions. He found coefficients ranging from only .01 to —.13. Klare (384) made a similar study, relating the percentage of "indefinite answers" — "Don't Know," "Can't Say," "Undecided," etc. — in split-run questions to Flesch formula scores. He found a significant relationship, but the subsequent product-moment correlation between scores and percentage of indefinite answers to 138 questions was only .25.

James Young (421) studied the relationship of readability and listening difficulty. He used four versions of a news story about UNESCO; they were rated at college level, 9–10 grade, 7–8 grade, and 5–6 grade by the Dale-Chall formula. High school students serving as subjects answered 20 objective questions and also indicated their judgments of understanding on a 5-point scale. The results showed no clear-cut evidence of decreasing comprehension with increasing difficulty. It should be mentioned, however, that the groups hearing each version were small, and also that no attempt was made to check test scores on a control group prior to the experiment. It seems highly possible that many of the questions might have been answered before hearing the newscast at all, especially in view of the high average comprehension score of 62.5% after only *one* hearing.

Francis Cartier (366), in a study that can be compared to Young's, came to an almost opposite conclusion. He prepared three versions of each of seven stories with Flesch Human Interest scores of 15, 30, and 60, respectively. The seven stories themselves varied by seven steps of difficulty from Flesch's "very easy" to "very difficult."

Cartier found that human interest had no significant effect upon listenability, as measured by a 15-item, multiple-choice test on each story version. This result held regardless of level of difficulty of the story. The difficulty predictions did appear to be fairly consistent with comprehension scores over the range used, although this was not the object of investigation in the study and was not separately analyzed.

William Allen (360) also found that comprehension can be affected by changes in readability. He wrote four commentaries for each of two films; as rated by the Flesch Reading Ease and Human Interest formulas, they were (1) fifth grade — very interesting, (2) fifth grade — dull, (3) seventh grade — very interesting, and (4) seventh grade — dull. Sixth-grade students took both a pre-test and a post-test, and effects were measured as gains between the two tests.

Allen's results showed that greater readability of commentaries produced increased learning of the factual content of the films; greater human interest produced increased learning only on the film that lent itself naturally to such humanizing. Three readability formulas, the Flesch Reading Ease, Dale-Chall, and Lorge were about equally effective in predicting comparative readability even though they differed from each other in grade-placement ratings. The individual style factor that showed the highest relationship to gain was sentence length, with a correlation coefficient of .61.

Orville Manion (400) again studied the relationship of readability measures to listener difficulty, but in a group discussion situation. The style factors from the 1948 Flesch, Lorge, and Dale-Chall formulas were related to three criteria of listener difficulty: "listener understanding during discussion," "listener understanding following discussion," and "clarification requested." It was found that no significant relationship existed between the style factors and the three criteria.

A final study of listenability was Rudolf Vancura's application (416) of the Flesch Reading Ease and Human Interest formulas to television programs. He measured five 100-word samples from the programs and then related the scores to Telepulse ratings. He found significant correlations between

TABLE 6

VALIDITY STUDIES USING LISTENABILITY CRITERIA

Author(s)	Bibli- ography Number	Publi- cation Date	Nature of Study	Results*
1. Chall and Dial	367	1948	Correlations of readability scores with understanding scores, interest judgments	.63–.74 (Positive)
2. Nuckols	300	1949	Readability and "Don't Know" answers to public opinion questions	Negative
3 Klare	384	1950	Readability and "Indefinite" answers to public opinion questions	Indeterminate
4. Young	421	1950	Readability and comprehension scores and judgments	Negative
5. Cartier	366	1951	Readability and comprehension test scores	Positive
			Human interest and comprehension test scores	Negative
6. Allen	360	1952	Readability and comprehension test scores	Positive
			Human interest and comprehension test scores	Indeterminate
7. Manion	400	1954	Readability and reader "judgments"	Negative
8. Vancura	416	1955	Readability and television viewer ratings	Negative
			Human interest and television viewer ratings	Negative

* See TABLE 2 footnote, page 133.

Reading Ease and Human Interest scores in several comparisons, but no correlations with Telepulse ratings were significant.

Table 6 presents a summary of validity studies using listenability criteria.* The results were judged as positive in

---

* Two references were uncovered too late in the process of preparing the book for publication to be included in the text or tables. These are number 363, by Beryl Blain, and number 403, by John Moldstad. The results of the former study should be considered negative evidence of validity, and the results of the latter indeterminate. These results are generally in line with those of the other studies, and therefore do not change the conclusions reached regarding listenability in any essential way.

3 cases, negative in 6, and indeterminate in 2. Once again, studies with more than one part make this total greater than the total number of studies. Removing the studies involving a human interest factor (Cartier, 366; Allen, 360; Vancura, 416) reduces the values to 3, 4, and 1. The relationship of readability scores to listenability criteria is thus not clear. While some studies indicate a significant relationship, others contradict this. As in the case of readership, further studies are needed.

Writer Criteria. Surely one of the most surprising kinds of relationships to be studied in the evaluation of readability formulas is that between the intellectual or educational level of writers and the readability of their writings. This relationship was first noted by Rowena Wyant (420), who reported a high positive relationship between the educational level of the writers of letters to U. S. Congressmen and the readability level of the letters themselves, as measured by Lorge's formula.

Lorge and Kruglov made two separate studies (394, 395) of essays written by eighth and ninth graders applying for admission to the Bronx High School of Science. They compared the Lorge formula scores for the essays to the writers' intelligence, and at first found no relationship. In their second study, however, they found a correlation of .47 between Lorge scores and intelligence of writers, and .46 between Lorge scores and judgments of merit made by six doctoral candidates.

A study of readability of letters and occupational level of writers was made by Arthur MacKinney and James Jenkins (399). They measured the Flesch Reading Ease score of letters entered in an industrial employees' contest, and then compared these to the occupational classification of the writers. They found a significant relationship, with employees in higher-level jobs writing in a generally more difficult style.

These studies are interesting not only for themselves but also because they indicate something of the breadth of possible application of readability formulas. Apparently there is a general tendency for the analysis of language difficulty to apply to listening and writing as well as reading. It is surprising, in view of this, that it has not been studied more carefully with respect to speaking; see, however, Siegel and Siegel's Flesch readability analysis (327) of the major preelection speeches of Eisenhower and Stevenson.

A special table has not been prepared to summarize the validity studies using writer criteria, as it has for the other criteria, because only 4 studies are involved. They may be characterized as yielding positive results in 2 cases, negative in 1, and indeterminate in 1.

A Summary Statement Concerning Validation Against Outside Criteria. All important studies of the validity of readability formulas that the writer was able to locate were included in this chapter. The summaries of the subsections on the various external validity criteria included a categorization of each study as positive, negative, or indeterminate evidence of validity. The assignment to a category was, of course, a judgment. While the judgment was generally based on the author's interpretation of his results, the summary figures derived provide only a rough picture, rather than a refined analysis, of probable validity for various purposes. Furthermore, it is possible that even the over-all figures may be somewhat optimistic, since a study with positive results is more likely to appear in a professional journal than one with a negative outcome.

Nevertheless, a look at summary figures can be useful in the attempt to answer the questions of when a formula will and will not work, and why. As before, it is preferable to list separately the data based on the nine studies using human interest factors. While the personal or impersonal nature of style is certainly part of some larger definition, most uses

TABLE 7

SUMMARY TABLE OF VALIDITY STUDIES*

CRITERION USED	NUMBER OF STUDIES WITH SPECIFIED RESULTS†		
	Positive	Negative	Indeterminate
Reading Speed (Efficiency)	6	0	0
Judgments	12	2	3
Readership	5	1	3
Comprehension (Retention)	11	8	2
Listenability	3	4	1
Writer Characteristics	2	1	1
Totals	39	16	10

* "Human interest" studies are not included.
† For a definition of the terms "positive," "negative," and "indeterminate," see TABLE 2 footnote, page 133.

of the term "readability" are restricted to an analysis of style *difficulty.* Because a separate concern for human interest lies outside the scope of this report, the results of the studies using it are not considered here. Eliminating these leaves 65 studies; they are summarized in Table 7 above. The over-all results are predominantly positive, with over twice as many cases judged positive as negative. If the further restriction is made that only modern studies be included (those appearing in 1946 or after), the results are even more clearcut: 35 positive, 9 negative, and 9 indeterminate.

More valuable to an understanding of the adequacy of readability formulas than this total picture, however, is an examination of the areas in which formulas work relatively well as opposed to areas in which formulas are less effective. The grouping of such diverse categories as the various validity criteria might otherwise obscure these differences in effectiveness.

Inspection of the results indicates that reading efficiency may definitely be increased by the use of more readable material. It would seem, in fact, that this is probably a major effect of increased readability.

The results of these studies also indicate that more read-able material as measured by formulas can be *judged* to be more readable by experts or by general readers. To be sure, studies show that such material is also consistently preferred by readers, generally because it permits easier reading. Where increases in readership due to increased readability are found, they doubtless stem from the increased efficiency afforded the reader and his correspondingly favorable at-titude toward, and judgment of, the material. So, again, a major effect on readership appears to lie in readers' readily judged preference for more readable material.

A final expected effect of increased readability is increased comprehension and retention. This would be expected be-cause readability was originally studied, and formulas were intended, as providers and predictors of desired comprehen-sion levels. Yet it is somewhat less certain than the other major effects. This is not to say that increases do not occur; they do, but more frequently under certain conditions of reading and listening than others. There is a distinct need to specify (beyond the suggestions already made on page 134) when an increase in comprehension or retention can be expected, and why it occurs. There is a similar need to understand why increased efficiency and preferability occur so consistently. Possible reasons for these results, based on this writer's analysis, will be taken up in the next two chap-ters. They cover considerations in written material, and the reader. Actually, these major areas are closely inter-related in any study of readability, and, in fact, the reader is logically of first concern. They appear in the opposite order simply for convenience of organization and discussion.

Part III

Basic Considerations in Readability

Why are readability formulas adequate or inadequate to certain measurement tasks? Some basic factors to be considered in readers and written material are suggested here, along with an analysis of the future research needed for a more complete answer.

9. Basic Considerations in Written Material

THE COMPLEXITY OF LANGUAGE makes analyses of basic considerations in written material possible at several levels. The research worker can simply start from the available studies of style factors found to be predictive of readability. These are certainly the primary source of information here. But it is also important to realize that these studies started with certain assumptions about the sizes and types of language units to analyze. Therefore, before considering style factors themselves, something should be said about such units.

Units of Analysis

The basic unit of analysis, both as a formula factor and as a measure of length of standard passages, is the "word." This would certainly seem to be an obvious and satisfactory one, since it is the one which is commonly used in language teaching. Adults, too, use it most frequently in formal and informal analyses. It is, however, certainly not the only unit possible.

A smaller unit is the letter, or to be somewhat more general, the type space. Hackman and Kershner (97) proposed this unit for future investigations because it is not subject to the variability in length found in words. The common standard passage of 100 words used in most analyses may vary considerably in number of letters of length. Since such aspects of reading as speed or other efficiency measures may depend upon length, a 100-word passage is no longer a strict standard. Hackman and Kershner therefore proposed use of standard passages of 2000 type spaces.

This writer has also found that 100-word passages may differ in length, using inches as a measure. This type of measurement, inches, would not be very satisfactory for analyses, however, because length also depends upon size and character of type. If this method of defining a standard passage is used, a table for equating type for length must be employed when passages with different type are to be compared. Furthermore, type faces differ in characteristics other than length, and these may also affect speed of reading, as Paterson and Tinker (11) and others have shown. Tables equating type for speed of reading would probably provide somewhat increased accuracy in measuring other effects of readability, but most users of readability formulas would find them undesirable because their use would add so much time and complexity to the measurement of standard passages.

Counting passages in terms of type spaces is also more time-consuming than counting them in word units. This should not necessarily eliminate a type-space count from consideration, especially if it adds sufficient accuracy of measurement. But even this is questionable. In the analyses made by this writer, it was found that differences in lengths of passages which differed in readability were due to the decreased length of more frequently used as compared to less frequently used words. Since word frequency is a major factor in most readability formulas, this procedure simply eliminates one of the effects of this factor and results in the inclusion of a larger number of frequent than infrequent words in a standard passage of 2000 type spaces. This procedure, at worst, prejudices the passage in favor of longer words, since there are fewer of them to read. At best, this procedure results in a *decreased* sensitivity of measurement of readability effects. Klare, Shuford, and Nichols showed this in an unpublished study in which they spaced out an "easy" version of material to the same length as the "hard" version, thereby equating the passages in terms of type spaces as well as number of words. The number of words read per *second* still significantly favored the easy version, but differences in number of words read per *fixation* were no longer significantly higher for the easy version, as they had been in unspaced material.

If type spaces and inches of length are not used as measures, larger measures are needed. The "syllable" is a possible measure of length, and it has been widely used as a formula factor. There seems to be little question that its popularity as a factor lies in the rather widespread ability of adults to count syllables rapidly and (more or less) accurately, and also in the fact that it eliminates need for a count of words on, or not on, a word-list. This is possible because it provides a measure of word length and thus, indirectly, of word frequency. On the other hand, the syllable is not a very respectable unit in linguistic analysis. An indication of the problems encountered is seen in the comparison of the number of syllables in "flower" and "flour." Syllables have been shown to correspond to breath pulses while reading, but, if oral reading is being considered, phonetic units are much more acceptable. Such units have been given very little attention in readability work. Flesch (31) used affixed morphemes (prefixes, suffixes, and inflectional endings), and Bloomer (21) has recently used sound complexity of modifiers, but no full-scale attempt has been made to use phonetic counts. The reason is not hard to find. A count of syllables is quick and easy for most adults, even more so than a count of letters, whereas a count of phonetic units is not. Some check should be made, however, on whether the more

difficult phonetic count might not be a more adequate predictive method where accuracy rather than speed is the
major concern of the analyst.

The "word" might also be criticized, since it is not a very
satisfactory formal unit for linguistic work. This is at least
partly because such work is done with oral material, however, and it is unlikely that analysts of written material will
ever discard it. It is simply too convenient, too easy and
reliable to count. Consequently, words have been used at
all levels of analysis, ranging from simple counts of running
words to formal categorizing of words in such terms as abstract or concrete. Somewhere between lie counts of number
of words on or not on given lists, and counts of words as
carriers of meaning.

Groups of words have also been used as formula factors,
chiefly in units like phrases and clauses. Much more common, however, have been sentence units. In fact, the sentence has been used more often than any other unit except
the word. And it, too, has been used at several levels of
analysis, from counts of number of words per sentence to
such analyses as counts of simple versus complex sentences.

No units beyond the sentence in size have been used in
readability studies, although Flesch does give some attention
to paragraphs in his 1958 formula. Some such length unit
as the paragraph is certainly possible, but apparently large
units meet with the objection of being unreliable in counting or subjective in categorizing. At any rate, it is clear from
a review of the available studies that the two most common,
and therefore most important, units have been words and
sentences.

Factor Analyses of Readability Elements

Another approach to the question of the most important
elements or factors in readability research is that of factor
analysis. A ready-made body of data for the factor analyst is

provided by Gray and Leary (41). As indicated in an earlier section, these authors presented correlations between the occurrences of 44 objective structural elements of expression in reading passages and comprehension scores of readers on these passages.

Two factor analyses of Gray and Leary's matrix appeared independently and at almost the same time. In the first, James Brinton and Wayne Danielson (422) reduced the 44 factors to 20 for convenience in analysis. (This is reasonable, since many of Gray and Leary's elements were very similar; for example, one element might consist of *number* of occurrences of a given element, while another might be a corresponding *percentage*.) A factor analysis was then performed, and six factors with correlations significantly different from zero were extracted. Of these, Factor I dealt with words and was labeled by the authors a "vocabulary" factor. Elements dealing with sentences had a high loading on Factor II, which is therefore a "sentence" factor. The remaining factors were found to be of lesser importance and were difficult to name. The authors suggest that Factor III has something to do with stylistics or devices of content and Factor IV with grammatical complexities, but indicate that further study is needed before anything very definite can be said about them.

The second study was made by Lawrence M. Stolurow and J. Robert Newman (465). These authors also eliminated some of Gray and Leary's elements, finally retaining 23 of the 44. Ten of these were found to account for 92.8% of the total variance; these were then rotated and two major factors emerged. Factor I was labeled "relative difficulty of words" and Factor II "relative sentence difficulty." These two accounted for 34% and 20%, respectively, of the total of 92.8%; no other factors accounted for more than 8.2% of the variance, and these were therefore not interpreted.

Thus the two studies yield essentially the same conclusions: (1) with few exceptions the 20 to 23 elements could be roughly grouped under two main factors, word and sentence difficulty; (2) of the two, word difficulty is relatively the more important; and (3), of the remaining factors, none was clear enough to be given a satisfactory name. This does not mean, of course, that the other factors should be forgotten; Brinton and Danielson feel that purer measures of them should be devised if possible, and that they should then be re-evaluated and perhaps used in new multiple-factor regression equations. It should be noted that Rudolf Flesch (438) feels his syllable count departs from the word factor and involves instead an "abstractness" factor. It is true that this count differs from more common methods of measuring the word factor; however, the nature of the correlations of scores derived from the formulas of Flesch and of others suggests that syllable and word counts have much in common.

Further factor analyses are certainly indicated when it is noted that Gray and Leary's data: (1) appear to have a very heavy weighting of elements that are rather obviously of word and sentence types; (2) consist of comprehension data for adult readers of somewhat limited ability; and (3) involve a measure of comprehension based on selection of a summary statement for a particular paragraph, and on selection of one of a list of details not in the paragraph, which is certainly a limited definition of comprehension. Despite whatever limitations these restrictions impose, it is still notable that word and sentence factors again emerge as most important. Any interpretation of the underlying reasons for the relative effectiveness of readability formulas in particular circumstances clearly must account for these factors.

The Word Factor

As indicated, the most important unit in the study of readability is the "word." It is a natural unit of analysis in written material; it is the most often used of all factors in readability prediction; it accounts for the greatest amount of variance in available factor analyses of readability elements. Nothing yet has been said, however, of the measurable characteristics of words that are important in readability.

Word Frequency and Recognition. So far as frequency analyses in the readability of English are concerned, a major landmark was the publication of E. L. Thorndike's *The Teacher's Word Book* (14). This count and its subsequent revisions in 1932 and 1944 (15, 16) made possible easy, reliable estimates of the frequency of most of the words used in English prose. Another study important to an understanding of the effectiveness of frequency was Davis Howes' demonstration of the relationship of English word frequency, or word-probability, as he called it, to the speed with which words are recognized, or "visual duration threshold" (Howes and Solomon, 444). His work, plus that of his collaborators and others, showed that this relationship was a reliable one. It was not perfect, but there was good reason to believe that a general (population frequency) count like Thorndike's could not provide frequency values for specific individuals (idiosyncratic frequency). A person with a major interest in psychology, for example, would encounter the word "psychology" or associated words much more frequently than they are found in general prose, with the result that frequency estimates like Thorndike's would be underestimates of such words for him. Experimental work bore this out; when artificial words not previously seen by subjects were used, and their frequency built up by controlling exposure to them, the relationship between frequency of occurrence and speed of recognition was found to be very high (Solomon and Postman, 463). In one study the correlation between frequency and recognition time was even found to be —.99 (King-Ellison and Jenkins, 447). Factors may be present in studies of controlled frequency of artificial words that are not present when English words are used; for example, a subject may be building up his tendency merely to *say* a given word or to *guess* it rather than to *recognize* it visually when frequency is controlled by repeated exposure in a short time. Even considering this possibility, however, the relationship between frequency of English words and recognition time cannot be explained away.

Given this relationship, it is not difficult to see why validity studies show the further relationship between readability and reading speed or efficiency. It seems clear that reading speed is increased by the use of frequently occurring words. This relationship can be explored even further. The question of why frequent words are recognized faster may, according to this writer, be explained in terms of the *amount* of a word that must be seen for recognition to occur. Luther Haseley (422), using a mask to expose successively larger amounts of words, demonstrated a close relationship between frequency and the amounts of the words necessary for recognition. Apparently the more frequently a word is seen, the less of it is necessary for recognition, a process referred to as "cue-reduction." It seems highly possible that reading speed is increased when frequent words are used because less of the word needs to be seen in a visual fixation before the word can be recognized.

Increased readability as measured by formula can thus be expected to produce increased reading speed or efficiency as a result of the use of more frequent words. But there is another factor involved. G. K. Zipf (466) is usually credited with first having shown that there is a relationship between the age (and thus the frequency of usage) of words and their length, words becoming shorter with time (and usage). Dramatic examples are seen in the reduction of "horseless carriage" to "car" or the use of letter abbreviations such as NRA or WPA in the alphabet days of the 1930's. But the same process, in less dramatic fashion, can be seen in words in general. Of great importance for the study of readability, it can be shown that length of word is related to speed of recognition (McGinnies, Comer, and Lacey, 449); the shorter the word, within limits, the more rapid the recognition time. The earlier objection to using the type space as a unit of measurement in readability was based on the fact that it counteracts the effect of this difference in length between frequent and infrequent words, and thus may unfairly prejudice measurement of the effects of readability.

In summary, more frequent words are recognized faster than less frequent both because the reader apparently needs to see less of them and because they tend to be shorter. These relationships appear tied to the results of the validity studies showing that readability affects reading speed or efficiency. The characteristic of words most often measured in readability studies is, directly or indirectly, that of frequency. Since recognition time and reading speed are themselves similar measures, it appears that relative frequency of occurrence of words may be the important factor in both.

There is some reason to believe that frequency may also play a part in the results of the validity studies using judgments as criteria. Studies have shown that judges tend to consider readability and reading ease rather closely related. Probably both shortness of words and apparent familiarity are responsible. It further seems likely that these characteristics of words are at least partly responsible for the results of the validity studies using readership criteria. Readers prefer material that is easy to read, as many studies show, and this preference must certainly be important in any measures of readership.

Word Frequency and Familiarity. While increased frequency of occurrence of the words used plays a clear-cut part in readability, there is a limit to its effects. Beyond some point of high frequency, for example, one additional exposure of the word is unlikely to have much effect upon the recognition of it, whereas at low frequency an added exposure may be highly effective. This suggests that "familiarity" does not bear a one-to-one relationship to frequency. This was found to be the case by Clyde E. Noble (456), who demonstrated that the familiarity-frequency relationship for words followed a hyperbolic "law of diminishing returns" (i.e., reduced effect with increased frequency). Edgar Dale (432) has also pointed out that familiarity and frequency are not perfectly related. The value of Dale's lists of words that are familiar to students in various grades can be seen in its successful use in his (Dale-Chall) formula and those of others. All this should not imply that the frequency factor is not important; it is still the base upon which familiarity rests. Rather, a measure of familiarity, when a good one is available, may be more accurately predictive of readability than a frequency count.

Frequency and Familiarity, Meaning and Learning. Word frequency can be counted upon to produce an effect upon reading efficiency. The next question is whether or not it can be expected to affect word meaning and comprehension. Irving Lorge has pointed out (104) that the more frequent words in the English language have a larger number of meanings than the less frequent; this seems to suggest that use of frequent words would lead to greater difficulty in comprehension rather than to greater ease. Apparently the mitigating factor here is a hierarchy of frequencies of word meanings in context, with the one or two commonest meanings usually occurring a disproportionately large number of times. Thus use of a highly frequent word most often will involve use of a highly frequent meaning.

At any rate, studies over the years have shown that frequency and familiarity are related to the ease with which words can be learned (Hall, 441) and can be remembered (Peters, 457). Noble (455) has graphed the relationship between familiarity and meaning, where meaning is defined basically in terms of number of associates to a stimulus word. He found a "diminishing return" relationship (negatively accelerated growth curve) of much the same sort as that between familiarity and frequency; in other words, an increase in meaning does not increase the familiarity of a highly familiar word nearly so much as that of a word of low familiarity. Noble also points to the primacy of the frequency factor when he hypothesizes that ". . . verbal stimuli acquire the attributes of m [meaning] and f [familiarity] as joint functions of frequency of stimulation [n]." (455, p. 96.)

One might expect that, if frequency is related to ease of learning and to meaning, it might also be closely related to comprehension. But the studies of the validity of readability measures which used comprehension and retention criteria do not show so clear-cut a relationship. Apparently, factors other than frequency play a major role in determining comprehension. Warren Seyfert (461), among others, has emphasized that frequency alone is not sufficient, and suggests such additional factors as level of abstraction and ambiguity. Even in the simpler matter of the learning of words in lists, C. H. Haagen's work (440) points to the importance of such additional factors as synonymity, vividness, and association value.

The Sentence Factor

The most obvious second factor to consider as a major contributor to readability is the sentence. Evidence for this comes from two sources: the use of a sentence factor in virtually all readability formulas, and the appearance of a sentence factor in the two factor analyses previously described.

Two characteristics of sentences have been studied, length, and structure or complexity. Of these, length has been used much more often, the measure virtually always involving a count of the number of words in the sentences of a passage. Structure has most often involved an analysis of sentences in terms of complexity, with number or percentage of simple sentences compared to number or percentage of complex and/or compound sentences. Considering that more complicated sentences are generally longer than simple sentences, it can be seen that structure (as usually measured) and length are themselves related. It has been found that the effect of length and structure differ with different patterns of sentences, with different individuals, and with different groups of subjects (Holland, 443); but length of sentences remains one of the basic factors in determining readability.

The question of why sentence length is an effective factor requires further consideration. It seems to this writer that one primary reason can be found in human "memory span," the ability to recall material correctly after only one presentation. A number of studies have shown that memory span differs with the age and intellectual ability of subjects and with the nature of the materials used. Subjects who are older (within the limits of the growth of mental ability) and brighter have a longer span than those who are younger and duller. The span is also longer, for example, for English words in sentence context than in unrelated lists, or for lists of English words than lists of nonsense syllables.

Miller and Selfridge (452) have shown recently that memory span (words recalled) is closely related to the extent to which the organization of verbal context approximates that of English. In human use of English words, any given word is related to the words preceding it in such a way that the word may not be chosen freely but rather depends upon the previous words to some extent. For example, the sen-

tence "The man went to town in his ————" may be completed only with a relatively small number of words such as
"car," "dream," or "consternation"; *most* English words are
not possible. Such dependencies may be removed, as in an
unrelated list of words, creating a low order of approximation to English. What Miller and Selfridge have shown
is that, *particularly* for longer lists (sentences), memory span
(words recalled) is a function of the degree of approximation
to English; they feel that these results are due more to the
fact that higher orders of approximation permit the use of
previous learning (a form of redundancy) than to any distinction between "meaning" and "nonsense." Marks and Jack
later questioned whether the results were not still due to
meaningfulness (450). Whatever the distinction here, it is
clear that memory span must be related to what has been
called the relative "redundancy" of English text. Comprehension of written material depends upon the length of
sentences used, as readability studies show, probably because
of human limits in the memory span. But it probably also
depends upon other factors in written material, such as
redundancy. The following section discusses these matters
more fully.

Other Factors in Written Material

One of the notable features of earlier readability work was
the search for factors other than words and sentences which,
when added to these two, could improve the predictive
power of formulas. The search for other factors has not been
abandoned, since they can be of potential value for formulas
intended for specific purposes. But the most highly predictive formula available, that of Dale and Chall, relies only
on the two factors already discussed, word familiarity and
sentence length. This might suggest that the search for other
factors *should* be abandoned, except that even the best for-

mula provides much less than perfect prediction of read-ability.

One of the factors in written material that has received far too little attention is that of redundancy. Redundancy has a precise mathematical definition in information theory; its use here is a more general extension of the concept. *Redundancy, in this case, refers to the extent to which a given unit of language is determined by nearby units.* Approximations to English, such as those used by Miller and Self-ridge (452), are ways of varying redundancy. In contextual material, it may be measured in terms of the extent to which (1) deleted letters can be correctly filled in, as measured by C. E. Shannon (Shannon and Weaver, 462) or Alphonse Chapanis (430); (2) deleted words can be filled in, as measured by Dearborn, Johnston and Carmichael (88), or by Wilson Taylor (119) and called "cloze procedure"; or (3) each successive word in a sample of prose can be predicted, as measured by Rubenstein and Aborn (459) and called "predictability."

The work of Chapanis raised some question as to whether or not readability and redundancy were related, but Taylor and Rubenstein and Aborn found relatively close relationships. It is possible that this is due to use of letter units by the former, versus use of word units by the latter. The further fact that readability analyses are made largely in word units may have something to do with this. At any rate, Rubenstein and Aborn found a correlation of .60 between Dale-Chall readability scores and predictability scores; they also found the further correlations of .73 between "amount learned" (amount of a passage memorized in a given study period) and predictability scores, and .75 between "amount learned" and Dale-Chall readability scores. This last correlation is, interestingly enough, approximately the same as that reported earlier between Dale-Chall scores and the comprehension score criterion used in developing the formula.

Redundancy, as predictability, is here seen to be rather closely related to readability. But inclusion of a redundancy factor in readability formulas is not being suggested; after all, use of such a factor would rob formulas of their usefulness as non-test predictors, since redundancy can only be estimated through a tryout of written material on subjects. Instead, it seems to this writer that the degree of redundancy will determine to some extent whether or not a formula will be a useful predictor of the readability of a passage. Wilson Taylor has pointed out that formulas will tend to seriously overestimate the readability of such writings as those of James Joyce or Gertrude Stein; the words may be familiar and the sentences short, but redundancy may still be very low. The failure of a writer such as Joyce or Stein to follow the "rules of the language" makes the writing more difficult than a formula would predict. (There is little need to apply formulas to writing of this sort, of course.)

Redundancy, along with memory span, should be considered in analysis of studies using listenability criteria. These studies, it will be recalled, yielded slightly more negative results than they did positive. Many of the studies used comprehension measures basically; since reading studies sometimes yielded negative results, it is not surprising to find listening studies doing the same. But a somewhat larger number of negative results might be expected in listening studies because of the temporal nature of speech; once heard, the message is gone and the listener must rely on his memory since, in most studies, the message is not repeated. In the case of reading, the reader in many cases is allowed to regress or even to re-read the message, placing a lighter burden on memory span. The point is, with messages of any great length, the listener is simply not able to retain enough details of what he has heard for satisfactory measurement.

When this happens, little other than negative results can be expected from comparison of more readable versus less readable versions of the message. With relatively simple, highly redundant material, increased readability appears to be a good indicator of increased listenability; with more difficult, less redundant material, positive results can be expected only when the material is fairly short or when repetition or some other method of increasing redundancy — and therefore amount learned — is used.

Furthermore, redundancy will vary not only with the materials or procedures used, but also with readers. A reader who has a rather complete background of experience in a particular field may find even an apparently difficult passage to be highly redundant; a formula would almost certainly underestimate the readability of the passage for him. As a matter of fact, experimentation shows this to be the case.

But a discussion of redundancy as a function of *readers* is getting into another major area, that of basic considerations in the reader that affect readability. Readability should properly not be spoken of in absolute terms, as though it were divorced from readers; rather, it is a relative matter, one that is concisely expressed in the question "readability for whom?" In discussing word and sentence factors, particularly as they concerned the recognition of words and the memory span, the reader *has* been considered. At least indirect reference is unavoidable. In the next chapter, however, the reader is given more direct consideration for the part he plays in determining readability.

10. Basic Considerations in the Reader

READERS DESERVE PRIMARY CONSIDERATION in determinations of readability. The final criterion of readability is the effect of a passage upon a particular reader, not its readability score. In this chapter some of the more important characteristics of readers which affect readability will be considered.

Reading Level

Many modern formulas are designed to provide readability scores calibrated in reading grade levels. These levels are in terms of materials of average difficulty for average students of a given grade, and are usually based on the results of standardized tests. In some cases, the criterion of understanding of a passage is correct answers to 75% of the comprehension questions, in other cases to 50%. This in itself is responsible for some formula error, at least insofar as differences among formula ratings are concerned. As indicated earlier, agreement on a standard level is needed. Apart from the manner of arriving at a given grade-level score, other problems are more directly concerned with formula validity.

Relation of Reading and Educational Levels. Where test score data are available for readers the determination of reading level is not a problem. Even when data such as present school grade of the reader are not at hand, reading level can at least be estimated. Where a reading test score is not available and where the reader is no longer in school (which is the situation for most adult readers), the determination of reading level is more difficult. Fortunately, reading level appears to correspond roughly to last school grade completed. This estimate is, of course, not perfectly accurate; persons who have finished the same school grade may still differ considerably in intellectual level and this may well affect reading level. Other factors, such as background and experience with the content of a given passage, will also affect readability for the specific reader.

All in all, it appears that prediction of readability level by formula will be most accurate for readers in the primary grade levels, and become increasingly inaccurate as secondary, college, and adult levels are reached. Some attempts at adjustment have been made by providing "corrected" values for formula scores at the higher levels, but these could hardly be expected to eliminate all error. There seems little doubt that some of the negative results of validity studies using comprehension criteria stem from inadequacies in the estimation of higher reading levels.

Material Above the Reader's Level. Another problem allied with the use of reading level is the assumption that a given level is an absolute value. It is not hard to see that a person can read material at a lower level than his own, but it should not be assumed that he cannot read *above* a given "reading level." On the contrary, this is done by most readers; take, for example, the reading of income tax instructions by adults at all grade levels. The notion of a level presumes simply that a reader will read above his level only with difficulty. He may have to re-read a number of times, and even then may not understand perfectly — but he *can* read above his level.

This, again, appears to have an effect upon whether or not validity studies using a comprehension criterion will show positive results. When the readability scores indicate that experimental versions of a passage to be compared are *much* harder and/or *much* easier than the reader's level, significant differences in comprehension can be expected. When the passages differ relatively little — that is, are only *slightly* easier and/or *slightly* harder than the reader's level — positive results are not so likely. Note, however, that both high-ability and low-ability readers can profit from readable material. Studies by Klare and associates with airmen at all levels of reading ability from just above minimum literacy up to the highest level used (probably approximating college, at least) showed gains in retention scores on more readable as compared to less readable versions of material. All this is being said here is that the gains between versions will be greatest when the range between easiest and hardest material is greatest; this appears to be true for the more able readers as well as for the less able.

Perhaps reading level should be thought of as a range of grades rather than a single grade. Certainly the level at which a person can and will read with understanding varies with the circumstances under which he reads.

Reader Experience

It was pointed out earlier that redundancy and readability are related, and that in turn the redundancy of any given material is always relative to a particular reader. A further characteristic of the reader which plays a large part in determining readability is background and previous experience with the subject matter in question. At one extreme, a subject who has memorized a passage will obviously be able to get high scores on the usual redundancy measure — filling in deleted blanks or predicting successive words correctly. At the other extreme, however, a subject who has never before seen the passage might still easily fill in a large number of blanks or predict a large number of words. In the first place, a reader's experience with the English language will usually permit him to supply certain words correctly; rules that govern the use of words and the construction of sentences make his attempts much better than guesses. In the second place, a reader's experience with the content or subject of the passage can help him. An expert in a field should be able to supply many more correct words than one who is not an expert. Related to this is the likelihood of a greater vocabulary and therefore a clearer notion of the meaning of the passage. No attempt has been made in this book to cover vocabulary studies as such; the interested reader may wish to examine Seashore and Eckerson's methods of measuring individual differences in general English vocabularies (460) and Chall and Dale's description (429) of the methods they used in establishing the familiarity of words. A general listing of references has been provided by Dale and Reichert in *Bibliography of Vocabulary Studies* (87).

The tendency for redundancy to depend upon the reader's experience with the English language and with the subject matter being discussed must be considered in evaluating the validity of readability formulas. Klare, Mabry, and Gustafson (386) have shown that when knowledge of a particular passage is high, experimental versions of material cannot be expected to produce differences in test scores. A technical lesson that was presumed to contain material new to trainees was used in experimental work; subsequent analysis, however, showed that trainees could answer test questions much beyond chance expectation even before reading the lesson. In such circumstances, test score differences for easy (readable) versus hard (less readable) versions did not appear. When, however, more nearly naïve trainees were used, significant differences between the more and less readable versions were found. This study suggests that the results of certain validity studies using comprehension or retention criteria may have been negative due to a high level of background experience on the part of subjects. Once again it is interesting to note that differences in reading *speed* were found whether or not the subjects were naïve regarding the material.

Motivation

It is one of the truisms of psychology that motivation, as well as ability, is necessary to achievement. This holds for reading as well as for other kinds of human behavior.

"Set to Learn." A number of studies show that perceptual habits in reading, once they are firmly established, become rather mechanical in nature. One such unpublished study, for example, showed that feeble-minded and normal boys "read" passages at approximately the same speed; it was only when they were tested for comprehension that the two groups were markedly different. Klare and associates also demonstrated the mechanical nature of such reading habits in a series of largely unpublished studies. College subjects were asked to read a short technical passage before an eye-movement camera and were then given a modified recall (fill-in) test. Words-read-per-second and words-read-per-fixation were also determined. It was at first found that the recall scores were so low that a useful statistical analysis could not be performed; differences between an easy (relatively readable) and hard (relatively unreadable) version of a passage (the reason for the study) obviously could not show up under these conditions. Exhortations to subsequent subjects to read more carefully were relatively ineffective. More or less by chance, however, certain subjects were asked to read a different passage and take a test on it immediately after their unfortunate experience with the first passage and test. It was found that test scores increased markedly, and the more readable version then produced significantly higher scores than the less readable. Further studies gave similar results, and the use of a passage and test preceding the experimental passage and test was said to produce a strong "set to learn" as opposed to the initially weak "set to learn."

Several important features of the situation should be noted. First, the more readable (easier) version was read significantly faster and with fewer fixations than the less readable (harder) version under *both* strong and weak sets; however, recall scores on the more readable version were significantly higher than on the less readable *only* under the strong set. This is in line with the findings from validity studies showing that increased readability *consistently* produces greater reading speed, but greater learning, retention, and comprehension only part of the time.

Second, the subjects under the weak set appeared to be reading in their habitual (rather mechanical) manner, presumably determined by previous reading experiences of a similar sort. When under a strong set, however, reading speed decreased at the same time that recall scores increased. Furthermore, speed and recall scores became much more closely related under the strong set than they had been under the weak. This may help to explain the contradictory results of various investigators, some of whom have found high speed-comprehension relationships and others low speed-comprehension relationships.

Finally, these results may well extend to everyday reading since "set to learn" is simply a specific kind of motivation. Readers may read successfully beyond their grade level, as in the case of income-tax instructions, when motivation is high, but not when it is low.

The Principle of Least Effort. A factor that is related to the reader's low "set to learn" and should be discussed under the heading of motivation is the "principle of least effort"

(Zipf, 466). This is the notion that a human will minimize the work — average rate of work — necessary to reach a certain goal. It is a general factor in human behavior and is not peculiar to reading, but it does show up very clearly in some aspects of readers' behavior. The studies by Klare and associates referred to earlier (386, 387, 388) in which "split" versions of passages were used provide some examples. Readers indicated preferences for one of two style variations used in a split version as being "easier to read" and "more pleasant to read." These two judgments were highly related, as represented by tetrachoric correlations of .86 to .97. In other similar studies where subjects were first asked which of the two style variations they preferred and then asked to give the reason for their choice, "easier to read" was most often selected from among the given alternatives. These studies demonstrated that "least effort" was the basis for the preferences given. Of further interest was the subjects' ability to choose correctly the more readable variation of the two being used. This judgment, furthermore, appeared to be based on the efficiency with which a version could be read.

There is evidence of the principle of least effort in other reading behavior. For example, readers have been known to choose the simplest of three versions of a free article on an interesting topic and they have been known to read more of an easier, compared to a harder, article, or to read it in larger numbers. In more general terms, it has been estimated that a reader will choose material around two grades below his level when he is reading for pleasure. All this is not to say that readers will never tackle something that is hard reading. But it does mean that they are not likely to unless their motivation is high. This may be when the topic is very interesting, or very necessary (e.g., to health), or when the "set to learn" is strong. In other words, the goal must be important if the energy required to reach it is great.

11. Future Research
   in Readability

Speculating on what future research in any field *will* be is tempting but often leads to disappointment. Things just do not seem to happen the way it appears they will. Suggesting what future research *should* be is a somewhat more satisfactory way of introducing speculations. The writer can still defend his statement that they ought to have happened a particular way even if they have not done so. More reasonably, there are usually either available research data or the inevitable final statements in dissertations and published studies on "further problems" that can serve as guides.

In the field of readability there are three directions future research might well go: (1) basic research on critical, underlying variables in the process of reading and learning from print, leading to some kind of a theoretical framework for understanding them; (2) attempts to identify and/or incorporate new factors important to accurate readability measurement into formulas; and (3) refinement of factors and methods now used in readability formulas. Each is taken up in turn below.

Basic Research

Readability research workers have almost always followed a largely empirical approach. If factors or methods, however arrived at, have worked well, they have been retained, and if not, they have been discarded. This procedure is a natural and even a necessary one because writing is so complex to analyze and because readability is essentially a practical matter. But the empirical approach is not enough by itself, because it does not provide much of a basis for understanding *why* something has worked (when it has).

The procedure is often inefficient because the potential user of readability principles and formulas has few guidelines to follow. The research worker, similarly, lacks a theoretical framework that can suggest future research. Basic research is needed to turn up some of the critical, underlying variables in readability as they affect the process of reading and learning from print. They may, of course, be established variables borrowed from relevant existing research, or they may be newly established ones. But, once they are known and something of their relationships determined, a new look at the problem of readability is possible.

In this book an attempt has been made to identify and emphasize critical factors of two different sorts (those in the language and those in the reader) as they affect reading behavior. The purpose was to provide a picture of the complex interrelationships that play a part in determining formula validity. Table 8 presents some of these relationships that appear to be important. It is only a first crude attempt to provide a framework which can incorporate existing research results and suggest procedures for future work.

Table 8 indicates that if reading efficiency is being studied, it will be a function of:

1. The reader's speed of recognition of the words used, as determined by their frequency (or familiarity) and their length. As frequency increases, recognition speed increases

TABLE 8
Some Suggested Relationships Among Readability Variables

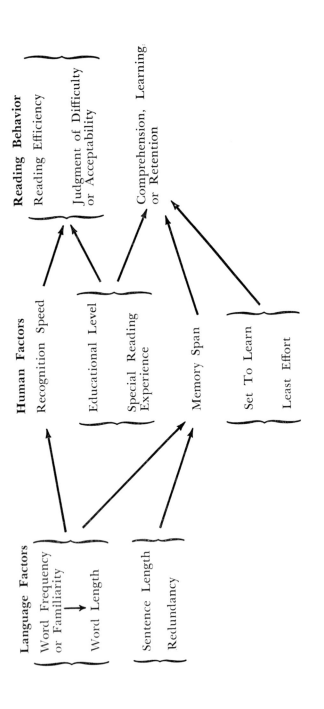

and reading efficiency becomes greater. Increased frequency also tends to decrease length, and shorter words, in turn, produce greater reading efficiency.

2. Educational level and special reading experience, or reading skill factors. As the educational level rises, reading efficiency becomes greater; similarly, when the reader's special experience with the subject matter of the written material is increased, so also is efficiency.

No assumption is made that these are the only important factors. Legibility of the type used certainly plays a part in recognition speed, but it is not included in the diagram because it was not considered in this book. There may well be other variables along with it which would be included in a larger view of the reading process or in a broader definition of readability than that used here.

If judgment of difficulty or acceptability of material is being studied, the same listed variables are of importance since these judgments seem so closely related to the reader's efficiency in reading the material. Once again, however, variables not included in this book may play a part. An example is the extent to which the reader is in agreement with the point of view expressed in the material. If it is contrary to his beliefs, he will doubtless find it "unacceptable" even if it is "readable."

If the comprehension, learning, or retention of material is being studied, the number of important variables is increased. These variables include:

1. Word frequency (or familiarity) and length. Increased frequency and shorter length of words mean that the reader will have a larger number of words within his memory span. This increased span is related to comprehension, learning and retention measures; so also is the

tendency for more frequent words to have more common (familiar) dictionary meanings.

2. Sentence length and redundancy. Short sentences and highly redundant material are important because of a reader's limited memory span. This, once again, affects comprehension, learning, and retention measures.

3. Educational level and special reading experience. As these increase, comprehension, learning, and retention measures tend to show a corresponding increase.

4. "Set to learn" and the principle of least effort, or motivational factors. Whether or not a reader has a strong "set to learn," reading efficiency may be increased in readable material; but only when it is strong will the effect of readable material be shown in increased comprehension, learning or retention scores. Apparently the operation of the principle of least effort may obscure any such increase unless "set to learn" is controlled.

This interpretation of the effects and interrelationships of readability variables may be used in the analysis of the results of the validity studies reported. Those studies using reading efficiency and judgmental criteria are examples of the measurement of the corresponding reading behaviors in Table 8. Readership is apparently a function of both reading efficiency and judgment behaviors; whether a person will read a given piece of material, or how much of it he will read, seems to depend upon these behaviors. The results of the validity studies using these criteria are predominantly positive.

In the case of the studies using comprehension, learning, or retention criteria, the results are positive only under certain conditions. This might well be due to the complex of factors affecting measurement of these criteria; one or more of these appear not to have been favorable to positive results in many of the cited studies. In the listenability studies, the preponderance of negative results may well have been due to the same reasons plus the increased need for redundancy in oral as compared to written presentation.

This interpretation is tentative and admittedly crude. Lumping such factors as recognition speed and memory span with the larger, more complex and sometimes less well-defined measures of educational level, special reading experience, "set to learn" and least effort is a matter of expediency here. Furthermore, the concept of memory span, usually measured on serially presented stimuli, needs revision to apply to contextual material. Perhaps the notion of "recoding," or reorganization of smaller related units into larger ones for a greater span (Miller, 451), should be included. Certainly the traditional usage of memory span would otherwise not seem to apply to large units of writing. The purpose of this approach to the understanding of readability, then, is not to present a rigidly refined, definitive picture. Rather it is intended to suggest (1) some of the variables a user of readability should consider, and (2) some notion of factors that need further investigation.

And this is not the only direction in which basic research might go. Powers and Kearl (458) suggest that basic research be done on such components of reading as the ability to recognize explicit statements; infer intent, purpose, or point of view; recognize isolated word meanings and word meanings in context; synthesize main ideas; and reason abstractly. These authors suggest also that new source materials (reading passages), methods of statistical analysis, and sampling effects be investigated. The need for new reading passages, and particularly for a good *adult* reading test to serve as a criterion, has also been emphasized by many other writers; similarly, studies of efficiency and reliability of analysts using various formulas have been mentioned. There is further agreement also on the need for identification and incorporation of new readability factors.

New Readability Factors

A wide range of factors important to readability but not now measured has been mentioned by various writers. There is perhaps most agreement among these writers that organization of material should not be neglected. This is emphasized by Lorge (448), Chall (425), and Dale and Chall (434). These authors also feel that attempts should be made to include a measure of conceptual difficulty in formulas. Dale and Chall particularly point to the need for some way of including an evaluative factor for content and format (physical features).

In this writer's opinion, the need for a study of content is of particular importance. Perhaps the greatest need is for some satisfactory *unit* of content. One of the reasons that research in readability is so difficult is that the research worker can never be completely certain that he has not also changed the content *(what* is said) when he has changed the readability or style *(how* it is said). Klare and associates have used technical experts as judges of whether or not content was changed in their experimental passages, but a more refined method of controlling content is needed. The unit called a "cont" developed by Carnap and Bar-Hillel (423) appears promising, but is of very limited applicability to contextual material at this time.

The failure of formulas to include or take account of the above factors does not stem from any lack of agreement on their importance. Rather, it arises from an inability to state these factors in the quantitative terms necessary for inclusion in formulas. Nevertheless, Chall (426, 427) considers these factors of sufficient importance to justify using qualitative methods. She feels that the first efforts would doubtless be unreliable, but that their importance, plus the possibility of further refinement, makes the effort worthwhile. In the desire to see basic research done and new factors uncovered these writers are not suggesting that the refinement of existing factors be abandoned. Rather, as indicated below, most of them feel these need continuing study.

Refinement of Existing Factors and Methods

Powers and Kearl (458) believe that refinement of existing readability factors and methods should be of at least three kinds: study of style factors other than words and sentences; examination of the exact relationships of words and sentences to difficulty — for example, whether or not they are linear (as is tacitly assumed); and, the use of new word-lists. One possible approach is to use specialized lists for specialized purposes, so that probable difficulty of words in a list can be based directly on the kind of materials to be analyzed rather than on general reading materials. The work of Standlee, Fattu, and Auble (464) on word frequency in Naval publications is an example. Another possible approach is to use longer word-lists based on the analysis of general materials. The use by Dale of his list of 3000 familiar words in the Dale-Chall formula raised its predictive accuracy over that which would have been possible with his 769-word-list. Further increases in length would doubtless provide a further increase in accuracy, though the size of the increase might well begin to fall off rather rapidly. Furthermore, application time would probably begin to increase to such an extent that most users would avoid formulas with long lists.

Chall (427) lists vocabulary and criterion passages as present factors needing further refinements. She and Dale (Dale and Chall, 433 and 434) both emphasize that variations in word meanings from those most commonly used deserve further attention. There is also a feeling that insufficient attention has been paid to the best uses of existing readability tools: when and where to use a specific formula, and the availability of separate norms for the readability of different types of material and different audiences (Chall, 424; Powers and Kearl, 458). As indicated earlier in this report, the present trend in formula development suggests that more attention is now being paid to specialized formulas. Apparently the general, all-purpose formulas have reached the state where practical application time cannot be decreased much more. The use of specialized formulas might have a further advantage, that of indicating the limitations of general formulas. Much evidence suggests that such formulas are often naïvely applied and the results of analysis simply accepted as accurate, even to the extent of specifying exactly how "hard" writers ought to make their writing.

Summary

The preceding pages provide some possible directions that readability research should go. But, to repeat, this does not mean that research *will* take these directions, and surely they are not the only ones possible. Readability formulas and principles are now widely used and generally accepted: the survey of users of just one formula, the Dale-Chall, made by Jeanne Chall (428) shows something of the extent to which this is true. This widespread use, plus the observation that formulas are often accepted as being more accurate and valid than they are, makes attention to improvement extremely important. Perhaps, as Chall suggests (427), one way to accomplish this efficiently would be to provide some method for the exchange of information that has been collected. Also, the general distribution of such summaries as that of Dale (431) should help keep users informed of the state of affairs and correct misconceptions about what formulas *can* and *cannot* be expected to do.

Part IV

Annotated and Classified Bibliography

The references cited in the text by name of author(s) and reference number are listed in detail in this section. The topic headings parallel, at least generally, the headings of the various chapters; a list of cross-references is provided at the end of most sections for items which fit under more than one heading.

The references themselves are arranged in alphabetical order within each category by last name of (first) author. Reference numbers have been assigned on this arbitrary basis. Each reference is briefly annotated.

Bibliographies

A. Introductory References

Nos. 1–19

1. Bear, M. V. "The Length of Word as an Index of Difficulty in Silent Reading." Unpublished Master's thesis, University of Chicago, 1927.

   With sixth-grade pupils, the percentage of monosyllabic words in reading material was found to be a fair index of the probable difficulty of the material. There was a close statistical correlation between word length and frequency of use, indicating that there may be an average word length which is desirable for reading material of a given grade level.

2. Bernstein, M. R. "Relationship Between Interest and Reading Comprehension." Unpublished Doctoral dissertation, Teachers College, Columbia University, April, 1953.

   In a study of adolescent reading interests and comprehension of matter read, it was found that "interest has a real relationship to comprehension in reading. It not only makes reading a pleasure, but operates effectively to enhance reading efficiency."

3. Burtt, H. E. "Typography and Readability," *Elementary English,* 26:212–21, April, 1949.

   The results of reported studies indicate that style and size of type, length of line, space between lines, spatial arrangement of page, color of printed material, and illumination of the printed page all affect legibility and, consequently, readability.

4. Gerwig, G. W. "On the Decrease of Predication and of Sentence Weight in English Prose," *University of Nebraska Studies,* 2:17–44, July, 1894.

   In an investigation of literary works from Homer to the time of the study, style within a single work was found to be uniform.

When arranged in order of descending predication and ascending number of simple sentences, the samples roughly approximated the chronological order in which they were written.

5. Gray, W. S. "Progress in the Study of Readability," *Library Trends*. Chicago: University of Chicago Press, 1937, pp. 237–54.

   This review of the progress made to 1937 in the study of readability is divided into three main areas: the origin of the readability movement; a survey of experimentation into simple reading materials for adults; and the study of elements of difficulty in reading material.

6. Gray, W. S. "Progress in the Study of Readability," *Elementary School Journal,* **47**:491–99, May, 1947.

   In this historical treatise of the progress to 1947 in the field of readability, the most important studies of readability are discussed. Results show that most of the work to 1947 has dealt with the vocabulary element, but more recent studies have explored such elements as number of sentences, sentence length, prepositions, content, and reading level.

7. Kitson, H. D. *The Mind of the Buyer*. New York: The Macmillan Company, 1921, pp. 58–63.

   The author analyzed four periodicals in terms of syllable length and sentence length, finding differences corresponding to the supposed "high-brow" and "low-brow" nature of the periodicals. This is an interesting early use of readability factors, although no readability formula was developed by the author.

8. Lorge, I. "Word Lists as Background for Communication," *Teachers College Record,* **45**:543–52, May, 1944.

   This theoretical study discusses the history of word counts and evaluates their importance. Some of the better known word counts and vocabulary lists are discussed, including Thorndike's *Teacher's Word Book,* Horn's word count, and Dale's vocabulary list.

9. Lorge, I. "Reading and Readability," *Teachers College Record,* **51**:90–97, November, 1949.

   The author summarizes some of the more widely used elements employed in readability formulae including vocabulary load, sentence structure, human interest, density of ideas, and concreteness of approach. Simpler versions of the same basic material were found to be more widely and thoroughly read than more difficult versions.

10. McCall, W. A., and Crabbs, L. M. *Standard Test Lessons in Reading: Teacher's Manual for all Books.* New York: Bureau of Publications, Teachers College, Columbia University, 1925.

    This manual describes the procedure for administering the *Standard Test Lessons in Reading* devised by the authors. The purposes of the tests are to teach pupils to comprehend rapidly many kinds of reading matter, to help them enjoy reading, and to motivate and improve oral expression.

11. Paterson, D. G., and Tinker, M. A. *How to Make Type Readable.* New York: Harper and Brothers, 1940.

    This book presents the results of a systematic investigation of the relationship between typographic factors and legibility. It presents a fairly comprehensive picture of the effect of ten factors: style of type face, type form, size of type, width of line, leading, margins, columnar arrangement, space between columns, color of print and background, and paper surface.

12. Sherman, L. A. "The Literary Sentence-Length in English Prose," (Ch. XIX), and "The Decrease of Predication," (Ch. XX), *Analytics of Literature.* Boston: Ginn and Co., 1893, pp. 256–68.

    The author attempts to determine why styles differ in readability by analyzing sentence length, predication and the use of simple sentences. Analysis shows that, historically, both sentence length and predications have decreased while the number of simple sentences has increased.

13. Strang, R. "Estimating the Difficulty of High-School and College Reading Material," (abstract), *Practical Values of Educational Research.* Official Report of the American Educational Research Association, Atlantic City, New Jersey, February 26–March 2, 1938. Washington: American Educational Research Association, May, 1938, pp. 50–51.

    The author reviews the literature on the improvement of reading of high school and college students, with suggestions for further inquiries. She lists the methods for determining difficulty — expert opinion, experimental evaluation and quantitative analysis of passages of known difficulty — and recommends that the clinical method be added to these.

14. Thorndike, E. L. *The Teacher's Word Book.* New York: Teachers College, Columbia University, 1921.

    This book provides a list of words whose range and frequency of occurrence have been estimated through a sampling of English texts. It is intended to provide an estimate of the commonness of words and to help teachers make decisions on the relative importance of words.

15. Thorndike, E. L. *A Teacher's Word Book of 20,000 Words.* New York: Bureau of Publications, Teachers College, Columbia University, 1932.

    This book extends, revises, and improves the author's original word-list of 10,000 words to 20,000 words rated according to their frequency and range of occurrence. Reliability of placement, both as to median probable placement accruing from more extensive counts and relative position within the list, is considered.

16. Thorndike, E. L., and Lorge, I. *The Teacher's Word Book of 30,000 Words.* New York: Bureau of Publications, Teachers College, Columbia University, 1944.

    This book lists the frequency with which 30,000 different English words occurred in four different word counts. The authors conclude that the book can be used as a guide in knowing how common a word is in standard English reading matter. Specific rules are given for teaching words.

17. Waples, D. "The Relation of Subject Interests to Actual Reading," *Library Quarterly,* 2:42–70, January, 1932.

    To determine the relation of subject interest to actual reading, the author studied the reading habits of factory workers and students. No significant positive relationship was found between the subjects of most interest and the subjects which the industrial groups read most. Accessibility is the most important influence on actual reading, "readability" the second most important.

18. Williams, C. B. "A Note on the Statistical Analysis of Sentence-Length as a Criterion of Literary Style," *Biometrika,* 31:356–61, February, 1940.

    The frequency distributions of sentence length in samples from the work of G. K. Chesterton, H. G. Wells, and George Bernard Shaw are examined. Statistical analysis revealed a significant difference in the means between Shaw and Wells. Between Shaw and Chesterton the difference in means was barely significant, but that between the standard deviations was quite evident. Authors apparently maintain a definite sentence length distribution in their works and may be identified through an examination of this distribution.

19. Yule, G. U. "On Sentence-Length as a Statistical Characteristic of Style in Prose: With Application to Two Cases of Disputed Authorship," *Biometrika,* **30**:363–90, January, 1939.

This study is concerned with the characteristic sentence length which distinguishes an author's style. Several works of disputed authorship were examined and compared with other works of the alleged authors. Results revealed that sentence length is a characteristic of an author's style.

See also 68, 87, and 433.

B. Readability Formulas

Nos. 20–79

20. Bergman, W. G. "Objective and Subjective Grade Placement of Supplementary Readers," *Reconstructing Education Through Research; Official Report.* Washington: American Educational Research Association of the National Education Association, 263–71, 1936.

Teachers' judgments, and an objective measure developed by the Research Department of the Winnetka public schools, were used to determine whether, as determined by vocabulary difficulty, supplementary texts placed in Detroit schools were suitable to the grades in which they were placed. The objective measure showed a much wider range of difficulty than did teachers' judgments.

21. Bloomer, R. H. "Level of Abstraction as a Function of Modifier Load," *Journal of Educational Research,* **52**:269–72, March, 1959.

In readers of primary to sixth-grade level, it was found that modifiers increased in number and difficulty of discrimination as grade levels of the books increased. As written materials become more abstract, they tend to become more specific.

22. Dale, E. "A Comparison of Two Word Lists," *Educational Research Bulletin,* **10**:484–89, December 9, 1931.

    The Thorndike word-list (1921), and a list prepared by the Child Study Committee of the International Kindergarten Union, are compared. Seven hundred and sixty-nine words are common to both lists. Two hundred and thirty words found in the first 1000 of Thorndike's list are not found in the Kindergarten list; most of the Kindergarten words are in the second 500 of Thorndike's first 1000 words. A large number of the common words are homographs (same spelling but different meaning).

23. Dale, E., and Chall, J. S. "A Formula for Predicting Readability," *Educational Research Bulletin,* **27**:11–20, January 21, 1948.

    A simple two-factor readability formula is presented. The factors employed are vocabulary load and sentence structure. Statistical analysis shows the formula to be a good predictor of readability. It was validated by applying it to other reading material.

24. Dale, E., and Chall, J. S. "A Formula for Predicting Readability: Instructions," *Educational Research Bulletin,* **27**: 37–54, February 18, 1948.

    This article presents specific information about the technique of applying the Dale-Chall formula for predicting readability. The necessary steps for using the formula worksheet are outlined and a sample case presented. The Dale list of 3,000 words is presented in full.

25. Dale, E., and Tyler, R. W. "A Study of the Factors Influencing the Difficulty of Reading Materials for Adults of Limited Reading Ability," *Library Quarterly,* **4**:384–412, July, 1934.

    This study attempts to determine the factors influencing the difficulty of reading matter for adults with limited reading skills. Results show that scores determining the difficulty of selections have high reliability. Because the study covered many factors, other conclusions were too diverse to be significant.

26. Dolch, E. W. "Vocabulary Burden," *Journal of Educational Research,* **17**:170–83, March, 1928.

    Textbooks for Grades 1 through 4 were examined for their

vocabulary burden with the aid of Dolch's *Combined Word Study List.* Results showed a wide variation of difficulty between books intended for the same grade and indicated that supplementary material should contain a large percentage of words from grades lower than the reader.

27. Dolch, E. W. "Graded Reading Difficulty," (Ch. XXI), *Problems in Reading.* Champaign: The Garrard Press, 1948, pp. 229–55.

In school readers for Grades 1 to 4, sentence length, word length, and word difficulty were found to increase from grade to grade. These three standards may be used to determine the "grade" of a book for children.

28. Edgerton, R. B. "How Difficult Are Children's Encyclopedias? I," *Elementary School Journal,* 45:379–85, March, 1945.

The author presents a shortened version of the Washburne readability formula and uses it to analyze sample passages from three children's encyclopedias. His findings are reported in Edgerton, R. B., "How Difficult Are Children's Encyclopedias? II," *Elementary School Journal,* 45:455–64, April, 1945.

29. Farr, J. N., and Jenkins, J. J. "Tables for Use with the Flesch Readability Formulas," *Journal of Applied Psychology,* 33:275–78, June, 1949.

To facilitate use of Flesch's "Reading Ease" and "Human Interest" formulas, the authors have tabled the values for them.

30. Farr, J. N., Jenkins, J. J., and Paterson, D. G. "Simplification of Flesch Reading Ease Formula," *Journal of Applied Psychology,* 35:333–37, October, 1951.

The authors present a revised method for the application of Flesch's readability formula, substituting the number of one-syllable words per hundred words for Flesch's syllable count per hundred words. Based on the substitution, a new Reading Ease regression equation is devised.

31. Flesch, R. F. "Estimating the Comprehension Difficulty of Magazine Articles," *Journal of General Psychology,* 28:63–80, 1943.

Analysis of magazine articles of increasing comprehension difficulty shows that (1) comprehension difficulty can be predicted by measuring the number of affixed morphemes and abstract words, and (2) with increased difficulty, diversity of vocabulary becomes less important as an element of comprehension difficulty in reading.

32. Flesch, R. F. *Marks of Readable Style: A Study in Adult Education.* New York: Bureau of Publications, Teachers College, Columbia University, 1943.

Flesch hypothesizes that the word-familiarity factor is not important in readability measurement, but that the sentence factor and the number of abstract words, affixed morphemes, and personal references are important. His formula is applicable to children's reading material as well as to adult material.

33. Flesch, R. F. "A New Readability Yardstick," *Journal of Applied Psychology,* **32:**221–33, June, 1948.

Flesch revises his original readability formula into two formulas including the following elements: average sentence length in words, average word length in syllables per 100 words, average percentage of "personal words" and average percentage of "personal sentences." The first two elements comprise his "Reading Ease" formula; the last two elements, his "Human Interest" formula.

34. Flesch, R. F. "Measuring the Level of Abstraction," *Journal of Applied Psychology,* **34:**384–90, December, 1950.

Flesch develops a formula to measure the level of abstraction of material by computing the ratio of definite (concrete) words to abstract words in test passages. The formula can also be used as a measure of readability as it replaces the "Human Interest" part in his earlier formulas.

35. Flesch, R. F. "Reply to Criticism by Jenkins and Jones," *Journal of Applied Psychology,* **35:**69, February, 1951.

Flesch, answering the criticism of Jenkins and Jones of his level of abstraction formula, states that it must not be evaluated solely on the basis of its numerical correlation with the criterion, but that readability is a complex quality of written prose involving age and education level, comprehension, readership and speed, recall, etc., of readers.

36. Flesch, R. F. *How to Make Sense*. New York: Harper and Brothers, 1954.

   The author presents the view that communication is life and that making sense is a matter of learning new habits. He expresses doubts about certain popular methods of improving communication and argues for specificity and skillful punctuation. He admonishes the writer to live, learn, and draw upon his subconscious in writing. An Appendix presents a new formula with two parts, one to measure realism and one to measure energy in writing.

37. Flesch, R. F. *A New Way to Better English*. New York: Harper and Brothers, 1958.

   The author conveys his notion of a "relaxed feeling" in writing. He concludes that the natural, spoken style gives fluency; the first person singular can be used successfully; dialogue and anecdotes make for readability; and the light touch should be used. He presents a new formula for readability based on these principles.

38. Forbes, F. W., and Cottle, W. C. "A New Method for Determining Readability of Standardized Tests," *Journal of Applied Psychology*, **37**:185–90, June, 1953.

   A new and simplified method is developed for determining the reading difficulty of standardized tests used in counseling. The Forbes method reduces measurement time considerably, is highly objective and easily applied.

39. Gillie, P. J. "A Simplified Formula for Measuring Abstraction in Writing," *Journal of Applied Psychology*, 41:214–17, August, 1957.

   A simplification of the Flesch Level of Abstraction formula, that combines the elements of definite articles and finite words with "nouns of abstraction." The revised abstraction formula gives similar results to those obtained by the lengthier Flesch formula and is easier to apply.

40. Gray, W. S., and Leary, B. E. "What Makes a Book Readable?" *Journal of Adult Education*, 6:408–11, October, 1934.

   This study examines some of the elements making a book readable and is specifically concerned with the reader of limited ability. The factors influencing readability are investigated and divided into four major categories. Through examination and testing, eight elements relating to readability are combined into a single instrument of prediction.

41. Gray, W. S., and Leary, B. E. *What Makes a Book Readable . . . : An Initial Study*. Chicago: The University of Chicago Press, 1935.

Some of the findings of this classic study of readability are that many adults cannot read a large part of available materials; experts rate content factors most important in readability; readers consider the ease or difficulty of materials a potent factor; some 44 structural factors are related to difficulty; and one factor may be used to measure difficulty of material, but a combination of significant factors is superior.

42. *Guide for Air Force Writing*. Air Force Manual 11-3. Maxwell, Ala.: Department of the Air Force, Maxwell Air Force Base, Air University, June, 1953.

A standard writing guide for Air Force writers and editors, this manual shows methods of applying the principles of plain talk to readable writing. Based upon the conclusions of several authors in the field of readability, it is designed to improve communication efficiency of Air Force personnel. Included in the Guide is a "Fog Count" readability formula developed by McElroy.

43. Gunning, R. *The Technique of Clear Writing*. New York: McGraw-Hill, 1952.

Intended to help writers make their work more readable, this book sets forth ten principles of clear writing developed by the author. The conclusions drawn include a statement of the value of using the Fog Index devised by Gunning. Special applications are discussed.

44. Hebb, D. O., and Bindra, D. "Scientific Writing and the General Problem of Communication," *American Psychologist*, 7:569–73, October, 1952.

The authors feel that the larger organization of scientific writing constitutes its difficulty and that too easy writing can be as great a stumbling block as too difficult writing. The basic problem of communication is helping the reader retain preceding information while adding to it bit by bit. The authors point out aids available to the writer in gaining the desired integration.

45. Jenkins, J. J., and Jones, R. L. "Flesch's 'Measuring the Level of Abstraction,'" *Journal of Applied Psychology,* 35:68, February, 1951.

Presenting five criticisms of Flesch's Level of Abstraction formula, the authors show why they feel it is not a better measure of readability than the Reading Ease formula. They conclude that for abstraction *per se* the new measure may have value, but as a measure of readability, existing instruments would seem to be as good or better.

46. Johnson, G. R. "An Objective Method of Determining Reading Difficulty," *Journal of Educational Research,* 21: 283–87, April, 1930.

Using a measure of the percentage of polysyllabic words in a given book to determine the difficulty of children's textbooks and reading matter, Johnson found that graded books show an increasing number of polysyllabic words from grade to grade. Difficulty is related to the proportion of polysyllabic words rather than to the actual length of such words occurring in a selection.

47. Kessler, E. "The Readability of Selected Contemporary Books for Leisure Reading in High School Biology," *Science Education,* 25:260–64, October, 1941.

The author analyzes 35 high school biology texts using the Gray-Leary readability formula elements. He concludes that the majority of the books belong in the "average" area and can be described as no more difficult structurally than the reading texts provided for junior high school reading.

48. Klare, G. R. "A Table for Rapid Determination of Dale-Chall Readability Scores," *Educational Research Bulletin,* 31:43–47, February 13, 1952.

Noting the problem of the time and effort necessary for application of readability formulas, Klare presents a table from which "a Dale-Chall readability raw score may be read directly by entering with the average sentence length and the Dale score values found by application of the formula. . . ."

49. Lewerenz, A. S. "Measurement of the Difficulty of Reading Materials," *Educational Research Bulletin,* Los Angeles City Schools, 8:11–16, March, 1929.

This study presents the Lewerenz measure of reading difficulty. From a 1000-word sample, the number of different words beginning with each letter of the alphabet is recorded. Totals for each letter and a grand total for the entire alphabet are found. The total for the five letters most involved in difficulty of material are made into a percentage of the grand total. Norms are consulted and percentage values of the five letters recorded. The average of the five values is the grade placement.

50. Lewerenz, A. S. "Vocabulary Grade Placement of Typical Newspaper Content," *Educational Research Bulletin,* Los Angeles City Schools, 10:4–6, September, 1930.

The results of an analysis of vocabulary difficulty and diversity of nonadvertising content of daily newspapers show a wide range of vocabulary difficulty. Comic strips and accounts of murders represent the simplest element; telegraph news and editorials, the most difficult.

51. Lewerenz, A. S. "Objective Measures for Selecting Reading Materials," *Educational Research Bulletin,* Los Angeles City Schools, 11:54–56, November, 1931.

Two objective measures are available for measuring vocabulary difficulty and diversity of textbooks. Books can be recommended to students based on their interest and reading ability. The reasons for presenting students with adequate and appropriate reading materials are stressed.

52. Lewerenz, A. S. "A Vocabulary Grade Placement Formula," *Journal of Experimental Education,* 3:236, 1935.

This is a general article on the topic of readability, in which the author tells of three measures he uses — vocabulary difficulty, vocabulary diversity, and vocabulary interest — but gives no further details.

53. Lewerenz, A. S. "Methods and Procedures for Evaluating Instructional Materials for Reading," *Claremont College's Reading Conference, Summer Session 1936.* Claremont, California: Claremont Library, 22–27, 1938.

Statistical procedures for the evaluation of textbooks are outlined, followed by a discussion of some of the existing aids to the objective analysis of reading materials. The importance of more extensive readability research is stressed; what has been accomplished to date is but an initial step in evaluating books and the children who read them.

54. Lewerenz, A. S. "Selection of Reading Materials by Pupil Ability and Interest," *Elementary English Review,* **16**:151–56, April, 1939.

Mental age, chronological age, and pupil achievement must all be considered when selecting books for students. Determining the reading comprehension level and vocabulary interest of a book is necessary in order to give the right child the right book.

55. Lively, B. A., and Pressey, S. L. "A Method for Measuring the 'Vocabulary Burden' of Textbooks," *Educational Administration and Supervision,* **9**:389–98, October, 1923.

Application of a vocabulary burden measure developed by Lively to texts from second grade to medical school levels indicated that vocabulary range increases from second grade up, is highest in newspapers and not particularly high in science books. Comparative difficulty also increased from second grade up, and from beginning science books to physiology texts.

56. Lorge, I. "Predicting Reading Difficulty of Selections for Children," *Elementary English Review,* **16**:229–33, October, 1939.

After reporting on six studies of reading difficulty, Lorge offers the suggestion that ". . . the most significant predictor of reading difficulty is some function of the vocabulary used." He then provides a formula using vocabulary, prepositional phrase, and sentence-length elements. *(See also* 57.)

57. Lorge, I. "Predicting Readability," *Teachers College Record,* **45**:404–19, March, 1944.

A formula is presented designed to obtain a prediction – the readability index – of written and spoken material in terms of grade level of reading. The formula predicts readability so that a passage is adjudged suitable for the grade corresponding with the readability index. *(See also* 56.)

58. Lorge, I. "The Lorge and Flesch Readability Formulae: A Correction," *School and Society,* **67**:141–42, February 21, 1948.

The readability formulas of Flesch and Lorge are corrected and tables presented which show the corrected data. "The correlation between the values estimated by the erroneous Lorge formula and the corrected Lorge formula is about .94 so that the relative difficulties by the new formula correspond pretty closely to those of the old."

59. Lorge, I. *The Lorge Formula for Estimating Difficulty of Reading Materials.* New York: Bureau of Publications, Teachers College, Columbia University, 1959.

    This booklet presents an introduction to the Lorge readability formula (1948 version) and directions for its use. There are three Appendices, the first containing a worksheet for use of the formula; the second an application to a sample passage; and the third the Dale List of 769 Easy Words.

60. McClusky, H. Y. "A Quantitative Analysis of the Difficulty of Reading Materials," *Journal of Educational Research,* **28**:276–82, December, 1934.

    The characteristics of college-level reading materials were studied. The results showed that easy material contains short sentences and simple vocabulary, while difficult material contains a technical and unfamiliar vocabulary and complex sentence structure.

61. Morriss, E. C., and Halverson, D. "Idea Analysis Technique." Unpublished (dittoed), on file Columbia University Library, 1938.

    Presents a method of analysis of reading difficulty based upon the consideration of words as representative of ideas (content words). Four classifications are given for content words: I. early words; II. localisms; III. concrete word-labels; IV. abstract word-labels.

62. Ojemann, R. H. "The Reading Ability of Parents and Factors Associated with Reading Difficulty of Parent Education Materials," *University of Iowa Studies in Child Welfare,* **8**:11–32, 1934.

    The distribution of reading ability among adults, the factors related to reading difficulty and the characteristics of materials at the various levels of difficulty are studied. Results show that reading material for adults with less than an eighth-grade education should contain simplified vocabulary and sentence structure, and few prepositional phrases.

63. Patty, W. W., and Painter, W. I. "Improving Our Method of Selecting High-School Textbooks," *Journal of Educational Research,* 24:23–32, June, 1931.

    In a study of the vocabulary burden of Indiana high school textbooks, it was found that the sophomore texts had the greatest vocabulary burden and that little difference obtained between texts of the other three grades.

64. Patty, W. W., and Painter, W. I. "A Technique for Measuring the Vocabulary Burden of Textbooks," *Journal of Educational Research,* 24:127–34, September, 1931.

    A technique is suggested for measuring the vocabulary burden of high school textbooks. The method is based upon samples from the texts, each sampled word given a weight according to its value in Thorndike's *Teachers' Word Book.* The method of determining the average-word-weighted-value and range of words of a book is explained.

65. Powers, R. D., Sumner, W. A., and Kearl, B. E. "A Recalculation of Four Readability Formulas," *Journal of Educational Psychology,* 49:99–105, April, 1958.

    The Flesch, Dale-Chall, Farr-Jenkins-Paterson and Gunning readability formulas are recalculated in order to modernize them and establish formulas derived from identical materials. All four recalculations agree with each other more closely than the original Dale-Chall and Flesch formulas did. For ease in using these formulas, see "New Diagrams for Calculating Readability Scores Rapidly," by R. D. Powers and J. E. Ross, *Journalism Quarterly,* 36:177–82, Spring, 1959.

66. Rosenzweig, S. "The Flesch and the Spirit," *American Psychologist,* 2:523–24, November, 1947.

    Defending the writing styles of Boring and James and arguing that the Flesch count fails to measure some important principles of writing, Rosenzweig suggests that since psychological writing deals with the whole human being and the concrete, vivid, and personal events of life, there is little danger of such writing "approaching the highest Flesch counts."

67. Spache, G. "A New Readability Formula for Primary-Grade Reading Materials," *Elementary School Journal,* 53:410–13, March, 1953.

    A regression equation which may be used to estimate the reading difficulty and grade level of primary grade reading materials is presented. Based on average sentence length and percentage of hard words in the material, the formula correlates favorably with other readability formulas, and formula estimates of reading difficulty agree closely with observed reading performances.

68. Stevens, S. S., and Stone, G. "Psychological Writing, Easy and Hard," *American Psychologist,* 2:230–35, July, 1947.

The Flesch readability formula (1943) is used to analyze nineteen psychology texts ranging from introductory texts to handbooks. The results show the fresh fertility of the psychological approach and the feasibility of it as a measure of readability. In general, the scores for the texts analyzed followed expectations.

69. Stevens, S. S., and Stone, G. "Further Comment [on "Psychological Writing, Easy and Hard," as discussed in "The Flesch and the Spirit," by Saul Rosenzweig, in the same issue of *American Psychologist*]," *American Psychologist,* 2:524–25, November, 1947.

The replies of Rosenzweig and of Flesch to the James-Koffka controversy, which arose when Stevens and Stone applied the Flesch count to a group of psychological writings, are discussed. To Rosenzweig's arguments they answer that (1) the distortions may prove too great for some purposes, insignificant for others; and (2) variability is a good style element.

70. Stone, C. "Measuring Difficulty of Primary Reading Material: A Constructive Criticism of Spache's Measure," *Elementary School Journal,* 57:36–41, October, 1957.

Primary reading material is found to rate lower in grade difficulty when the Stone revision of the Dale List of 769 Easy Words is employed with Spache's formula. Stone implies that his list increases the accuracy of the Spache formula for measuring reading difficulty.

71. Thorndike, E. L. "Improving the Ability to Read," *Teachers College Record,* 36:1–19, 123–44, 229–41, October, November, December, 1934.

Analyzing reading materials for Grades 4 to 9, Thorndike concludes that vocabulary can be increased by frequently introducing new words and repeating them often; the difficulty of a book can be determined with the Thorndike Inventory of English; and school dictionaries need to reduce facts and lengthen definitions if they are to be functional. A new method of improving reading ability that stresses the use of graded supplementary material is introduced.

72. Tribe, E. B. "A Readability Formula for the Elementary School Based Upon the Rinsland Vocabulary." Unpublished Doctoral dissertation, University of Oklahoma, 1956.

From an analysis of standard reading tests administered to elementary school children, Tribe develops a readability formula based upon Rinsland's *A Basic Vocabulary of Elementary School Children*. The two major factors contributing to structural difficulty in reading are vocabulary and average sentence length.

73. Twedt, D. W. "A Table for Use with Flesch's Level of Abstraction Readability Formula," *Journal of Applied Psychology,* **35:**157–59, June, 1951.

A convenient method for counting words and syllables, and a table to simplify use of Flesch's Level of Abstraction Readability Formula, are explained. The typewriter space bar is used for scoring counts; Twedt's table then gives readability scores for the counts.

74. Vogel, M., and Washburne, C. "An Objective Method of Determining Grade Placement of Children's Reading Material," *Elementary School Journal,* **28:**373–81, January, 1928.

A measuring device for checking the structural difficulty of children's reading matter is introduced. Results of application of the measure to 152 children's books showed that it was possible to analyze elementary reading material in terms of structural difficulty to determine the correct placement of the material.

75. Washburne, C., and Morphett, M. V. "Grade Placement of Children's Books," *Elementary School Journal,* **38:**355–64, January, 1938.

The authors revise their earlier formula for grading children's books and improve its application. The revised formula is applied to a sample of children's books selected by children's librarians; the results are compiled in *The Right Book for the Right Child.*

76. Wheeler, L. R., and Smith, E. H. "A Practical Readability Formula for the Classroom Teacher in the Primary Grades," *Elementary English,* 31:397–99, November, 1954. A readability formula devised for grading primary reading materials is outlined. The formula is based on the analysis of average sentence length and percentage of polysyllabic words.

77. Wheeler, L. R., and Wheeler, V. D. "Selecting Appropriate Reading Materials," *Elementary English,* **25:**478–89, December, 1948.

    The causes of reading difficulty and various methods of determining this difficulty are considered. Among the causes discussed are adaptability, organization, illustrations, sentence structure, and format. Vocabulary is stressed as the chief cause of reading difficulty. Practical suggestions for selecting reading materials for school children are offered.

78. Yoakam, G. A. "Revised Directions for Using the Yoakam Readability Formula." Unpublished study, University of Pittsburgh, 1948.

    Revised directions for applying the 1939 Yoakam readability formula are given. Ten pages selected from a book comprise a sample analysis. After all computations are completed, the Reading Difficulty Scale is used to grade the book.

79. Yoakam, G. A. *Basal Reading Instruction.* New York: McGraw-Hill, 1955.

    This book contains the author's views on basic procedures in teaching teachers how to teach reading. Part 1 of the Appendix (pp. 329–43) contains short descriptions of the nature, derivation, validation, use, sampling, and application of the Yoakam readability formula; Part 2, forms for use with the formula; Part 3, readability studies completed or in preparation at the University of Pittsburgh; and Part 4, annual reports of reading conferences at the University of Pittsburgh.

See also 309, 311, 314, and 316.

C. *Other Measures of Readability*

Nos. 80–127

80. Becker, E. "An Analysis of Thirty-One Preprimers." Un-published Master's thesis, University of Pittsburgh, 1936.

A vocabulary analysis of 31 preprimers showed no agreement among authors of preprimers about vocabulary makeup. Little agreement was found between vocabularies and standard word-lists; repetition was limited; and more recently published books tended to have fewer words outside the standard word-lists and fewer different words.

81. Bongers, H. *The History and Principles of Vocabulary Control, Parts I, II, and III.* Holland: Wocopi-Woerden, 1947.

A study of the history of word counts, plus a detailed com-parison of recent English word-lists, leads Bongers to develop his own 3,000 word K.L.M.-List. The author feels that his list covers more of the words in English texts than do the other recent lists.

82. Brown, R. "Vocabularies of History and Reading Text-books," *Bulletin of the Department of Elementary School Principals,* 10:408–11, April, 1931.

In a study comparing sixth-grade history textbooks with sixth-grade readers, it was found that history texts offer a heavier vocabulary burden than do readers where presumably one of the goals of teaching reading is the teaching of vocabulary. Brown suggests (1) rewriting history texts to downscale diffi-culty, (2) placing texts in advanced grades, or (3) drilling children on words in various texts.

83. Burk, C. "A Study of the Influence of Some Factors in Style of Composition on the Interest, Comprehension, and Rate of Reading of Fourth-Grade Pupils," *Journal of Experi-mental Education,* 4:303–52, June, 1936.

Examination of fourth-grade children's rate of reading, interest, and comprehension reveals that pupils are not consistently more or less interested in a single type of sentence or form of story. There is some indication, however, that they are more interested in stories containing short simple sentences and written in direct conversational form.

84. Curtis, F. D. *Investigations of Vocabulary in Textbooks of Science for Secondary Schools.* Boston: Ginn and Company, 1938.

    Investigations of the vocabulary used in junior and senior high science textbooks indicate that the writers of science texts should employ simpler vocabulary and use glossaries of important terms.

85. Cutright, P., Halvorson, G. P., and Brueckner, L. J. "A Study of One Factor in the Grade Placement of Reading Materials," *Elementary School Journal,* **29**:284–96, December, 1928.

    A method of measuring the difficulty of comprehension of reading materials and determining the proper grade placement of the materials is presented. The method employs vocabulary, comprehension, and pupil reading ability tests, related to each other by a method developed in Otis' *Statistical Method in Educational Measurement.*

86. Dale, E. *Familiarity of 8000 Common Words to Pupils in the Fourth, Sixth, and Eighth Grades.* Columbus, Ohio: Bureau of Educational Research, Ohio State University. (Mimeographed; not available.)

    This is a list of words based on the criterion of familiarity to children rather than the more common one of frequency of occurrence in print. Familiarity was determined on the basis of words being checked as known by readers. The list of approximately 3,000 words familiar to fourth graders is the one used in the Dale-Chall readability formula.

87. Dale, E., and Reichert, D. *Bibliography of Vocabulary Studies* (Revised Edition, 1957). Columbus, Ohio: Bureau of Educational Research, Ohio State University, 1957.

    This is a compilation through 1955 of all published vocabulary studies and a large number of unpublished theses and dissertations. It is a revision of the earlier 1949 issue, and contains 2,601 titles arranged in 26 groupings.

88. Dearborn, W. F., Johnston, P. W., and Carmichael, L. "Improving the Readability of Typewritten Manuscripts," *Proceedings of the National Academy of Sciences,* **37**:670–72, October 15, 1951.

    Print as a means of communication is studied, and several

methods of stressing words to emphasize meaning are presented. Use of stress methods in experiments showed an increase in comprehension as a result.

89. Dearborn, W. F., Johnston, P. W., and Carmichael, L. "Psychological Writing, Easy and Hard for Whom?" *American Psychologist,* **7**:195–96, June, 1952.

From investigation of the "peak stress" as a possible criterion of readability, evidence is offered that comprehension can be quantified by noting words stressed in reading aloud. A typical experiment is cited to show that scores for "peak stress" tests correlate with reading tests as reading tests correlate with each other.

90. DeLong, V. R. "Primary Promotion by Reading Levels," *Elementary School Journal,* **38**:663–71, May, 1938.

A plan of more efficient teaching of reading in the primary grades is offered. The plan retains the mastery of a basic vocabulary as a primary goal, but eliminates failure of promotion and needless re-reading of certain books as means of accomplishing this end. All available reading material in Grades 1 and 2 was rated according to word count and placed on the appropriate grade level.

91. Dewey, J. C. "A Case Study of Reading Comprehension Difficulties in American History." Unpublished Doctoral dissertation, State University of Iowa, 1931.

An investigation of the nature and limitations of comprehension in reading history at the eighth-grade level indicates that a larger percentage of correct answers is obtained from oral interviews than from written tests. Choosing correct pictures relating to certain contexts does not insure adequate understanding.

92. DiVesta, F. J. "The Effect of Methods of Presentation and Examining Conditions on Student Achievement in a Correspondence Course," *Journal of Applied Psychology,* **38**: 253–55, August, 1954.

In a study to determine the most effective method of presenting correspondence course materials, it was found that no particular presentation style — popular manner, formal expository manner, or study guide units — was more effective than another in terms of student achievement. Students who took open-book examinations had higher scores than those taking closed-book examinations.

93. Dolch, E. W. "Fact Burden and Reading Difficulty," *Elementary English Review,* **16**:135–38, April, 1939.

   Results of a study to determine reading difficulty of geography, history, science, and health textbooks at the elementary level indicate that geography texts were most difficult, followed by history, science, and health, in that order. As the texts became lighter in fact burden, the material became more story-like. However, fact burden did not always reflect the true picture of the text.

94. Dolch, E. W. "The Use of Vocabulary Lists in Predicting Readability and in Developing Reading Materials," *Elementary English,* **26**:142–49, 177, March, 1949.

   Problems of using vocabulary lists to determine the difficulty of reading material are discussed. While vocabulary is the basic element in reading difficulty, sentence length, multiple meanings, size of the list appropriate to the level of material, and the purpose of the list must also be considered.

95. Engleman, F. E. "The Relative Merits of Two Forms of Discourse When Applied to Children's Factual Content Reading Material," *Journal of Educational Research,* **29**:524–31, March, 1936.

   Comparison of the value of conversational and narrative-expository styles of writing at grade levels 4 and 7 shows that factual material written in a conversational style is preferred more frequently than narrative-expository style. Girls at grade 7 level preferred conversational style, while boys at this age had no decided preference.

96. Flesch, R. F. "Psychological Writing, Easy and Hard for Whom? Further Comment on the 'Peak Stress' Method," *American Psychologist,* **7**:593–94, October, 1952.

   Flesch argues that, in the "peak stress" method of measuring difficulty, the greatest agreement on which word to stress will occur in analysis of expository material because the simple, logical presentation and declarative sentences give only a limited degree of freedom with regard to "peak stress," whereas the informal style gives more freedom for personal interpretation, tone, and emphasis.

97. Hackman, R. C., and Kershner, A. M. *The Determination of Criteria of Readability.* Technical Report for Contract

NR 153-024, between the Office of Naval Research and the University of Maryland, 1951.

In a study to develop satisfactory criteria for readability research, criterion passages were selected on the basis of reader judgments of difficulty and reading time. The major conclusions were that a sampling unit of 2000 type spaces is superior to a word sample; reader judgment and reading time can be used as satisfactory criteria to differentiate "hard" and "easy" passages; and the passages could be used as criteria for the development of a prediction equation.

98. Hayes, J. D. "A Grade Placement Study of Primary Reading Material." Unpublished Master's thesis, University of Southern California, 1934.

A comparison of author and teacher grade placements of primary reading materials indicates that authors' placement of primer stories is much too advanced; the farther the reading matter is removed from the primer level, the closer the author-teacher agreement; and teachers agree with each other to a high degree on grade placement.

99. Keboch, F. D. "Variability of Word-Difficulty in Five American History Texts," *Journal of Educational Research,* **15**: 22–26, January, 1927.

A study to determine the variability of word difficulty in five seventh-grade history texts showed that all five texts ranked close in word difficulty.

100. Klare, G. R., Mabry, J. E., and Gustafson, L. M. "The Relationship of Patterning (Underlining) to Immediate Retention and to Acceptability of Technical Material," *Journal of Applied Psychology,* **49**:40–42, February, 1955.

Using an aircraft mechanics' lesson, the authors investigated the relationship of patterning of technical information to immediate retention. It was found that the patterning gave somewhat greater immediate retention among more able subjects but not among less able subjects. Patterning seemed to have little effect on either the speed with which material was read or on its acceptability.

101. Klare, G. R., Nichols, W. H., and Shuford, E. H. "The Relationship of Typographic Arrangement to the Learning

of Technical Training Material," *Journal of Applied Psychology*, 41:41–45, February, 1957.

This study was an attempt to relate two newly developed typographic arrangements to reading efficiency, acceptability, and immediate retention test score. Results showed, among other things, that the new arrangements aided the more able subjects, but not the less able, in achieving higher immediate retention test scores.

102. Klare, G. R., Shuford, E. H., and Nichols, W. H. "The Relation of Format Organization to Learning," *Educational Research Bulletin,* 37:39–45, February 12, 1958.

This study was an attempt to relate three levels of "format organization" to efficiency (speed) of reading, acceptability (reader preference), and immediate retention (comprehension) score. Results indicated that a higher level of format organization did not affect efficiency, but was judged more acceptable by readers and aided the more able, but not the less able, in achieving higher immediate retention test scores.

103. Kyte, G. C. "Calibrating Reading Material," *Elementary School Journal,* 25:533–46, March, 1925.

Materials recommended for use in third-grade readers were analyzed to determine if they were appropriate for third-grade use. Results showed that 22 of the 53 selections were not appropriate for third-grade use, some being too difficult and others too easy.

104. Lorge, I. *The Semantic Count of the 570 Commonest English Words*. New York: Bureau of Publications, Teachers College, Columbia University, 1949.

A study to discover the relative frequency of occurrence of the various meanings of the commonest 570 English words showed a relationship between frequency of occurrence and number of meanings a word can carry. The commonest words in English carry a large number of meanings.

105. Lorge, I., and Thorndike, E. L. *A Semantic Count of English Words,* Vols. 1 and 2. New York: The Institute of Educational Research, Teachers College, Columbia University, 1938. (Microfilm)

This count of the relative frequency with which the various

dictionary meanings of English words occur in print was made primarily for the use of teachers and textbook writers, in the stated hope that it would help them free their speaking and writing from undesirable rarities of word meanings.

106. McCullough, C. "What is a Good Book to a Ninth-Grader?" *English Journal*, 25:381–87, May, 1936.

A study of the reading interests of ninth-grade students showed that both boys and girls seem to favor books about boys and girls rather than books about adults or animals. Girls may read books about boys, but boys do not read books about girls. Adventure and heroism are the top-ranking interest factors for boys; hardship and heroism the girls' main interests.

107. McKee, P. "Word Lists and Vocabulary Difficulty in Reading Matter," *Elementary English Review*, 14:241–45, November, 1937.

The vocabulary burden of reading matter cannot be judged by its correspondence with vocabulary of word-lists. The author suggests that word-list users also consider the element of conceptual meaning as against visual recognition, the importance of word frequency, the multiple meanings of words, and the wisdom of removing all unfamiliarity from content.

108. Marcum, D. M. "Experiences, Concepts, and Reading," *Elementary School Journal*, 44:410–15, March, 1944.

Analysis of primary-grade reading materials, in an effort to determine a basic list of concepts needed by children using such reading materials, indicated that unfamiliar concepts can confuse reading as much as difficult vocabulary and that the teacher can teach concepts by providing experiences.

109. Mathews, C. O. *The Grade Placement of Curriculum Materials in the Social Studies*. Columbia University Contributions to Education, No. 241. New York: Teachers College, Columbia University, 1926.

Results of a study to determine how well students in Grades 4 through 12 comprehend various types of social studies materials showed that the ability to comprehend the materials increased gradually from the fourth to the twelfth grade. Episodes were comprehended better than other types, while graphs were least understood.

110. Mehl, M. A. "A Vocabulary Study of First Grade Readers,"
     Unpublished Master's thesis, University of Colorado, 1931.
     Primers and first readers were analyzed to determine the
     number of concepts they contained and to show, with the use
     of standard word-lists, how these concepts prepare for current
     and future reading. Numbers of different words and concepts
     and the frequencies of each were determined. It was found
     that more recent readers were improved with regard to the
     number of different words and their repetition.

111. O'Rourke, E. V., and Mead, C. D. "Vocabulary Difficulties
     in Five Textbooks in Third-Grade Arithmetic," *Elemen-
     tary School Journal*, 41:683–91, May, 1941.
     After evaluating the vocabulary-difficulty of five third-grade
     arithmetics, the author concludes that, in the case of proper
     nouns, children are meeting an unwarranted number of new
     persons and places in the texts. These constitute stumbling
     blocks in getting the real message of the problems across.

112. Peterson, E. M. *Aspects of Readability in the Social Studies*.
     Teachers College Studies in Education. New York: Bureau
     of Publications, Teachers College, Columbia University,
     1954.
     Two high school textbook passages were revised so that a
     version with increased interest and one with more logical or-
     ganization were developed for each. Tests of several kinds
     revealed that the interest and organization versions resulted in
     superior comprehension as compared to the original version,
     and that the interest modification version was preferred to the
     original and organization versions.

113. Robinson, F. P. "The Effect of Language Style on Reading
     Performance," *The Journal of Educational Psychology*,
     38:149–56, March, 1947.
     The results of this study, designed to show how markedly read-
     ing comprehension may be affected by the complexity of lan-
     guage structure, were not significant. However, it is suggested
     that vocabulary is not the only determinant of paragraph com-
     prehension and that language structure, intelligence, and
     training are factors which must be considered.

114. Smith, H. E. "The Validity of Teachers' Judgments of
     Difficulty in Curricular Materials," *Journal of Educational
     Psychology*, 21:460–66, September, 1930.

The validity of difficulty-judgments by experienced and inexperienced teachers and by experts in the given fields of different types of subject matter are examined. Comparison of these judgments with actual difficulty revealed that the validity coefficients ranged from high to low, but were higher than those found by previous investigators.

115. Stadtlander, E. L. "A Scale for Evaluating the Difficulty of Reading Materials for the Intermediate Grades," Abstracts of Theses, Vol. XV, 1939, *University of Pittsburgh Bulletin*, **36**:347–52, January 10, 1940.

A scale is presented for determining reading difficulty for material for the intermediate grades, and for determining where children at various grade levels no longer comprehend vocabulary. It is shown that it is possible to construct material by summing index numbers of words on the Thorndike Word-List, and to control the vocabulary within the comprehension range of various grade levels.

116. Staiger, R. C. "Certain Language Factors in the Readability of Primary Reading Textbooks," *Journal of Educational Research*, **48**:589–96, April, 1955.

The influence of certain language factors on the readability of materials used in language instruction in the first through the third grades is examined. Results of the study reveal that words typically introduced in third readers; different words among the Thorndike 1000 commonest words; and words per paragraph were significant factors in the difficulty of language materials.

117. Stone, C. R. "Measures of Simplicity and Beginning Texts in Reading," *Journal of Educational Research*, **31**:447–50, February, 1938.

Beginning reading books are compared for simplicity by using the three factors of the ratio of new words to total words, average new words per page, and per cent of sentences complete in one line. Stone concludes that this method determines the simplicity of material with a high degree of reliability.

118. Stone, C. R. "A Vocabulary Study Based on 107 Primary-Grade Books," *Elementary School Journal*, **42**:452–55, February, 1942.

A graded vocabulary in primary-grade reading is formulated, in which the words appearing most widely are listed and graded on the basis of their use as new words in the readers and on the basis of data available from other sources. Findings illustrate the accelerating rate of vocabulary growth among ten levels of reading.

119. Taylor, W. L. "Cloze Procedure: A New Tool for Measuring Readability," *Journalism Quarterly*, 30:415–33, Fall, 1953.

The Cloze procedure for readability measurement and experiments demonstrating its use are described. It is found that Cloze scores ranked passages in the same way as the Flesch and Dale-Chall formulas; that there was effective discrimination between different levels of readability; that random deletion yields reliable results without attention to meaning or function of deleted words; and that Cloze scores can be used to measure reading ability.

120. Taylor, W. L. "Recent Developments in the Use of 'Cloze Procedure,'" *Journalism Quarterly*, 33:42–48, 99, Winter, 1956.

Developments in the use of Cloze procedure since its introduction are reviewed. The method is briefly described, and details are given showing how Cloze procedure can measure comprehension, intelligence, and existing knowledge and learning; how it can be applied to the Korean language; how it can be applied to the "listenability" of spoken messages; and how it can be related to entropy scores.

121. Taylor, W. L. " 'Cloze' Readability Scores as Indices of Individual Differences in Comprehension and Aptitude," *Journal of Applied Psychology*, 41:19–26, February, 1957.

To test the validity of Cloze scores as readability measures, Cloze results are compared with comprehension tests on an Air Force supply article. Correlation coefficients are computed and all are found to be positive and significant. Score differences attributable to learning are also significant. Random deletion yields more stable, reliable, and discriminating results than the deletion of easy and hard words.

122. Von Qualen, V. D., and Kambley, P. E. "Children's Interests in Science as Indicated by Choices of Reading Material," *School Science and Mathematics*, 45:798–806, December, 1945.

Analysis of the scientific interests of elementary pupils as indicated by their choice of reading materials ranked thirteen interest areas as follows: Most Liked — Ancient Animals, Science and Industry, Transportation, General Science, Living Animals, and Electricity and Magnetism; Least Liked — Conservation, Light, Cloth, Astronomy, Weather, Plants, and the Earth's Crust.

123. Ward, J. L., and Stevenson, P. R. "The Vocabulary of a History Text," *American School Board Journal,* **71**:65, 131, July, 1925.

The vocabulary used in a modern history text is compared with the vocabulary of general reading by obtaining a count of all words and their frequencies in the first 106 pages of the text. It is suggested that the 327 words not found in Thorndike's list of 10,000 most commonly used words might well constitute an essential history vocabulary for which special instruction should be given.

124. Washburne, C. W. "A Scientifically Graded Book List for Children," *Teachers Journal and Abstract,* **1**:41–46, January, 1926.

Eight hundred schoolteachers assisted in the compilation of a graded list of 700 books read and enjoyed by children of varying degrees of reading ability. The list provides data regarding numbers of boys and girls reading and liking the books; age and grade level for which they are suitable; grade range of interest and a popularity index of the books.

125. Washburne, C., and Vogel, M. "What Books Fit What Children?" *School and Society,* **23**:22–24, January, 1926.

The results of an investigation of the books read and enjoyed by children of various ages and degrees of reading ability are presented. Such information as average age of pupils, average reading score, grade range of the middle 50% of students, number of readers falling within one grade of the median, and an index of popularity may be used to determine what books to assign children of varying ages, grades, and reading abilities.

126. Wilson, M. C. "The Effect of Amplifying Material Upon Comprehension," *Journal of Experimental Education,* **13**:5–8, September, 1944.

The results of a study to determine the effect of amplification of general comments upon reading comprehension of intermediate-level children show that amplification of material tends to improve comprehension.

127. Witty, P. A., and LaBrant, L. L. "Vocabulary and Reading," *School and Society*, 31:268–72, February 22, 1930.

In a study measuring vocabulary demands presented by adult reading materials, 12 well-known books are analyzed and the words in each are classified according to the Thorndike word-list of 10,000 words. It was found that over 90% of all words in the books came from the 5,000 most commonly used words, with the "so-called classics" presenting no greater vocabulary difficulty than the popular modern novels analyzed.

See also 2, 3, 11, 14, 15, and 16

D. *Applications of Readability Measures*
1. Education

Nos. 128–228

128. Adelman, M. "Difficulty of Four Original and Four Simplified Novels, as Judged by the Lewerenz, Winnetka and Lorge Formulae." Unpublished Master's thesis, College of the City of New York, 1941.

The grade placements of four original well-known novels were compared with the simplified versions of the books to determine the factors making a book difficult for the average reader. The simplified books were found easier in all cases. More hard, uncommon, and polysyllabic words were found in the originals than in the simplified versions.

129. Allard, J. A. "Difficulty of Poems Commonly Presented to Elementary School Pupils" (abstract of a Doctoral dissertation). *University of Pittsburgh Bulletin*, 42:9–18, February 10, 1946.

Six hundred and seventy-three poems were presented to 50,000 pupils in order to determine the reasons for children's likes and dislikes in poetry and to determine the vocabulary difficulty of poems written for and by children. Results indicated that difficulty of poems influences choice and that vocabulary difficulty specifically was significant. Child poets used a vocabulary corresponding closely to their respective grades in school.

130. Anderson, W. "Readability of Readers," *American Psychologist,* 11:147–48, March, 1956.

    Flesch Readability and Human Interest formulas were applied to five psychology readers to determine the difficulty and interestingness of books for psychology undergraduates, and of psychological writing in general. All the books were scored *Difficult,* with wide ranges of difficulty within books. Articles were *Mildly Interesting* to *Dull.* Readability did not necessarily imply interestingness.

131. Andrews, D. I. "A Study of the Vocabulary and Readability of a Third-Grade Classroom Periodical," Report of the Proceedings and Address, Forty-Ninth Annual Meeting, April 15–18, 1952, *Bulletin,* National Catholic Education Association, 49:221–25, August, 1952.

    Third-grade editions of a classroom periodical were analyzed to determine the comprehensive value of the periodical. Application of the Flesch formula showed that average affix count was excellent, sentence length was good, and human interest was satisfactory. The Winnetka formula showed the periodical to have a grade level of 2.98, a very superior interest rating, and a large majority of words appearing among the first 1,500 of the Thorndike list.

132. Ayer, A. M. *Some Difficulties in Elementary School History.* Contributions to Education, No. 212. New York: Teachers College, Columbia University, 1926.

    A study to determine whether the material offered in elementary history is comprehended by pupils showed a large degree of incomprehension of fifth-grade history paragraphs by both fifth- and seventh-grade pupils. Results were generally better when the paragraphs were simplified. A great deal of history material tested was found sufficiently difficult for high school use.

133. Baker, W. M. "A Study of the Vocabulary Load of Six Arithmetic Texts Approved for Use in Kentucky High Schools." Unpublished Master's thesis, University of Kentucky, 1932.

    Six high school arithmetic texts were analyzed to ascertain whether they differed significantly in their vocabularies. It was found that intra-book word counts established the reliability of the sampling method and that inter-book counts established the essential similarity of difficulty among the books. The ninth-grade book ranked easiest and the rest close together, furnishing no basis for a choice in terms of vocabulary difficulty.

134. Berger, H. I. "The Difficulty of Third Grade Readers," *Elementary School Journal,* 47:391–95, March, 1947.

A study to determine the effect of vocabulary burden upon the reading skills of third-grade children revealed that many of the new words introduced in the third grade are used too infrequently to permit continued progress in the reading skills.

135. Beust, E. "The Publisher's Role in Promoting Growth in Interpretation," *Promoting Growth Toward Maturity in Interpreting What Is Read,* ed. W. S. Gray. Supplementary Educational Monograph No. 74. Chicago: University of Chicago Press, 1951, pp. 240–44.

To show how the textbook performs the dual function of teaching reading and applying reading ability to the learning of subject matter, a description is presented of what is being done on the levels of mental capacity, language ability, and experiential background to ensure understanding and communication by textbook users.

136. Brayfield, A. H., and Reed, P. A. "How Readable Are Occupational Information Booklets?" *Journal of Applied Psychology,* 34:325–28, October, 1950.

Analysis of the readability of occupational information literature revealed that approximately two-thirds of the material examined ranked as *Very Difficult* by Flesch's Reading Ease measure and almost equal proportions were ranked as *Dull* and *Mildly Interesting* by the Human Interest measure.

137. Broening, A. M. "Literary Merit and the Winnetka Formula for Grading Children's Books," *The Role of Research in Educational Progress,* Official Report, American Educational Research Association, a Department of the National Education Assn. Washington: American Educational Research Association, 148–52, 1937.

How the Winnetka formula may be used without lessening the literary merits of children's books is discussed. The author states that the essence of a literary work is not measured by formulas but by ideas and feelings expressed in the use of words. The reader's own experience is the key to literature.

138. Bryson, L. "Readability Laboratory," *Library Journal,* **61**:455, June, 1936.

     The origin and growth of work in readability problems is reviewed and the techniques used at the Readability Laboratory at Columbia University for establishing readability of materials are discussed. The author concludes that the Laboratory's techniques can and have been used to establish whether materials are readable and what makes them readable, and that this knowledge helps in the writing of readable materials.

139. Bryson, L. "What Are Readable Books?" *The Educational Forum,* **1**:397–402, May, 1937.

     The reasons for readability research are shown and various approaches to the problem are described. It is concluded that some of the factors involved in readability have been isolated, pointing the way for future research.

140. Burkey, J. E. "The Readability of Elementary Science Materials," *Dissertation Abstracts,* University of Pittsburgh, **14**:1328, September, 1954.

     Forty-one science texts were analyzed with Yoakam's formula to determine their readability; technical and general vocabularies were distinguished and gradations within texts determined. It was found that 18 of the 41 were scored the same by the formula and by publishers' estimates of difficulty. The 16 most difficult texts contained 35% technical words among the words scaled.

141. Caliver, A. "Literacy Education Project Draws to a Close," *School Life,* **32**:74–75, February, 1950.

     The author reports on the Literacy Education Project conducted under the sponsorship of the Office of Education for the purposes of developing instructional materials, preparing qualified teachers, and stimulating civic interest in the problem of illiteracy. The author concludes that the purposes of the study were accomplished, and he reports on the materials produced by the Project.

142. Carpenter, H. M. *Gateways to American History: An Annotated Graded List of Books for Slow Learners in Junior High School.* New York: H. W. Wilson Company, 1942.

     The Lorge formula for readability was used in the development of an annotated, graded list of books for slow learners in junior high school and recommended for use by teachers and librarians in the selection of books not listed in the bibliography.

143. Carr, E. R., Wesley, E. B., and Murra, W. F. "Social Studies," *Encyclopedia of Educational Research.* New York: The Macmillan Co., 1950, pp. 1213–38.

    In this survey of social studies, the section on grade placement is pertinent to readability studies. It is pointed out that research is beginning to develop lists of social science vocabulary and concepts, and that word counts based on the Thorndike list point to a great deal of difficulty in social studies texts. The problem of large numbers of difficult terms used infrequently can be approached through the substitution of less difficult words and the amplification and expansion of materials to provide for repetition.

144. Chall, J. S. "Graded Reading Paragraphs in Health Education." Unpublished Master's thesis, Ohio State University, 1947.

    Health education materials for specified levels of reading ability were constructed and given to subjects from Grade 3 through graduate level. Results showed that the graded reading materials were appropriate for the grades intended. It was concluded that these materials could be used as samples for other fields, provided the material used was similar to that used in the study.

145. Charters, W. W., Jr. "Pre-Testing a College Textbook," *Educational Research Bulletin,* **29**:85–95, 112, 1950.

    The use of research techniques in constructing a college text is discussed to show how textbook writing is amenable to improvement through research. In an "exploratory study," the author, by means of interviews and student editing of a preliminary manuscript, gathered information regarding organization, interestingness, reading ease, etc., and used it in his final revision of the book.

146. Clarke, J. "Readability: A Practical Problem," *Library Journal,* **66**:383–85, May 1, 1941.

    The complexity of the problem of readability is pointed out and it is suggested that numerical formulas are not reliable or complete indices of readability. According to criteria for readability developed by the Readability Laboratory at Columbia University, material should be informative, lucid, at the proper level for the reader, and offer rewards and satisfactions.

147. Courtier, A. M. "Criteria for the Selection of Primers," *Elementary English Review*, 16:271–78, November, 1939.

     The necessary requirements for conducting an adequate primary reading program are discussed. An analysis of the vocabulary burden of 20 primers showed that repetition is more prevalent in primers today than prior to 1930, that not only should vocabulary be controlled but the book should have interest appeal, that the book should contain child-interest stories of the action type, and that sentences should be simple, gradually lengthening through the book.

148. Cramer, J. F. "Relative Difficulty of Junior High School Social Studies Texts," *Journal of Educational Research*, 26:425–28, February, 1933.

     Two criticisms of a unified junior high school social studies course — that there was too much material to cover in the allotted time and the vocabulary of the special unified text was too difficult — are evaluated. The author concludes that allotting additional time to the combined courses provided ample opportunity to cover the work and that the unified texts were actually easier than those which they replaced.

149. Crooks, K. B. M., and Smith, C. H. "The Reading Problem in College Science Instruction," *Science Education*, 41:54–57, February, 1957.

     Twenty college science texts were analyzed with Flesch's "Method of Readability" to determine whether Reading Ease was related to failures in courses using the texts. Of the 20, two scored *Fairly Difficult* and the others *Difficult*. All scored *Dull* on the Human Interest scale. It was concluded that the average college freshman encounters unnecessary problems in science courses due to the style of writing in science texts.

150. DeBoer, J., and Yoakam, G. E. "Textbooks and the Educative Process: A Discussion," *Elementary English Review*, 22:333–36, December, 1945.

     Discussing Yoakam's article, "The Reading Difficulty of School Textbooks," it is suggested that in aiming at the average readers in a class, individual differences within the average are not considered. It is concluded that textbooks and basal readers have been important in their attention to vocabulary, child-interest themes and comprehensive reading skill, but that without individual attention, the child's reading difficulties are multiplied.

151. Edgerton, R. B. "How Difficult Are Children's Encyclopedias? II," *Elementary School Journal,* 45:455–64, April, 1945.

   Analysis of three children's encyclopedias to determine their reading difficulty revealed all three to be far too difficult for their intended elementary school audiences. *Junior Britannica* ranked easiest, followed in order by *Compton's Pictured* and *World Book.*

152. Edgerton, R. B. "How Difficult Are Children's Encylopedias? A Second Report," *Elementary School Journal,* 55:219–29, December, 1954.

   In a ten-year follow-up to determine what had been done to bring children's encyclopedias within the reading range of elementary pupils, the vocabulary load and sentence length in three children's encyclopedias were analyzed. It was found that the three, between 1943 and 1953, showed an over-all gain in reading ease of three full grades, from Grade 10 to Grade 7.

153. Egan, M. "An Experiment in Advisory Service and Graded Reading in the CCC Camps," *Library Quarterly,* 7:471–91, October, 1937.

   In a study to determine the need or desire for more personal library service, the practicability of individual guidance, and the type of book most wanted, the author found a widespread reading deficiency in relation to amount of previous schooling. Reading grade level affected ability to understand and enjoy books in spite of difficulties caused by unfamiliar vocabulary or content.

154. Faison, E. W. J. "Readability of Children's Textbooks," *Journal of Educational Psychology,* 42:43–51, January, 1951.

   Analysis of 38 textbooks for Grades 5 through 8 using Flesch's Reading Ease and Human Interest formulas showed that, for reading ease, all books fell within the range from *Fairly Difficult* to *Easy,* and all averages for individual grades were in the *Interesting* human interest range.

155. Fihe, P. J., Wallace, V., and Schulz, M. *Books for Adult Beginners, Grades I to VII* (rev. ed.). Chicago: American Library Association, 1946.

Readability formulas were used in grading a selected, diversified list of books for the illiterate and near-illiterate. It was found difficult to compile a suitable list for Grades 1–4. The Flesch formula, despite the time necessary for application, was valuable for Grade 5 and on.

156. Flesch, R. F. "What Can You Do About Readability?" *Wilson Library Bulletin,* 15:752–54, May, 1941.

The problem of readability is outlined for the librarian, and a brief account of work in the field is given. Three practical suggestions for approaching the problem are advanced: horizontally classifying books as "easy," "difficult," and "in-between"; making books accessible under broad subject classification; and obtaining data from prospective readers which will enable librarians to get the right books into the hands of the right reader.

157. Flesch, R. F. "Readability — A New Approach," *The Library Journal,* 67:213–15, March 1, 1942.

Progress toward a workable readability formula and its application to library service is reported. The elements of morpheme count and sentence length were found more useful than previous indices. A convenient way is presented for librarians to compare comprehension difficulty of a given book with the magazine level scale devised in the study.

158. Gardner, W. E. "Aspects of Books that Affect Readability and Use — In Social Studies," Ch. XVII of *Materials for Reading,* Proceedings of the Annual Conference on Reading held at the University of Chicago, 1957, ed. H. M. Robinson. Chicago: University of Chicago Press, in conjunction with *School Review* and *Elementary School Journal,* 19:170–74, December, 1957.

The effects of content, style, and format upon the reading ease of social studies books is discussed. It is concluded that "because the social studies deal with complex generalizations and concepts, the handling of the content has the greatest influence on readability, although the three aspects are most certainly interrelated." Readability formulas are discounted because of their quantitative nature.

159. Gholston, L. B. "Reading Difficulty of Science Textbooks Adopted for the State of Alabama as Determined by the

Lorge Formula." Unpublished Master's thesis, Alabama Polytechnic Institute, 1947.

Results of Lorge Three-Factor Formula analysis of science textbooks adopted in Alabama showed that the books did not conform to grades for which they were intended. Grade 2, 3, and 4 texts were found especially difficult, while junior high and senior high school texts showed little increase in reading difficulty.

160. Glott, R. "An Investigation of the Verbal Matter in Recently Published Arithmetic Textbooks and Workbooks for the Intermediate Grades," *Dissertation Abstracts,* University of Pittsburgh, **16**:477–78, March, 1956.

Arithmetic texts and workbooks used in Grades 4 through 6 were studied to determine their readability levels and the extent of gradation within them. It was found that the samples used ranged from *More Difficult* than the publisher's estimate to *Easier.* The language of problems was more difficult than developmental and explanatory material and extreme internal variations in difficulty were found.

161. Goodman, D. G. "A Study of the Readability of High School Business Law Textbooks," *Dissertation Abstracts,* **17**:61–62, January, 1957.

Determination of the grade placement of 28 high school business law texts revealed that the majority of the texts were within the comprehension of the average twelfth-grader and over half of them were not too difficult for the average eleventh-grader. Only a slight difference in difficulty was noted between legal and nonlegal words used.

162. Ham, C. "Aspects of Books that Affect Readability and Use — In Literature," Ch. XVII of *Materials for Reading,* Proceedings of the Annual Conference on Reading held at the University of Chicago, 1957, ed. H. M. Robinson. Chicago: University of Chicago Press, in conjunction with *School Review* and *Elementary School Journal,* **19**:167–70, December, 1957.

Discussing the question, "What makes a book readable?" the author suggests that interest, experience, purpose, and reader needs are not accounted for in readability predictions. The author turns to literary criticism for the answers, discussing interest or preference as it relates to personal taste, and concludes that almost every book is readable to someone. The reader determines readability, not the book.

163. Hildreth, G. "All in Favor of a Low Vocabulary," *Elementary School Journal,* **43**:462–70, April, 1943.

Investigating the question of whether reduced vocabulary in primary reading books promotes better learning or retards development of reading skills, the author concludes that low vocabulary in early reading experience teaches the child to use reading as a tool from the start and that is it easier to enrich a reading program than to lighten the load for slow learners and problem readers.

164. Hildreth, G., and Wagner, G. "Putting the Know-How of Readability to Work," *Midland Schools,* **68**:16–17, 42, May, 1954.

Noting that few teachers have time to analyze books with readability formulas, the authors suggest that it is important for teachers to understand readability principles and apply them. Testing of reading ability is a way teachers can help in this work. Elements of difficulty or ease which teachers must watch for are listed.

165. Hockett, J. A. *The Vocabularies and Contents of Elementary School Readers.* State of California Dept. of Education Bulletin. Sacramento: California State Dept. of Education, May 1, 1938.

Detailed information is presented regarding the relative vocabulary burden and difficulty of elementary reading materials, along with a guide classifying such materials on a variety of topics. Tables summarize the vocabulary data obtained for books on each grade level.

166. Hockett, J. A. "The Vocabularies of Recent Primers and First Readers," *Elementary School Journal,* **39**:112–15, October, 1938.

Basic vocabulary data on six primers and six first readers are presented. Trends noted in an earlier study of primers and first readers toward lighter vocabulary loads were found to be continuing and it was noted that the average primer is shorter and has a less extensive vocabulary load than the average first reader.

167. Hockett, J. A., and Neeley, N. G. "The Vocabularies of Twenty-Eight First Readers," *Elementary School Journal,* 37:344–52, January, 1937.

A study of 28 widely used first readers revealed that the typical reader contains more than 9000 words of reading matter, slightly less than 600 different words and 15.6 running words to each different word. About half of the words are repeated more than five times and about a fourth appear more than 15 times. The trend is toward smaller vocabularies, increased repetition, and greater use of word-lists.

168. Horn, E. *Methods of Instruction in the Social Studies.* New York: Charles Scribner's Sons, 1937.

This book is a survey of methods of teaching social studies subjects, based upon a canvass of the literature up to approximately the time of publication. Of greatest relevance to readability is the section, "Reading Difficulty in Relation to the Difficulty of Ideas," pp. 157–71, which includes references to the work of Gray and Leary, Vogel and Washburne, Dale and Tyler, Ojemann, Thorndike, Ogden, Dale, and Horn. The author concludes that style factors are important in reading difficulty, but conceptual difficulties are even more important.

169. Hoyman, H. S. "Are High School Health Texts Too Difficult?" *Journal of School Health,* 25:274–82, December, 1955.

Analysis of data on 20 high school health texts showed that many "current high school health texts may be too difficult"; that the texts differed in readability; and that specific texts could be designated as too difficult for given grades or given reading abilities. No progression of reading difficulty was found from the beginning to end of any text.

170. Jenson, L. "Evaluation of Reading Difficulty in Encyclopedia Content in Grades Five Through Eight." Unpublished Master's thesis, University of Minnesota, June, 1939.

To determine the relation between reading comprehension and comprehension of the content of four encyclopedias, 281 students in Grades 5 through 8 took standard reading tests and tests on sample paragraphs from the encyclopedias. It was found that a student must have seventh- to ninth-grade reading ability to understand the material and that compactness and unfamiliar concepts and information caused trouble while familiarity and simplicity contributed to ease of reading.

171. Johnson, D. A. "The Readability of Mathematics Books," *The Mathematics Teacher,* **50:**105–10, February, 1957.

Examination of three seventh-grade and three eighth-grade arithmetic texts, two elementary algebra texts, three plane geometry texts and seven supplementary mathematics books showed that seventh- and eighth-grade books were most difficult, algebra texts at about the right level, and geometry books occasionally a grade level below that for which they were written. Variation was found among grade levels and within books; problem material was found easier than expository or enrichment material.

172. Johnson, E. M. "How to Make News Materials Written for Children Readable," *A Report of the Tenth Annual Conference on Reading.* Pittsburgh: University of Pittsburgh Press, 149–56, 1954.

The use of readability factors to improve the quality and amount of reading done by children and adults is discussed. It is shown that editors can write best for children when they know the problems and interests of the particular group for which they are writing. Having a full knowledge of vocabulary load, sentence length, and paragraph structure is vital.

173. Jones, H. "Readability and the Results of Applying a Readability Formula to Health Textbooks," *A Report of the Tenth Annual Conference on Reading.* Pittsburgh: University of Pittsburgh Press, 56–66, 1954.

The aspects of readability, as applied to the formal learning situation, are discussed. While readability formulas are not absolute measures and have, in some cases, glaring faults, they can be of use in finding the readability of various materials. Used in the classroom, formulas can help the teacher determine whether the material used is appropriate.

174. Kearney, N. C. "Sentence Length in 121 Representative First-Grade Readers," *Journal of Educational Research,* **38:**447–61, February, 1945.

Detailed data on sentence length in 42 pre-primers, 38 primers, and 42 first readers were obtained. It was found that sentences get longer from pre-primer to first reader and that there were very few extremely long sentences. It was concluded from the study that sentence length may not wholly account for reading difficulty, but that it may serve as a guide for teachers in further study.

175. Kempfer, H. "Simpler Reading Materials Needed for 50,000,000 Adults," *School Life*, **32**:115, 127, May, 1950.

To show that the reading level of most publications is too difficult for most adults, 56 librarians and evening school principals were queried about levels at which a shortage of appropriate materials occurs, acuteness of need at third-, fourth-, and fifth-grade levels, and fields in which the need is most felt. The greatest gap in materials occurred between the barely literate and facile levels. Respondents felt the need for materials was great, particularly in the field of nonfiction.

176. Larrick, N. "Readability Formulas and Books for Children," *Publishers' Weekly*, **160**:1708–12, October 27, 1951.

Basic misunderstandings about readability formulas are discussed and aspects of several well-known formulas elaborated on. Formulas measure difficulty of words read *by* the child and not *to* him. The speaking vocabulary of a child is larger than his reading vocabulary. Formulas do not restrict vocabulary to certain words for certain grades, but consider that the more words not on a word-list, the more difficult the material.

177. Leary, B. E. "Determining Difficulty of Reading Materials," *School Life*, **23**:275–76, 295, April, 1938.

Discussing the inadequacy of reading materials for slow learners and methods derived to determine the difficulty of reading materials, the author points out that there is a lack of materials for slow readers at all levels, particularly for adults. Familiar words and simple sentences have been shown to aid in comprehension. Vocabulary has been the focus of most readability studies, which have seldom proceeded to the study of ideas, where the main concern should lie.

178. Lewerenz, A. S. "An Experiment in Evaluating Books Read and Enjoyed by School Children," *Educational Research Bulletin*, Los Angeles City Schools, **9**:10–14, September, 1929.

Evaluation of 36 elementary-level library books showed that very popular books were given a comparatively low interest value by pupils. Girls showed greater interest in the books they read than did boys, who liked series books and the story element. Children read books below their actual reading level for recreation.

179. Lewerenz, A. S. "Objective Measurement of Diverse Types of Reading Materials," *Educational Research Bulletin,* Los Angeles City Schools, 9:8–11, October, 1929.

The results of examination of different kinds of reading material using the Lewerenz formula showed that primary readers vary in difficulty; readers of a series do not always advance progressively in difficulty; and ninth-grade reading ability is necessary to understand the material on an editorial page of a daily paper.

180. Lewerenz, A. S. "Reading Material Evaluated by Means of the Vocabulary Grade Placement Formula," *Educational Research Bulletin,* Los Angeles City Schools, 11:98–119, April, 1932.

A list of reading materials is presented which were evaluated for difficulty by means of the Vocabulary Grade Placement Formula. Some 260 titles were analyzed and summarized into three categories: (1) Vocabulary Difficulty and Diversity Grade Placements, (2) alphabetically listed titles by grade, and (3) alphabetically listed titles by subject.

181. Lewerenz, A. S. *Books Evaluated by Means of the Vocabulary Grade Placement Formula — Revised to March, 1937.* Los Angeles: City School District, 1937.

Over 2,700 books are evaluated by means of the Vocabulary Grade Placement Formula and listed for the purpose of enabling teachers and librarians to select books more adequately for individual students. Vocabulary Difficulty and Vocabulary Diversity are the elements determining Grade Placement. Several types of material were noted in which a definite trend in Difficulty and Diversity was evident.

182. McCallister, J. M. "Aspects of Books that Affect Readability and Use — In Science," Ch. XVII of *Materials for Reading,* Proceedings of the Annual Conference on Reading held at the University of Chicago, 1957, ed. H. M. Robinson. Chicago: University of Chicago Press, in con-

junction with *School Review* and *Elementary School Journal,* **19**:167–70, December, 1957.

Showing that readability of science books include reacting to facts as well as understanding them, the study concludes that a book is readable and useful in teaching science when it stimulates five types of scientific thinking: understanding and retaining information; apprehension of relationships; problem-solving; application; and observation and interpretation of natural phenomena.

183. MacLatchy, J. H., and Wardwell, F. "Common Pre-Primer Words," *Educational Research Bulletin,* **27**:199–206, 226, November 10, 1948.

Forty-two pre-primers were analyzed, the words listed and number of different words determined. Words were grouped in the following lists: number of pre-primers using word, number of primers using each of 104 pre-primer words, words used in four or fewer pre-primers and also found in ten or more primers, and pre-primer words found in four or fewer pre-primers. A 71-word pre-primer vocabulary was developed for use as a goal in pre-primer teaching.

184. Mallinson, G. G. "The Readability of High School Science Texts," *The Science Teacher,* **18**:253–56, November, 1951.

A study of vocabulary and difficulty of high school science texts showed many to be too difficult, as a whole or in part, for high school students. It is suggested that teachers and publishers use readability formulas to check grade levels of their texts, and that they provide glossaries of technical terms and sufficient context for, and repetition of, unfamiliar terms to permit the student to increase his vocabulary and lower the difficulty of the material.

185. Mallinson, G. G. "Textbook and Reading Difficulty in Science Teaching," *The Science Teacher,* **25**:474–75, December, 1958.

It is suggested that teachers and "reading experts" are not able to estimate consistently the grade levels of science texts; in some cases, they are four grade levels off the estimates of readability formulas. Therefore, formulas should be used as criteria of reading difficulty in the selection of texts.

186. Mallinson, G. G., Sturm, H. E., and Mallinson, L. M. "The Reading Difficulty of Textbooks in Junior High School Science," *School Review*, 58:536–40, December, 1950.

Results of a Flesch formula (1943) analysis of the reading difficulty of science texts used in Grades 7 through 9 showed that the level of books in these grades was suitable for all but the poorest readers. The range of difficulty was greatest in Grade 9. No evidence was found that the easiest portions of the books were at the beginning of the text.

187. Mallinson, G. G., Sturm, H. E., and Mallinson, L. M. "The Reading Difficulty of Textbooks for High-School Physics," *Science Education*, 36:19–23, February, 1952.

Sixteen high school physics texts were evaluated for their levels of reading difficulty using the Flesch formula (1943). The average grade levels of the books and the reading difficulty of individual texts were found to vary widely. Differences between easiest and hardest books were found to be significant, justifying the conclusion that the level of difficulty is a valid criterion for evaluating high school physics textbooks.

188. Mallinson, G. G., Sturm, H. E., and Mallinson, L. M. "The Reading Difficulty of Textbooks for High-School Chemistry," *Journal of Chemical Education*, 29:629–31, 1952.

Evaluation of 22 high school chemistry textbooks using the 1943 Flesch formula indicated that levels of reading difficulty of the texts and the grade levels of the texts varied greatly. Earlier passages were found to be no lower in difficulty than the later passages. Although some texts would be too difficult for less able students, the reading difficulty is not too great for most students.

189. Mallinson, G. G., Sturm, H. E., and Mallinson, L. M. "The Reading Difficulty of Textbooks for General Physical Science and Earth Science," *School Science and Mathematics*, 54:612–16, November, 1954.

Eleven general physical and seven earth science texts were studied to determine their levels of reading difficulty, using the 1943 Flesch formula. Conclusions indicated that levels of difficulty varied within books and that books written to be used in a specific grade varied greatly in their level of difficulty. Earlier passages were not consistently less difficult than later passages.

190. Mallinson, G. G., Sturm, H. E., and Mallinson, L. M. "The Reading Difficulty of Unit-Type Textbooks for Elementary Science," *Science Education,* **39**:406–10, December, 1955.

The results of an analysis of unit-type science texts at the fourth- through sixth-grade levels indicated that publishers' evaluations of the grade levels of their texts are not accurate. A great range of difficulty often appears within a single text or within a unit of texts. Integration among science areas in unit-type materials is less likely than in a conventional text.

191. Mallinson, G. G., Sturm, H. E., and Mallinson, L. M. "The Reading Difficulty of Some Recent Textbooks for Science," *School Science and Mathematics,* **57**:364–66, May, 1957.

Analysis of recent science texts to see if reading difficulties found in textbooks in 1953–54 had been corrected revealed continued variation among the levels of reading difficulty of science texts. Many of the books are written above the students' levels, average grade levels conceal many hard passages, and, generally, recent texts are as variable as their predecessors.

192. Mallinson, G. G., Sturm, H. E., and Patton, R. E. "The Reading Difficulty of Textbooks in Elementary Science," *Elementary School Journal,* **50**:460–63, April, 1950.

An evaluation of science textbooks used in Grades 4 through 6 indicated that none of them amounts to easy reading. The textbooks were found too difficult for even the average fourth-grader; too difficult throughout the grade for the slower fifth-graders; and only slightly difficult in the sixth grade, but still too difficult for the slow readers in that grade.

193. Manwiller, C. "Problems Involved in the Readability of Instructional Materials," *A Report of the Tenth Annual Conference on Reading.* Pittsburgh: University of Pittsburgh Press, 83–93, 1954.

The areas of evaluative studies, difficulty of materials, typography, physical factors, illustrations, regressive eye movements, and textbook analyses are suggested for more thorough investigation in readability research. The author feels that concentration should be made on evaluative studies, typography and textbook analyses.

194. Moreau, R. "Simplified Classics," *Journal of Adult Education,* 11:161–65, April, 1939.

Reader comprehension of the original and simplified versions of *Les Miserables, Treasure Island* and *Robinson Crusoe* was measured. Both *Les Miserables* and *Robinson Crusoe* proved to be easier to understand in the simplified version, while both versions of *Treasure Island* were equally hard to comprehend. All subjects felt that the simplified versions helped them to understand the original texts.

195. Morphett, M. V., and Washburne, C. (Eds.) *The Right Book for the Right Child,* 3rd ed. New York: The John Day Co., 1942.

This is an annotated, graded list of 1,359 books for children. The titles were selected and the annotations made by children's librarians. The gradings for difficulty were made with the Washburne-Morphett formula of 1938 by the Research Department of the Winnetka Public Schools, under the supervision of the authors.

196. Ogdon, D. P. "Flesch Counts of Eight Current Texts for Introductory Psychology," *American Psychologist,* 9:143–44, April, 1954.

Eight new books to be used as introductory psychology texts were evaluated on the basis of Flesch Reading Ease and Human Interest formulas, with the results that none of the eight could be classified as *Easy* or *Interesting.* Two were *Fairly Difficult,* the rest *Difficult.* Five were *Mildly Interesting,* the others *Dull.* No significant correlation was found between Reading Ease and Human Interest scores.

197. Overholser, O. V. "Grade Placement of Reference Books." Unpublished Master's thesis, Colorado State College of Education, June, 1935.

The grade placement of *Britannica Junior* material on place-geography was compared with that of *Compton's* and *World Book.* The *Britannica Junior,* while graded at a lower level than *Compton's* and *World Book,* was too difficult for the grades in which place-geography is most studied. Grade placements of 10th, 12th, and 10th were found for *Compton's, World Book,* and *Britannica Junior* respectively.

198. Oxhandler, A. "What Makes an Occupational Information Pamphlet Popular?" *Occupations,* **29**:26–29, October, 1950.

    Evaluation of 11 pamphlets in the field of home economics to determine what makes occupational information materials popular and whether they can fulfill their purpose and still be attractive and popular led to the conclusion that the pamphlet that looks easy to read and from which information can be easily obtained was the more popular.

199. Pittler, F. A. "An Analysis of the Relationship Between the Readability of Textbooks and the Abilities of Students in a Junior High School," *Dissertation Abstracts,* **16**:48, 1956.

    Analysis of the relationship between readability of junior high school textbooks and the abilities and needs of students showed that slow learners have more success with books at the third- and fourth-grade levels and that the required texts did not meet the needs of these students. The student's total needs should be considered when planning a reading program.

200. Porch, A. K. "Reading Difficulty of Adopted Textbooks in Social Studies for the State of Alabama, Grades 3 to 12." Unpublished Master's thesis, Alabama Polytechnic Inst., 1946.

    The results of a study to determine the readability level and technical vocabulary development of 12 social studies texts used in Grades 3 to 12 showed that while there is a progression of reading difficulty from grade to grade, it is erratic. Some texts are too difficult and some too easy for the grades using them. Technical vocabulary built up from Grade 3 to 12, with the greatest number of new terms introduced in the seventh grade.

201. Powers, S. R. "The Vocabularies of High School Science Text-Books," *Teachers College Record,* **26**:368–82, January, 1925.

    Comparison of the vocabulary difficulties of high school science texts indicated that the vocabulary burdens of the texts are unnecessarily high; that general science texts are no higher than those prepared for the average ninth-grade pupil in other science fields, and that biology texts are hardest, even though chemistry is studied by third- and fourth-year students while biology is studied by second-year students.

202. Pressy, L. C. "The Determination of the Technical Vocabularies of the School Subjects," *School and Society,* **20**: 91–96, July 19, 1924.

To find out what technical words appear in textbooks in each of several fields and to obtain some idea of their comparative importance, 100 textbooks were studied. Lists of technical words were compiled and later checked for importance. The longest total list was for home economics. Vocabulary size was the most important finding, pointing up the difficulties encountered in learning and teaching specific subjects.

203. Rader, G. "The Vocabulary Burden of a Junior High School Textbook in Biology," *Educational Research Bulletin,* 1:223, 231–32, December 20, 1922.

Systematic study of the vocabulary burden of a junior high school biology textbook showed that it contained 1,600 words considered difficult or technical, 600 of which did not appear on the Thorndike List of 10,000 words. It is concluded that this burden of new words is unwarranted when the chief purpose of the course is teaching the subject matter.

204. Robinson, T. E. "Reading Difficulty of History Textbooks." Unpublished Master's thesis, Rutgers University, 1940.

Quantitative comparison of eight elements of reading difficulty found in history books used in Grades 4 to 7 indicated that books are often too difficult for their grade, particularly the seventh grade. This is due largely to the absence of uniform standards for determining difficulty and accounts for the uneven progression from level to level which interferes with learning to read by minimizing cumulative effects.

205. Rue, E. *Subject Index to Books for Intermediate Grades.* Chicago: American Library Association, 1940.

A list of books covering some 4,000 subjects and about 20,000 entries. While the book was planned to meet only the needs of the intermediate grades (4–6), the books have also been graded for difficulty. The gradings listed in the book have been based on the author's experience primarily, but Washburne-Morphett and Lewerenz formula ratings have also been used.

206. Rue, E. *Subject Index to Books for Primary Grades.* Chicago: American Library Association, 1943.

     A graded list of books for the primary grades in which over 300 readers, 130 unit readers, and over 250 books of the nonreader type are indexed. This book is a revision of the 1938 *Subject Index to Readers.* The gradings for difficulty were made by librarian consultants, with the aid of Winnetka formula ratings.

207. Seay, M. F., and Clark, H. F. "Criteria for Use in the Preparation and Evaluation of Reading Materials," *The School Curriculum and Economic Improvement.* Bulletin of the Bureau of School Service, 13:68–78, Lexington: University of Kentucky, September, 1940.

     Content and mechanical make-up are suggested as criteria in preparing and evaluating readers for the elementary grades. Primer stories should contain a great deal of repetition, material should be checked against recognized vocabulary lists, and vocabulary range should be as wide as possible without going beyond the pupil's ability.

208. Seegers, J. C. "Vocabulary Problems in the Elementary School — A Digest of Current Research," *Elementary English Review,* 16:157–66, 199–204, 234–39, 279–82, 320–26, April, May, October, November, December, 1939, and 17:28–43, January, 1940.

     Some of the major findings of research dealing with elementary school vocabulary, including lists for spelling, reading and oral vocabulary, are discussed; studies of textbook and subject difficulty are reviewed; factors related to vocabulary development are inspected; and suggestions are made for vocabulary development.

209. Spache, G. "Problems in Primary Book Selection: I. The Selection of Pre-Primers; II. Supplementary Pre-Primers; III. Primers and Supplementary Primers; IV. First and Second Readers," *Elementary English Review,* 18:5–12, 52–59, 139–48, 175–81, January, February, April, May, 1961.

     In devising scorecards for evaluating primary reading books, numerical standards for vocabulary content and physical make-up were derived from studies in the field. Scorecards are given for pre-primers, supplementary pre-primers, primers, supplementary primers, and first and second readers, along with tables showing the application of the scorecards.

210. Stauffer, R. G., Brown, A., and Gettings, T. R. "Reading Vocabulary Study: First Reader Programs," *Delaware School Journal,* **16**:6–9, 15, May, 1951.

Tabulations of the total number of words introduced at different levels in the primary program of seven series of basic readers showed differences in both the number of new words introduced at the various levels and the specific words presented. Agreement between number of new words presented increased as the difference between levels increased and intra-level differences were greater than inter-level differences among the series.

211. Stevens, N. E. "The Moral Obligation to be Intelligible," *Scientific Monthly,* **70**:111–15, February, 1950.

With tongue in cheek, the author points out that gobbledygook in scientific writing is the surest way to gain respect and prestige. Arguing against such practice, he calls upon the opinions of several authors to support his arguments that it is unnecessary, unwise, and dishonest. He notes that public interest is vital to scientific endeavor and can be gained only if the public understands what the scientist is doing.

212. Stevenson, E. N. "An Investigation of the Vocabulary Problem in College Biology," *Journal of Educational Psychology,* **28**:663–72, December, 1937.

Estimating the vocabulary burden of a one-year survey course in biology, the author found that over 1,000 unfamiliar words were contacted in the first quarter of the course and that this excessive burden had a negative influence on understanding, achievement, and interest. The use of student judgments of difficulty and importance of words is defended by comparing their opinions with a standard list of scientific terms.

213. Strang, R., Checkovitz, A., Gilbert, C., and Scoggin, M. *Gateways to Readable Books.* New York: The H. W. Wilson Co., 1944.

An annotated, graded list of over 700 books for slow readers of high school age. The book actually is a composite based on other bibliographies selected by librarians. The gradings for difficulty were based on estimates given in other lists, use of the Lorge formula, and judgments of experienced persons.

214. Sward, B., and Harris, D. B. "Reading Ease, Human Interest Value, and Thematic Content of *St. Nicholas Magazine*: A Study of Children's Literature," *Journal of Educational Psychology,* **42**:153–65, March, 1951.

Comparison of the Reading Ease, Human Interest, and content of an early and a recent children's magazine showed that despite improved format of more recent stories, a fairly uniform level of Reading Ease and Human Interest obtained. Little alteration of content was discerned over the years. The trend seems to be toward treatment of children as "little adults" who solve adult problems using adult means.

215. Tague, J. V. "Readability of Texts," *High Points,* **35**:16–20, October, 1953.

The vocabulary difficulty of a biology and a history text at the high school level was studied, using the Thorndike-Lorge Word List. The history text presented difficulties largely attributable to the use of abstractions and figurative language. One per cent of the words used in the history text were unusual, 2.2% of those in the biology text were unusual. In the latter case, only .7% of the unusual words were not scientific terms.

216. Thorndike, E. L. "The Vocabulary of Books for Children in Grades 3 to 8," *Teachers College Record,* **38**:196–205, 316–23, 416–29, December, January, February, 1936–37.

The numbers, frequencies, and importance of words outside the Thorndike 20,000 found in 120 books recommended for pupils in Grades 3 to 8 were considered. The vocabularies of juvenile books were found to be excessively large and to contain extremely rare words occurring infrequently.

217. Thorndike, R. L. "Words and the Comics," *Journal of Experimental Education,* **10**:110–13, December, 1941.

The reading experience which comic books provide from the standpoint of range and difficulty of vocabulary was examined. Approximately 40,000 words were encountered in the study, of which 3,043 were not in the first 1,000 of the Thorndike list and 649 not on the list at all. Of the 649, about 25% were slang, 28% standard words and the rest "home-made compounds, contractions, and proper names."

218. Tompkins, M. D. "What Is a Readable Book?" *Booklist,* **30**:195–97, March, 1934.

    A workable classification of readers as a step towards determining what is meant by a "readable" book is suggested. Groups I to III are characterized by books and authors the group members might be expected to read with profit; books for Group IV have the vocabulary and sentence structures of seventh-grade readers, and Group V is composed of books for adults who have just learned to read.

219. Walchak, F. A. "Trends in the Readability of School Readers," *A Report of the Tenth Annual Conference on Reading.* Pittsburgh: University of Pittsburgh Press, 138–48, 1954.

    Ninety-six basic readers used in Grades 4 through 6 were studied to determine if readability had improved in the past 30 years. Results showed that the heavy vocabulary burden present in early fourth-grade readers had been remedied in many cases, but that this was not true for fifth-and sixth-grade readers. Readability can be improved by more careful gradation of reading materials.

220. Washburne, C., and Vogel, M. *Winnetka Graded Book List.* Chicago: American Library Association, 1926. (This book also appears in a reprint edition as *What Children Like to Read,* Rand, McNally and Co., 1926.)

    This is an annotated, graded list of about 700 books, with an additional index of popularity among readers. The annotations were made by children who had read the books; the gradings for difficulty were determined by the median reading ability of readers who read and liked the books. Of particular interest is the correlation coefficient of .80 between median reading grades and the "zero-value" factor of the Lively-Pressey formula.

221. Witherington, H. C. "Readability of Textbooks in Educational Psychology," *Journal of Educational Research,* **46**: 227–30, November, 1952.

    An examination of eight college textbooks in educational psychology was made using the Dale-Chall formula. The texts were found to vary in difficulty from Grades 10 to 12 with the average level at eleventh grade. Students enrolling in educational psychology courses read at a level somewhat higher than tenth grade. It was concluded that the texts examined were written at about the grade level for which they were intended.

222. Wood, L. N. "Readability of Certain Textbooks," *Elementary English,* **31**:214–16, April, 1954.
Twelve intermediate grade textbooks were rated with the Yoakam and Dale-Chall formulas, and the results compared and correlated with the judgments of 32 teachers. The formulas were within three-tenths of a grade apart on results, and the teachers' judgments were found to be substantially in accord with the formulas.

223. Woody, C. "Intrinsic Difficulties of Certain Reading Materials," *Peabody Journal of Education,* **17**:149–60, November, 1939.
Samples from a high school literature text and social studies texts for Grades 6 and 10 were examined in the light of three difficulties involved in reading. Results showed vocabulary load for the literature text was excessive, for the social science texts, adequate. Sentences in the texts were no longer than those written by students. Students were found to have an inadequate experience for understanding the material.

224. Wulfing, G. "Technique for Evaluation of Children's Encyclopedias." Unpublished Master's thesis, Stanford University, October, 1938.
Reading difficulty and the extent to which illustrations clarify and supplement the text of four children's encyclopedias were evaluated. The majority of the 32 articles examined were found too difficult to be understood by the average child in Grades 4 to 6. Vocabulary placement for the articles ranged from 4.96 to 10.82.

225. Yoakam, G. A. "Problems Involved in Differentiating Materials to Provide for the Individual Reading Needs of Children," *A Report of the Ninth Annual Conference on Reading.* Pittsburgh: University of Pittsburgh Press, 97–104, 1953.
Stressing the need for finer differentiation in textbook grading, the author discusses four possible solutions suggested by readability research: materials on different levels of difficulty within age groups; objective and accurate grading of text-

books; easier sequences in reading, writing, spelling, language, and arithmetic; and use of a variety of books of different difficulty levels for social studies, science, and health topics.

226. Yoakam, G. A. "Why Readability is a Problem for Teachers," *A Report of the Tenth Annual Conference on Reading.* Pittsburgh: University of Pittsburgh Press, 11–17, 1954.

Why readability is still a problem to teachers is discussed and suggestions are made as to how teachers can deal with the problem. Texts vary widely in readability, and it is suggested that teachers use formulas to examine texts and survey material for both subject content and readability.

227. Yoakam, G. "Unsolved Problems in Reading," *Elementary English,* **31**:427–30, November, 1954.

Some unsolved problems in the teaching of reading are discussed and the development of the teaching of reading traced. The author feels that a most notable recent accomplishment is the accelerating interest in readability research and the recognizable effect it is having upon authors and publishers.

228. Zahnizer, K. "The Readability of Economic Textbooks," *Dissertation Abstracts,* **16**:84, January, 1956.

An examination of 30 economics texts showed an average grade placement of 10.75 by the Yoakam formula, and 10.94 by the Flesch formula. There were 346 different economics terms isolated, most of which appeared consistently in the texts and were slightly more difficult than terms not in economics. About one economics word in 16 appeared inconsistently in the texts.

See also 47, 68, 82, 84, 91, 98, 107, 108, 111, 114, 118, 351, 352, 355, 359, 379, 402, 445, 454, and 460.

2. Business and Industry

Nos. 229–247

229. Carlucci, C., and Crissy, W. J. E. "How Readable are Employee Handbooks?" *Personnel Psychology,* 4:383–95, Winter, 1951.

Flesch Reading Ease and Human Interest formulas were applied to 23 employee handbooks to determine whether they were readable for their intended audience. Attractiveness, content, and typography were also examined. It was found that many of the handbooks were inappropriate for their purpose, covered fewer topics than desired, and needed some typographical improvements.

230. Davis, K., and Hopkins, J. O. "Readability of Employee Handbooks," *Personnel Psychology,* 3:317–26, Autumn, 1950.

Seventy-one employee handbooks were analyzed with the Flesch formulas and compared in terms of employer types and company sizes. The national average was *Difficult* for readability, and in the lower levels of *Interesting* for human interest. Size was a factor among the largest companies, but was less important than type of employer in both analyses.

231. England, A. O. "Employee Magazines are Hard to Read," *Personnel Journal,* 30:94–97, July, August, 1951.

The use of the Flesch formula to analyze employee magazines is discussed and improvements suggested. The 50 publications examined were found, on the average, to be difficult to read and understand. Industrial editors should know their audience and the difficulty of their writing. Personnel files and the Flesch formula are suggested as means of providing answers to these questions.

232. Farr, J. N. "Readability and Interest Values in an Employee Handbook," *Journal of Applied Psychology,* 34:16–21, February, 1950.

Analyzing and revising a proposed employee handbook, the author found that the existing book was much too difficult for the intended audience. Flesch's rules were applied in the revision; it was shortened in word and page length. Attention was given to page layout with fewer words per page and simple illustrations. A comparative analysis of the original and revised handbooks revealed a rise in both readability and human interest in the latter.

233. Farr, J. N., Paterson, D. G., and Stone, C. H. "Readability and Human Interest of Management and Union Publications," *Industrial and Labor Relations Review,* 4:88–91, October, 1950.

Fifty management and union publications were analyzed using

Flesch's formulas to determine whether they were written simply enough to be understood by employees and members. Results showed all scores fell below 70 (suitable for readers with high school or college educations). None of the publications rated *Dramatic,* and only two rated *Highly Interesting.* Means showed management publications to be *Fairly Dull* and *Mildly Interesting;* union newspapers were *Difficult* and *Dull.*

234. Flesch, R. F. "Making the Narrative Readable," Ch. 15 of *Modern Corporate Reports to Stockholders, Employees and the Public,* ed. L. Doris. New York: Prentice-Hall, Inc., 194–98, 1948.

Discussing methods to make annual corporate reports more readable, the author concludes that short paragraphs, frequent subheadings, large type, and short lines make for readability; sentences of 20 words or less insure readability; business English, legal jargon, and other unfamiliar terms must be avoided; and first person singular and plural add a personal touch contributing to readability.

235. Flesch, R. F. and Kheel, T. W. "Plain Talk for the Rank and File," *Conference Board Personnel Management Record,* **10:**565–66, December, 1948.

To show how and why plain talk should be used in labor-management communication, the confusion resulting from technical language in labor negotiations is demonstrated. Examples of rewriting contract clauses into ordinary language are given, illustrating that short sentences and words, explanations and step-by-step presentation can eliminate the difficulty in understanding contracts and remove the barrier between management and labor.

236. Jenkins, J. J. "Will It Be Read — And Understood?" *Modern Management,* **9:**7–8, April, 1949.

After pointing out that cooperative employee response can be obtained only if written communication is read and understood, the author gives the results of the revision of a managment letter to employees using Flesch's principles. Revision reduced the letter in length by sixty words; it gained in Reading Ease from *Fairly Interesting* to *Very Easy,* and increased in Human Interest from *Mildly Interesting* to *Highly Interesting.*

237. Lambie, J. M., Jr. "Financial Reports Can Be Written So People Can Understand Them," *Journal of Accountancy*, 84:40–45, July, 1947.

   The failure of financial communications is discussed; examples are given and the reasons for difficulty or ease of these communications are investigated. It is suggested that it is structure rather than hard words that most complicates communication. Efforts being made by various groups to simplify the language of financial communications are outlined.

238. Lauer, J., and Paterson, D. G. "Readability of Union Contracts," *Personnel*, 28:36–40, July, 1951.

   To report on the readability of union contracts and to show how difficulty may be reduced, 20 typical union contracts were analyzed by means of the Flesch formulas. It was found that the mean Reading Ease score of the contracts was *Very Difficult*, requiring a college education for understanding, and that none of the contracts fell into *Fairly Difficult* or easier categories.

239. Pashalian, S., and Crissy, W. J. E. "How Readable Are Corporate Annual Reports?" *Journal of Applied Psychology*, 34:244–48, August, 1950.

   Flesch analysis of the readability of 26 annual corporate reports revealed that, on the whole, the general level of Reading Ease was *Difficult* and the Human Interest value *Dull*. The reports contained language beyond the experience and comprehension of 75% of U.S. adults. There was a narrow range of Flesch scores between reports of different firms within the same industries.

240. Paterson, D. G. "Development of a General Information Sheet for Potential Applicants," *Personnel*, 24:317–20, March, 1948.

   An original job-applicant information sheet and a revision based on Flesch's principles were compared. With revision, difficulty was downgraded from "hard to read" to "easy to read." Responses of colleagues and students of personnel psychology and industrial relations to a questionnaire provided suggestions regarding attractiveness, information, directness, and incisiveness of the sheets. These suggestions were used in a final revision of the form.

241. Paterson, D. G., and Jenkins, J. J. "Communication Between Management and Workers," *Journal of Applied Psychology,* **32**:71–80, February, 1948.

> Flesch readability measurements of an information sheet for potential job applicants were reduced by revision according to Flesch's principles from *Hard* (academic, high school, or some college) to *Easy* (pulp magazine, fifth grade). The original sheet was found too difficult for its intended audience.

242. Paterson, D. G., and Walker, B. J. "Readability and Human Interest of House Organs," *Personnel,* **25**:438–41, May, 1949.

> Flesch formulas were applied to 34 internal and external house organs to determine their readability and human interest. It was found that readability levels were too difficult for employees with less than high school freshman or sophomore ability and that Human Interest averaged *Interesting.* Analysis of content showed that the material was being edited by advertising and promotion people and was not slanted toward personnel viewpoints.

243. Paterson, D. G., and Walker, B. J. "Experts Review NIEA Publications," Reporting, **2**:12–14, November-December, 1949. Dayton: International Council of Industrial Editors, Inc.

> The readability and human interest of 34 house organs entered in the NIEA 1948 contest were compared with 42 house organs entered in the 1949 contest and with six women's magazines, using the Flesch formula. As in 1948, the 1949 house organs were too difficult for rank-and-file employees, although some improvement was noted. Human Interest scores were higher, but allowed for much improvement. For both Reading Ease and Human Interest, the women's magazines scored higher than the house organs.

244. Raney, E. T. "How Readable Is Your Employee Publication?" *Personnel Psychology,* **2**:437–59, Winter, 1949.

> To show that content and readability analysis will insure that publications contain the desired message in understandable form, 27 management publications and 4 union newspapers

were examined. It was concluded that the content was not that which management would most like to stress and that the publications were too difficult to read.

245. Schenkel, K. F., and Paterson, D. G. "What Was Wrong With My Suggestion?" *Personnel,* **27**:212–15, November, 1950.

The readability of 15 letters rejecting employee suggestions was measured using the Flesch formula and recommendations made for improving tone and readability. It was found that the average Reading Ease score was *Difficult* (comparable to *Harper's*) and the average Human Interest score was comparable to that of *Reader's Digest.* Since the intended readers averaged seventh and eighth grade in education, the letters were declared too difficult and uninteresting.

246. Tiffin, J., and Walsh, F. X. "Readability of Union-Management Agreements," *Personnel Psychology,* 4:327–37, Winter, 1951.

The Flesch Reading Ease formula was applied to 59 union-management agreements to determine their readability. It was found that most of the agreements were at high school and college levels of readability, with one-third at the college level. The mean Reading Ease score was at the high school or "some college" level.

247. Wearne, D. "The Readability of House Magazines," *Bulletin of Industrial Psychology and Personnel Practice,* 5:28–32, December, 1949.

Flesch Reading Ease and Human Interest formulas were applied to 83 Australian house magazines. Reading material in which management directs information to employees was found, in general, too difficult to read and only mildly interesting.

See also 390.

3. Journalism and Mass Communications

Nos. 248–267

248. Alden, J. "Lots of Names — Short Sentences — Simple Words," *Printers' Ink,* **211**:21–22, June 29, 1945.

Advertisements in nationally known magazines were examined, using the Flesch formula, to determine their human interest.

The American Mutual Liability Insurance Company's ads rated highest of the materials examined. Western Electric ads also contained good human interest. However, Metropolitan Life, Campbell's Soup, Monsanto Chemical, and Kelvinator advertisements included little human interest.

249. Allias, M. T. "The Reading Difficulty of a Selected Set of Leading Mass Magazines," *Dissertation Abstracts,* **17**:57–58, January, 1957.

The Yoakam formula was used to determine the vocabulary load of mass magazines. The magazines ranged in reading grade level from 8.0 to 13.6, the median difficulty for the list being 10.8. Science fiction magazines were above the overall median difficulty; behavior type magazines were below.

250. Barnes, A. M. "Is Your Paper Easy to Read?" *Iowa Publisher,* **19**:3–7, July, 1947.

The Flesch formula was applied to several types of writing to show how it may be used to measure and control readability. It is concluded that the formula cannot be used as a mechanical device for producing readable material, but it can be used as a check and a guide to that end.

251. Brown, R. V. "Foreign News Written Over Heads of Readers," *Editor and Publisher,* **79**:28, December 28, 1946.

In a study of foreign news writing, it was found that the average foreign news was written for a reader with 14 years of school, although the average adult has had less than nine years. Editorial writers were found to be more easily understood than reporters. The importance of clear writing to make foreign news significant and interesting was stressed.

252. Burton, P. W., and Swanson, C. E. "Can Mass Audiences Read Institutional Advertising?" *Journalism Quarterly,* **25**:145–50, 156, June, 1948.

Institutional advertising was analyzed to see if it could reach most readers. "Potential" and "typical" audiences were determined, and it was found that 77 of the 100 advertisements examined could reach 40% or less of the U.S. adult population.

253. Craig, J. C. "The Readability of Best Sellers," *Report of the Ninth Conference on Reading.* Pittsburgh: University of Pittsburgh Press, 144–59, 1953.

Some 200 "best-selling" books of all types published between 1662 and 1945 were examined to determine their readability in general and their vocabulary load in particular. It was found that most best-sellers are too difficult for the average reader to understand, that only a few of the "great books" can be read by the average person and that about one-third of the classics are too difficult for over 80% of the population.

254. Dolch, E. W. "The Bible Is Easy Reading," *Elementary English Review,* **15**:297–98, December, 1938.

The vocabulary burden of the Gospel of St. Mark was determined. Results showed that almost one-half of the words were familiar to preschool children, nine out of ten were known to grade school children and all but 13 of the words were found in the 20,000 commonest words listed by Thorndike.

255. Dunlap, C. C. "Readability of Newspaper Items and of Basic Reading Material," *Elementary School Journal,* **51**:499–501, May, 1951.

A comparison was made between newspaper samples and samples taken from an eighth-grade reader to demonstrate the process of determining readability levels. Findings indicated that both samples covered a wide range of reading levels and that these levels were comparable between the two. Both samples were very similar according to the elements measured by the Dale-Chall formula.

256. Flesch, R. F. "How Copy Writers Can Use Readability Tests," *Printers' Ink,* **212**:85–86, August 31, 1945.

To sell the idea of readability formulas in improving the writing of advertising copy, the need for simple prose which will appeal to the customer rather than the client is stressed. In support of this point, five imaginary "cases" of the application of readability principles to a radio commercial, an institutional ad, a subway ad card, stockholders' reports, and employee instruction manuals are given.

257. Flesch, R. F. "How To Write Copy That Will Be Read," *Advertising and Selling,* **40**:113, 178–82, March, 1947.

To show that readership of advertising copy follows readability and an "easier-than" relation to editorial copy, the readability of ads in magazines and newspapers for which readership reports were available was determined. It was concluded that the most readable ads are the most read and that ad copy must be more readable than the editorial copy with which it appears in order to be read.

258. Flesch, R. F. *The AP Writing Handbook.* 1951.

The handbook, a summation of the readability campaign conducted by the Associated Press in 1948–50 with Dr. Flesch as consultant, presents rules and suggestions for readable and clear writing. The principles of readability are briefly described in action, together with examples for many of the points made.

259. Getzloe, L. "U. S. Press Does Well in Foreign News Volume, But Less Readable Than 1945," *The Ohio Newspaper,* Ohio State University, 28:1–4, November, 1946.

Results of a study of world-affairs reporting by the American press showed that foreign news received adequate coverage, but was less readable than in the previous year. The United Press rated most readable; the New York *Times* was most difficult. Summaries were found more readable than detailed reports and editorials were still easier.

260. Griffin, J. F. "What Did You Say?" *Catholic World,* **177**: 264–67, July, 1953.

The Reading Ease and Human Interest of the column "Sursum Corda" by Father James M. Gillis were compared with those of nine other New York columns. Father Gillis ranked highest in both Reading Ease and Human Interest: *Standard* for Reading Ease and *Very Interesting* for Human Interest. Scores of the other writers ranged from *Fairly Difficult* to *Difficult* for Reading Ease; from *Interesting* to *Mildly Interesting* for Human Interest.

261. Gunning, R. "Gunning Finds Papers Too Hard to Read," *Editor and Publisher,* **78**:12, May 19, 1945.

To demonstrate the work of "Readable News Reports" in measuring the difficulty of news and prescribing for its simplification, eight metropolitan dailies and the United Press world-wide service were studied for readability. It was found that while news writing is too difficult, it is possible to simplify it. "Readable News Reports" was able to help a paper produce simple, concise, and clear writing and to cut the reading difficulty of UP copy by five grade levels.

262. Johnson, E. J. "Readability in News Writing: Report on an Experiment by the United Press," *United Press Association*, 1945.

     Readable News Reports, an analysis of United Press news reports, showed that copy needed improvement in readability. Subsequent improvement of five grade levels was made in UP copy. The results and recommendations to the UP staff through a series of memoranda from the vice president and general manager of UP are here collected and reprinted.

263. Nieman Reports. "Readability Isn't Enough," *Reading, Writing and Newspapers: A Special Issue.* Cambridge: Harvard University, 4:46–50, April, 1950.

     This study shows that readability is not enough, and that the rules of English can be violated without destroying communication. The attributes of "good" writing are discussed, placing major emphasis on the tools of the craft. Grammar so correct that it excludes everything illogical, plus exact word usage, will insure not only readability but good writing as well.

264. "Readability and the News: An Account of Three Years' Work," *Readable News Reports* (unnumbered advertising pamphlet), 1947.

     The development of readability in the news field since 1945 is presented, and the need for more readable copy is stressed. Examples of good and bad copy are given, indicating what *Readable News Reports* can do to improve readability. Some common misconceptions about the use of readability yardsticks are also indicated.

265. "Say It Simply," *Time,* 51:52, February 16, 1948.

     Examination of Associated Press copy by Flesch showed that the AP reports were monotonous, the leads less readable than the stories, and that the stories ranked from *Fairly Poor* to *Poor.* The AP instructed its staff to simplify their copy in accordance with Flesch's criteria. The reporters found it difficult to do, but some improvement was noted.

266. "Some Add Shortening to 5-W Lead Recipe," *Editor and Publisher,* 80:24, February 22, 1947.

     Analysis of the front pages of 18 newspapers revealed a trend toward conciseness in news writing. The average length of leads was 33 words and leads usually contained one sentence only.

The average sentence contained 23 words; the average paragraph 35 words. Several short paragraphs are used rather than one long one. Average sentence lengths of wire and local leads were about the same, although wire leads tended to be longer and their paragraphs to be shorter.

267. Trenchard, K. I., and Crissy, W. J. E. "Readability of Advertising and Editorial Copy in *Time* and *Newsweek*," *Journal of Applied Psychology*, 36:161–63, June, 1952.

To find trends in reading ease and human interest of advertising and editorial copy of prewar and postwar issues of *Time* and *Newsweek*, 10 issues for each year from each magazine for the periods of 1936-40 and 1945-49 were studied. Advertising and editorial copy in both publications were found within the comprehension of the readers. Trends toward more difficult ad copy and easier editorial copy were found.

See also 354, 361, 370, 380, 396, 397, 398, 404, 405, 413, 414, 415, and 421.

4. Legal and Governmental Writing

Nos. 268–293

268. Bennett, S. S. "The Lawyer's Use of Words," *Georgia Bar Journal*, 5:5–10, February, 1943.

To indicate the importance of careful use of language in legal matters, several cases and legal situations in which careless language usage caused needless confusion are reviewed. It is pointed out that the use of too many words, overuse of technical language, and failure to note the importance of word and phrase position in a noninflexional language like English, all contribute to legal obscurities.

269. Cavers, D. F. "The Simplification of Government Regulations," *Federal Bar Journal*, 8:339–56, July, 1947.

A memorandum suggesting simplification of regulations issued by the Office of Price Administration is discussed. The use of the second person rather than the third person, shorter sentences free of numerous clauses and phrases, popular speech, and the avoidance of superfluous and polysyllabic words are suggested.

270. Chaffee, Z., Jr. "The Disorderly Conduct of Words," *Columbia Law Review*, **41**:381–404, March, 1941.

To ascertain whether semantics can be used to supplement the efforts of judges and law books to solve problems of legal interpretation, *The Meaning of Meaning* by Ogden and Richards and *The Tyranny of Words* by Chase were compared with various books on meaning by jurists. It was concluded that the work of semanticists may be used to clarify the alternatives which must be considered when meaning is a factor in a legal matter.

271. Cowing, A. G. "They Speak His Language," *Journal of Home Economics*, **37**:487–89, October, 1945.

The problems involved in writing at an appropriate grade level for a given audience are outlined, the farm audience described, and examples of how rewriting is done are presented, using Lorge and Flesch formulas. It is pointed out that "only about one-fourth of our farm readers would get the full meaning of" some bulletins.

272. Cowing, A. G. "Readability for Farm Families," *Land Policy Review*, **10**:29–31, Spring, 1947.

Defending the use of readability formulas to broaden communications with farm families, the article points out the need for attention to readability, how it is being accomplished and what it has been able to do. The need for reaching these readers and the methods for doing it are stressed. Simple writing for all educational levels is called for as a time-saving measure.

273. England, A. O. "Getting Your Message Across by Plain Talk," *Journal of Applied Psychology*, **34**:182–85, June, 1950.

A campaign directed at management and promoting the use of plain talk in government and armed forces communications is discussed. The Flesch formula was applied to "literally hundreds" of publications, uncovering evidence that as many as 90% of readers have some difficulty with some publications. Noticeable improvements in communications resulted from this campaign.

274. England, A. O. "Influence of 'Plain Talk' on AMC Communications," *Journal of Applied Psychology*, **35**:381–82, December, 1951.

To show the improvement resulting from the use of plain talk in AMC publications, a comparison was made between the estimated percentage of employees with the educational level necessary to read the style of writing used in January, 1950, and again in January, 1951. It is concluded that more employees can easily read the majority of the more recent publications. Productive time saved is translated into dollars and cents.

275. Fattu, N. A., and Standlee, L. S. "Analysis of Reading Difficulty of Selected Navy Materials," *Technical Bulletin* No. 54-3, March 1, 1954, Bureau of Naval Personnel; Bloomington, Indiana: Indiana University Institute of Educational Research.

In an assessment of the readability of eight Navy publications using the Flesch Reading Ease and Human Interest formulas, it was found that only four of the eight rated below high school level in difficulty, two were equivalent in difficulty to college material, and two to high school. The publications rated *Interesting* in two cases, and *Mildly Interesting* for the rest. It was concluded that the publications were too difficult for Navy recruits.

276. Flesch, R. F. "The Science of Making Sense," *American Mercury,* **60**:194–97, February, 1945.

To show how government publications can be written in simpler language, a formula for cutting sentence length and prefix-suffix density in half is given. Suggestions include throwing out unnecessary words ("such" and "which"); turning verbal nouns back into verbs; putting rules before exceptions; converting negative statements into positive ones; and rewriting legal definitions in understandable form.

277. Flesch, R. F. "More About Gobbledygook," *Public Administration Review,* **5**:240–44, Summer, 1945.

Attacking the problem of bureaucratic language, the author discusses some of the causes for "officialese" and shows how the Flesch formulas furnish a means by which such writing can be improved. Five suggestions for a campaign to bring plain English back to government writing are offered.

278. Flesch, R. F. "Teaching Bureaucrats Plain English," *College English,* **7**:470–74, May, 1946.

To show how readable writing can be taught to a class of adult students, the content of a United States Department of Agriculture course is outlined, showing how the backgrounds of language and the psychology of reading were used to heighten understanding of the Flesch formula. Supplementary reading for such a course and rules-of-thumb for applying the elements of the formula are given.

279. *Gobble-de-gook or Plain Talk?* AMC Manual 11-1. Dayton: Headquarters Air Materiel Command, Wright-Patterson Air Force Base, 1950.

To guide USAF writers in achieving a style easily read and understood, the handbook presents arguments for, and instructions in, readability based on Flesch's *The Art of Readable Writing*. It is posited that plain talk will insure understanding by the audience, give the writer a measure of the difficulty of his style, cut down paper work, save time and money and "get you out of the gobble-de-gook rut."

280. Hegg, J. O., and Weaver, D. O. "Evaluating the Reading Difficulty of Training Literature," *Air Training Command Informational Bulletin,* 19–22, Winter, 1952–53.

A technique devised to evaluate the readability of Air Force training literature is explained step-by-step and a number of materials analyzed with it. Results indicate that the literature is written above effective comprehension for the middle two-thirds of the students.

281. Irvine, P. "Plain Talk for Government Writers," *Public Personnel Review,* **10**:140–46, July, 1949.

Stressing the importance of clarity in government writing, the author gives a report on what readability research has done and is doing for various other media. Flesch's readability elements are translated into rules for clear and concise writing, and it is shown that application of these rules in rewriting government communications will make copy more understandable.

282. Klare, G. R. "Air Force Technical Training as a Problem in Communication: An Introductory Survey," Memorandum Report C-4, Task C, October 1, 1952. Urbana, Illinois: University of Illinois, unpublished.

A preliminary survey of possible relevant variables in a communication schema is presented. Flesch and Dale-Chall formulas were applied to four Air Force "Student Study Guides," which scored at beginning college level and ranged from seventh grade to college graduate. Airmen graded between eleventh and twelfth grades should be able to handle the materials, with difficulty only at the extremes.

283. Klare, G. R. "Technical Supplement to Memorandum Report C-4," Task C, October 1, 1952. Urbana, Illinois: University of Illinois, unpublished.

The procedure and results of a study reported in Klare, G. R., "Air Force Technical Training as a Problem in Communication: An Introductory Survey," are described. Practical suggestions for efficient analysis, and suggested solutions to the problems of inter-analyst reliability and representativeness of samples arising in the survey, are listed.

284. Littler, R. "Reader Rights in Legal Writing," *Journal of the State Bar of California*, 25:51–54, 59–67, January, February, 1950.

The author points out that much typical, wordy, and obscure legal writing is not understood and not necessary, and insists that the law is not too technical a field to be simplified in its writing. While the author does not feel that conversational dialogue style is appropriate in legal writing, he believes that the mattter deserves thought, and disagrees with Flesch that "rhetoric" and figures of speech must be abandoned.

285. Martinson, H. M. "TVA Improves Its Communications," *Public Administration Review*, 14:52–54, Winter, 1954.

Following a workshop to give TVA writers instruction and practice in writing clearly and efficiently, it was found that TVA communications were clearer, carried greater appeal, were read by more people, and were more clearly understood and better remembered by the readers.

286. Michaelis, J. U., and Tyler, F. T. "A Comparison of Reading Ability and Readability," *Journal of Educational Psychology*, 42:491–98, December, 1951.

In a study comparing the readability of certain United Nations publications prepared for high school use, grade levels were determined by three readability formulas (Dale-Chall, Flesch, and Lorge). A great deal of disparity in grading was found between the formulas. The material sampled appeared to be too difficult for high school students.

287. Peerson, V. I. "Evaluating the Readability of Training Literature," *Training Analysis and Development Informational Bulletin,* 4:48–52, Spring, 1953.

Eleven different readability criteria were considered for use in improving Air Force training literature. Hard words, percentage of affixes and prefixes, and average sentence length were selected as significant in discriminating between hard and easy passages.

288. *See the Light Before You Write.* Rantoul, Illinois: Headquarters Chanute Air Force Base, TP–75100–107C, December, 1950.

To provide Air Force personnel with a method for determining the difficulty of writing and a guide for preparing readable training materials, a step-by-step account of the use of the Flesch formula is given. It is recommended that the writer know the reading ability of his audience, know the difficulty of his writing, match the two together, write one level easier than the general reading ability of the audience, emphasize only one idea in a sentence, and explain technical ideas simply.

289. Snyder, M. "Notes on Some Extensional Methods for Putting Scientific Information Into Readable Forms," *General Semantics Bulletin,* 71–76, Winter-Spring, 1952.

The importance of preparation and acquaintance with the topic and the audience for whom one is writing is stressed for making scientific information functionally available to the segment of the population with sixth-grade reading ability. Of the first 16 issues of a soil conservation bulletin using these principles, only one was at seventh-grade reading level, ten were at sixth-grade level and five rated fifth-grade level .

290. Standlee, L. S., and Fattu, N. A. "Readability of Navy Publications," *Journal of Educational Research,* **49**:471–73, February, 1956.

Eight Navy publications were studied to determine whether fourth-grade reading ability was sufficient to enable a Navy enlisted man to read official publications. Flesch Reading Ease scores ranged from sixth grade to college level. Since all of the publications were above fourth-grade level, it was felt that that level was not "functional."

291. Stephenson, H. W., Jr. "Plain English," *U. S. Army Combat Forces Journal*, 38–39, September, 1950.

Citing the need for more readable Army training literature and giving good and poor examples, the author offers the following suggestions for writing: keep your sentences short; write spoken English, using short, common words; use the active voice; use more verbs; and cut out the deadwood — the prepositions, conjunctions, and adverbs.

292. U. S. Civil Service Commission. *How Does Your Writing Read?* Washington: U. S. Government Printing Office, 1946.

Step-by-step instructions are given for analyzing material according to the Flesch method, and a scale for measuring readability is included. Government writers direct their efforts to an audience of eighth- and ninth-grade reading ability. An average of 17 words per sentence, no more than 150 syllables per 100 words, and about six personal references per 100 words are recommended.

293. White, D. M. "Are Our 'American Scriptures' Readable?" *School and Society*, **68**:154–55, September 4, 1948.

Results of analysis of five historical American documents using the Flesch readability formula showed that all five rated very low on the readability scale. Particularly noticeable was the low rating on sentence length. It was suggested that sentences could be shortened without changing the word content and in this way produce a more readable and usable piece of Americana.

5. Psychological Tests and Questionnaires

Nos. 294–304

294. Hampton, P. "Language Difficulties of the Bernreuter Personality Inventory," *Journal of Educational Psychology*, **32**:471–73, September, 1941.

A study was made to determine whether changing words in the Bernreuter Personality Inventory to more understandable synonyms would make the Inventory more applicable to persons who did not have a high school or college education. It was discovered that when some words, which were misunderstood by 1 to 20% of the subjects, were changed to simpler synonyms, no synonym was misunderstood by more than 3% of the subjects.

295. Hanes, B. "Reading Ease and MMPI Results," *Journal of Clinical Psychology*, 9:83–85, January, 1953.

In an investigation of the reading problem of penitentiary inmates with the Minnesota Multiphasic Personality Inventory, prisoners from each of five grade levels were asked to give the meaning of MMPI questions. About 17% of the questions were incorrectly defined and only 34% were correctly defined. Subjects with lower reading ability showed greater degrees of question incomprehension; subjects with reading grades above the fifth-grade level responded more frequently with incorrect definitions.

296. Harker, J. B. "A Dictation Test for Quick Administration," *Personnel Journal*, 28:180–84, October, 1949.

The use of the Flesch formula in constructing a dictation test for stenographic applicants is described, and the procedure necessary to apply the formula outlined. For the purpose of standardizing dictation tests, the average number of syllables per 100 words is the most important measure.

297. Johnson, R. H., and Bond, G. L. "Reading Ease of Commonly Used Tests," *Journal of Applied Psychology*, 34:319–24, October, 1950.

The readability levels of 19 intelligence tests were determined using the Flesch Reading Ease formula. Results showed that many current tests may not be suited to their purposes. While some of the tests nearly matched the reading levels for the assigned groups, others did not. This would imply that re-evaluation of the practices in test selection, administration, and interpretation is needed.

298. Maloney, P. W. "Reading Ease Scores for File's *How Supervise?*" *Journal of Applied Psychology*, 36:225–27, August, 1952.

Flesch's Reading Ease formula was applied to File's *How Supervise?* to determine whether it was too difficult for supervisors to comprehend. Results showed the test to be at a difficult level for most supervisors; and a great deal of the material was beyond high school readability. In contrast, less than one-fourth of a national sample of foremen were high school graduates.

299. Mathews, N. "An Analysis of Vocabulary Difficulties Found in Text Directions of Standard Achievement and Diagnostic Tests in Grades Seven to Twelve." Unpublished Master's thesis, University of Pittsburgh, 1933.

Achievement and diagnostic tests were examined to determine the vocabulary used in test direction and the difficulties it presents to pupils in Grades 7 to 12. Results gave a test direction vocabulary that was scattered throughout the Thorndike Word List. The majority of words were common to all tests in the "mechanics" of the directions. The difficulty of a word had no relation to its position in the word-list and over half the words were equally difficult for all grades.

300. Nuckols, R. C. "Verbi!" *International Journal of Opinion and Attitude Research,* **3:**575–86, Winter, 1949–1950.

The Flesch index of readability was used to determine the difficulty of opinion poll questions and whether the effects of language difficulty tend to produce constant response error. Results indicated that many questions are too abstract or wordy for people with little or no formal education. A negative relationship exists between increasing wordiness and the number of "don't know" answers.

301. Patty, W. W. "Reading Difficulty Differences of Health Knowledge Tests," *Research Quarterly,* **16:**206–15, October, 1945.

The results of a study to determine if two frequently used health education tests vary significantly in reading-vocabulary difficulty showed that the words of one test were from 28 to 39% easier than those of the other. An index of reading familiarity, which considers the number of words and the number of different words as well as commonness of reading use, is the most discriminating measure of vocabulary burden.

302. Pierce-Jones, J. "The Readability of Certain Standard Tests," *California Journal of Educational Research,* **5:**80–82, March, 1954.

The readability of four aptitude tests was analyzed by means of the Flesch Reading Ease formula. It was found that the Kuder Preference Record and the Judgments Characteristic of a Socially Competent Person were more difficult than the Bell Adjustment Inventory and the Minnesota Multiphasic Personality Inventory. Difficulty ranged from fifth to eighth grade and was principally related to vocabulary diversity.

303. Smith, J. E. "Use of Readability Techniques in Constructing a Problem Check List," *Educational Research Bulletin,* **31**:129–33, 140, May 14, 1952.

    Application of readability techniques to the construction of a problem check list found 90% of the words in the check list on the Dale list, and less than 1% not among Thorndike and Lorge's 10,000 most frequently used words. Average sentence length was six words. Disadvantages were found in the techniques because they represented limited areas of experience, and used statements rather than sentences.

304. Stefflre, B. "The Reading Difficulty of Interest Inventories," *Occupations,* **26**:95–96, November, 1947.

    Six well-known interest inventories were studied to determine their reading grade placement. Results showed a vast difference in reading difficulty among the inventories, based on grade placement as determined by the Lewerenz formula. Actual grade placements obtained may be considered tentative, but of more importance was the establishing of the relative difficulty of the inventories.

See also 38, 326, 358, and 384.

6. Writing

Nos. 305–323

305. Chall, J. "Improving the Readability of Health Education Materials," *A Report of the Tenth Annual Conference on Reading.* Pittsburgh: University of Pittsburgh Press, 49–55, 1954.

    It is suggested that to improve the readability of health education materials the writer must know the audience for whom the material is written and the purpose of the material. Technical and general word-lists can help the writer determine whether he is writing at a suitable level for the audience. A closer approximation can be made if a pretest of the material is possible.

306. Dale, E. "Communication of Ideas to Adults," *American Educational Research Association,* Official Report, 96–101, 1949.

    Reporting on communications problems experienced during a four-year period by the Committee on Teaching Materials of the National Tuberculosis Association, the author concludes that pamphlets may be written at the seventh-grade level and not offend the able reader and that readability formulas will give a rough estimate of the reading grade level but will provide no automatic methods for writing readable materials.

307. Dale, E., and Hager, H. *Some Suggestions for Writing Health Materials.* New York: National Tuberculosis Association, 1950.

A report by the NTA's Committee on Materials suggests that concern for the audience, the purpose, the logic, the breakdown, the vocabulary, the summarization, and the individualization of approach will produce more readable writing in the organization's educational publications.

308. Dale, E., and Chall, J. S. "Techniques for Selecting and Writing Readable Materials," *Elementary English,* **26**: 250–58, May, 1949.

Suggesting some techniques for selecting and writing readable materials, the author places emphasis on the reader and the material's purpose. Procedures used to define audience and purpose are outlined and the writer and/or teacher is referred to publications which help in analyzing materials to fit a prospective audience's abilities, interests, and intellectual maturity.

309. Flesch, R. F. *The Art of Plain Talk.* New York: Harper and Brothers, 1946.

The 1943 Flesch readability formula is presented in simple language, and examples are given to show the formula's application to the writing of the researcher, librarian, teacher, editor, and writer. The formula provides a difficulty score which can be related to census figures, plus grading statistics to help tailor writing to readers. Many active verbs and as few adjectives, prepositions, conjunctions, and adverbs as possible make for readable writing.

310. Flesch, R. F. "How to Say What You Mean," *Science Digest,* **20**:37–39, November, 1946.

Explaining how to speak and write understandably, the author suggests that an average sentence length of 17 words should be understandable to the average reader. Active verbs should be used to brighten speech, and compound prepositions and conjunctions should be avoided, if possible.

311. Flesch, R. F. *The Art of Readable Writing.* New York: Harper and Brothers, 1949.

     The art of scientific rhetoric is discussed in a follow-up to *The Art of Plain Talk.* Emphasis is placed on the human interest aspect of the dual Flesch formula and the reader is referred to Flesch's article, "A New Readability Yardstick," for the scientific derivation of this new 1948 formula.

312. Flesch, R. F. "Shirt-Sleeve English in One Easy Lesson," *Reader's Digest,* **67**:46–48, August, 1950.

     The concept of shirt-sleeve English — the language of everyday speech — is presented, and it is pointed out that advertisers and public relations men are quick to see the value of down-to-earth language in their work. Four rules-of-thumb for writing shirt-sleeve English are presented: go slow on rare and fancy words; don't worry too much about avoiding repetition; don't worry too much about avoiding slang; and don't worry too much about being grammatical.

313. Flesch, R. F. "Let's Face the Facts About Writing, A Look at Our Common Problems," *College English,* **12**:19–24, October, 1950.

     Asserting that college composition, as it is being taught, does not prepare the student to do the kinds of writing he will meet in his work, the author concludes that the essay form is extinct and that attention to practical writing must replace it. Such skills as abstracting, digesting, the writing of letters, reports, and pamphlets, and even the organization of materials for the printer, must be taught.

314. Flesch, R. F. *How to Test Readability.* New York: Harper and Brothers, 1951.

     A manual for readability testing, this book gives detailed instructions in sampling, counting, computing scores, and interpretation of scores for both the Reading Ease and Human Interest measures. A brief section on how to raise readability, including answers to the 44 questions most commonly asked about readability, is included.

315. Flesch, R. F. *How to Write Better.* Life Adjustment Booklet. Chicago: Science Research Associates, 1951.

     A detailed description of the process of getting an idea, thinking and planning, mechanics of beginning and ending, use of easy, clear and interesting language, and making revisions is presented. The principles of everyday language, conversational tone, personal reference, and the use of action verbs and adverbs are especially stressed.

316. Flesch, R. F. "First Aid for Word Trouble," Ch. 7 of *The Art of Clear Thinking*. New York: Harper and Brothers, 51–58, 1951.

Flesch offers the following short-cut device for estimating concreteness or abstractness of everyday speech and writing: concrete words are those referring to people, things, and events; all others are abstract. Flesch concludes that abstract words can be useful when backed by concrete references, but are otherwise undesirable.

317. Gowers, Sir E. *Plain Words: Their ABC*. New York: Alfred A. Knopf, 1954.

A number of readability precepts are stated and illustrated to help improve the writing of those who use words as tools of their trade, in administration or business. The author concludes that British official writing is not especially bad; it is just especially important that it be good. First published in Great Britain.

318. Hanlon, M. "Science Stories for Children," *School Science and Mathematics,* **56:**32–38, January, 1956.

Demonstrating how a story with a first-grade vocabulary and a fourth-grade interest level can be written, the author notes that stories about animals and children seem to be most popular with children between the second and eighth grades. In evaluating a story, some points to consider are a minimum of new words surrounded by familiar context, the author's personal experience with the subject, and an interesting title.

319. Irvine, P. "We Saw It First," *American School Board Journal,* **120:**31–32, February, 1950.

If school administrators wish to reach their intended audiences, they must write at an appropriate level of difficulty. It is suggested that the Flesch formula be used as a check and guide for writing. Specific recommendations are: keep average sentence and paragraph length short; use familiar words; and emphasize the human aspects of the subject.

320. Lieberman, E. "The Art of Writing Educational Reports and Articles," *Education Digest,* **17**:44–45, April, 1952.
Some of the weaknesses of educational writing are pointed out. Two particular weaknesses are faulty sentence structure and the use of too many abstract forms. Those engaged in educational writing are urged to avoid using outlines; not to fill sentences with subordinate clauses and phrases; and to be simple and brief.

321. "Readable," *New Yorker,* **22**:14–15, August 17, 1946.
Lorge's readability formula was applied to the Gettysburg Address and to the early speeches of Franklin D. Roosevelt. The Gettysburg address was rated at 6.7 and Roosevelt's speeches at 7.2, appropriate for the second half of the sixth grade and the first half of the seventh grade, respectively.

322. Strang, R. "Principles of Readability Applied to Reporting Research," *Teacher's College Record,* **49**:449–51, April, 1948.
In the belief that research worth doing is worth reporting readably, six "principles" to use in accomplishing this are offered, including a brief mention of the Flesch and Lorge factors for plain talk and a plea for "appeal," "personalization," "patterning," "emphasis," and "dilution."

323. Van de Water, M. "Problems Faced by a Writer in Communicating Research Findings in Child Development," *Child Development,* **19**:67–75, February, 1948.
To indicate some of the problems of communicating scientific findings to the general public, the author gives a review of the difficulty of science news writing. It is recommended that the science reporter concern himself with content rather than style, imagine himself writing to a definite person, know his reader, avoid useless words, and keep it short.

See also 36, 37, 43, 278, and 285.

7. Speech

Nos. 324–328

324. Goldstein, H. *Reading and Listening Comprehension at Various Controlled Rates.* Columbia University Contribu-

tions to Education No. 821. New York: Teachers College, Columbia University, 1940.

Two hundred eighty subjects, when compared in reading and listening comprehension at various rates of presentation, showed that, in general, listening comprehension is superior to reading comprehension for easy materials at slow speeds. Increasing speed of presentation reduces both modes of comprehension.

325. Harwood, K. A. "An Experimental Comparison of Listening Comprehensibility with Reading Comprehensibility." Abstract of a Doctoral dissertation, University of Southern California, 1950. *Speech Monographs,* **18**:123–24, June, 1951.

To determine the relationships between written and spoken language of various levels of difficulty, a series of language samples graded for readability were aurally and visually presented to two similar groups. "Taken as a whole, the series . . . was only insignificantly more comprehensible when presented for reading than when presented for listening." More difficult samples were significantly more comprehensible when presented for reading than when presented for listening.

326. Payne, S. L. "Can You Make It Brief?" Ch. 8 of *The Art of Asking Questions.* Princeton: Princeton University Press, 129–37, 1951.

Sixteen interchangeable pairs of questions were used to determine the reasons why some questions are tight (show no significant differences in answers to the alternate wordings) and some are loose (show significant differences). The study concludes that, in a verbal statement of two ideas, the last one stated tends to have greater drawing power, and that brevity and simplicity in wording are important elements in tight questions.

327. Siegel, A. I., and Siegel, E. "Flesch Readability Analysis of the Major Pre-election Speeches of Eisenhower and Stevenson," *Journal of Applied Psychology,* **37**:105–6, April, 1953.

In order to test whether Stevenson was "speaking over the heads of his audiences," six of his pre-election speeches were analyzed using the Flesch Reading Ease and Human Interest formulas. As a basis for comparison, six of Eisenhower's speeches delivered on corresponding days were analyzed. Eisenhower's speeches were found to be 1.5 points more difficult and 2.8 points more interesting.

328. Silvey, R. "The Intelligibility of Broadcast Talks," *Public Opinion Quarterly*, 15:299–304, Summer, 1951.

A study measuring the extent to which broadcasts are understood by listeners and identifying the qualities which produce intelligibility showed that comprehension depends upon intellectual capacity to the extent that material appropriate for the top third of the audience is not very meaningful to people of average intelligence and little or nothing is derived by below-average individuals.

See also 360, 363, 366, 367, 400, 403, 416, and 421.

8. Foreign Languages

Nos. 329–336

329. Feer, U. "A Study on the Application of Readability Formulas to Satirical Writing and to Foreign Language Texts." Unpublished Honors paper, Ohio University, Athens, Ohio, 1956.

Flesch's Reading Ease and Level of Abstraction formulas were used to compare Voltaire's *Candide* in the original French with English and German translations. A "definite word" count apparently did not measure the abstract quality of satire. All three versions scored Fairly Concrete; the differences between them were small and consistent. The German word length measures were consistently longer than either the French or English.

330. Flesch, R. F. "How Basic is Basic English?" *Harper's*, 188:339–43, March, 1944.

To show that Basic English is not a successful simplification of English, a set of criteria for simplicity was derived from an inspection of Chinese and Pidgin English. Appraisal of Basic English in the light of these criteria showed that Basic English is neither basic nor English.

331. Nannetti, G. "Something to Read: Latin America Works for Freedom Through Books," *Americas*, 4:13–15, March, 1952.

Reporting on the Latin American literacy campaign, the author argues that many social problems could be solved with the aid of books. The dearth of reading materials begins where primary school ends; the literacy campaign furnishes adults with the mechanics of reading through the use of children's books. It then sends them into a world devoid of adult reading materials at the appropriate level so that the habit of reading cannot become established. The Organization of American States and UNESCO are working to provide simple texts to fill the need.

332. Shiba, S. "A Study of Readability Measurement — Application of Cloze Procedure to Japanese Language," *Japanese Journal of Psychology,* **28**:67 (Japanese text), 69 (English abstract), August, 1957.

Testing the validity of applying Cloze Procedure to the Japanese language, the author found that the method is applicable to the language. He suggests that "letter" rather than "word" deletion be used because word deletion requires more powerful discrimination. The value of 10–15% deleting frequency and the use of 30 subjects are also recommended.

333. Spaulding, S. "Two Formulas for Estimating the Reading Difficulty of Spanish," *Educational Research Bulletin,* **30**:117–24, May 16, 1951.

Two proposed formulas for rating Spanish materials according to reading difficulty were tested. The difficulty ratings of 20 selections according to both formulas were compared with the ratings of independent judges. The first formula was a more accurate measuring device, employing the frequency-index calculation, but required more time. The second formula was easier because of the simplicity of the density measure, but was not as accurate.

334. Spaulding, S. "Trial Run: OAS–UNESCO Booklets for Adults Who Have Just Learned to Read," *Americas,* 4:20–22, December, 1952.

A study was conducted in Costa Rica and Mexico to gather specific details for guidance in the preparation of materials for adult new-literates. It was found that thought must be given to the lighting conditions available to prospective readers; that drawings must be absolutely realistic to avoid confusion; that some expressions used in the test booklets were foreign to native readers; and that the topics of pediatrics and television would be of interest, as well as the liquor problem. Chief concerns uncovered were water supply, childbirth, and recreation.

335. Spaulding, S. "A Spanish Readability Formula," *Modern Language Journal,* **40**:433–41, December, 1956.

A reading difficulty formula and the required steps for its application to Spanish materials are presented. The formula is explained and the procedure for applying it outlined, including how to choose samples, how to determine average sentence length, how to determine density, and the rules for computation.

336. Tharp, J. B. "The Measurement of Vocabulary Difficulty," *Modern Language Journal,* **24**:169–78, December, 1939.

To describe the application to French texts of a proposed *Index of Difficulty* combining *Density* and *Frequency* factors, data from an investigation of eight stories and analysis of twelve elementary readers are presented. No significant results were available, but it was considered possible to combine the spread of density and the burden of frequency into one measurement. Results of the second study showed that some elementary texts may have too high vocabulary to remain elementary.

E. *Sampling and Analyst Reliability*

Nos. 337–348

337. Chase, W. L. "Determination of Grade Placement of History Material," *Journal of Educational Research,* **28**:593–96, April, 1935.

To test the Vogel-Washburne technique for determining grade placement of children's reading material, a current history text was examined. Results of the examination showed a variance of one-half reading grade between two samples from the same page of the text, indicating, in the author's opinion, the unreliability of the technique.

338. Dolch, E. W. "Sampling of Reading Matter," *Journal of Educational Research,* **22**:213–15, October, 1930.

The reliability of samplings of reading matter to determine the proportion of difficult words was studied. Three books were entirely examined. Two different samples taken from every tenth page of the books were also examined. Results of the examination showed that the samplings tended to rate books much higher than the true values based on the entire book.

339. Dunnette, M. D., and Maloney, P. W. "Factorial Analysis of the Original and the Simplified Flesch Reading Ease Formulas," *Journal of Applied Psychology,* **37**:107–10, April, 1953.

A factorial experiment was conducted to study the effects of difficulty of reading material, type of count performed, reading ability of persons performing the counts, and sex, on the accuracy and time taken by naive subjects to perform readability counts. It was found that one-syllable words can be counted in about three-fourths the time required for counting syllables. Boys performed the former count more accurately than the latter, while no difference was found for girls.

340. Elliott, C. J. "A Critical Analysis of the Objective Method of Measuring Reading Difficulty," *Pittsburgh Schools,* **15**:201–9, May–June, 1941.

Five methods of determining reading difficulty are analyzed in an effort to find evidence of agreement between the methods and to see if objective measurement may claim reliability (as a measure of difficulty). Analysis of 28 school readers by the five methods varied; there was little agreement about the elements which contribute to ease or difficulty of material.

341. England, G. W., Thomas, M., and Paterson, D. G. "Reliability of the Original and the Simplified Flesch Reading Ease Formulas," *Journal of Applied Psychology,* **37**:111–13, April, 1953.

Defending attacks on the Farr, Jenkins, and Paterson simplification of the Flesch Reading Ease formula, the authors sought to show the reliability of both the original and simplified Flesch formulas. Samples taken from house organs were counted by 13 pairs of analysts; the results showed that both the original and the simplified formulas were highly reliable.

342. Farr, J. N., Jenkins, J. J., Paterson, D. G., and England, G. W. "Reply to Klare and Flesch re 'Simplification of Flesch Reading Ease Formula,' " *Journal of Applied Psychology,* **36**:55–57, February, 1952.

Refuting the arguments of Klare and Flesch who attacked their simplification of the Flesch Reading Ease formula, the authors present data from new and old method counts of samples taken from house publications. They found that the new formula took less computation time than the old formula, and did not introduce a systematic bias at extremes of difficulty but was, in fact, more sensitive at these extremes.

343.   Flesch, R. F. "Reply to 'Simplification of Flesch Reading Ease Formula,'" *Journal of Applied Psychology,* **36**:54–55, February, 1952.

Criticizing the Farr, Jenkins, and Paterson proposal that one-syllable words be counted instead of all syllables when using his Reading Ease formula, Flesch compares the average number of syllables and one-syllable words per 100 standard words. It was found that results for both formulas are roughly equivalent around the standard score but diverge toward either end of the scale. Flesch concludes that the new formula under-rates ease and difficulty and is a cruder, rather than a more precise, measure.

344.   Hayes, P. M., Jenkins, J. J., and Walker, B. J. "Reliability of the Flesch Readability Formulas," *Journal of Applied Psychology,* 34:22–26, February, 1950.

The independent analyst-to-analyst reliability of the Flesch readability formulas is examined. Results show that reliability for word length, sentence length, and reading ease was high for the materials used; for personal words, fair, and personal sentences, lower than desirable.

345.   Klare, G. R. "A Note on 'Simplification of Flesch Reading Ease Formula,'" *Journal of Applied Psychology,* **36**:53, February, 1952.

The advantages claimed for the Farr, Jenkins, and Paterson simplification of the Flesch Reading Ease formula are questioned. The author points out the difficulty in recognizing and selecting one-syllable words. He also points out that most writing contains a majority of one- and two-syllable words and asks whether the few polysyllabic words encountered would account for a saving of time. It is suggested that counting error may be magnified using the simplified method.

346.   Leifeste, B. V. "An Investigaton of the Reliability of the Sampling of Reading Material," *Journal of Educational Research,* 37:441–50, February, 1944.

Investigating the reliability of sampling, the author determines the minimum sampling necessary for adequate and consistent measurement of texts checked by the "Yoakam Technique for Grading Books." Results showed that a combination of several samplings for one book produced greater reliability than a single sampling and that the largest sampling seemed to show the greatest reliability.

347. Powers, R. D. "Sampling Problems in Studies of Writing Style," *Journal of Applied Psychology,* **38**:105–8, April, 1954.

Random samples from USDA reports were taken to compare two types of sampling: "cluster" (sampling by sentences) and word sampling. Results indicated that clustered sampling overestimated the percentage of "short," "structural," and "easy" words.

348. Ward, J. L. "Measuring the 'Vocabulary Burden,'" *American School Board Journal,* **71**:98, September, 1925.

Checking the accuracy of Pressey's sampling method for measuring vocabulary burden of textbooks, the author used the method to measure the vocabulary burden of a history text. He then made an actual count of these factors in the first 100 pages of the book. Ward concludes that Pressey's method is "a waste of time, money and energy" when applied to history texts.

See also 41, 282, and 283.

F. *Validity*

1. Comparative Data

Nos. 349–359

349. Aber, L. A. "A Comparison of the Readability Levels of Broadcasts by Certain National and Local Newscasters." Unpublished Doctoral dissertation, University of Pittsburgh, 1953.

The Flesch, Dale-Chall, and Yoakam readability formulas were applied to 600 samples from actual radio news broadcasts in order to determine their reading level. Results showed that, in general, newscasts are too difficult for the average listener. The Flesch and Dale-Chall formulas correlated higher than any other combination of formulas on the grade-levels of the 40 newscasters.

350. Beal, A. B. "An Evaluation of Techniques for Determining
the Difficulty of Primary Grade Readings." Unpublished
Master's thesis, Boston University, 1937.

This study was undertaken to develop a criterion against which
methods of determining the difficulty of primary-grade reading
materials might be evaluated and to evaluate certain grade-
placing techniques already formulated. It was found that in
oral reading, complex sentences slow up the reader but have a
negligible effect on comprehension. In silent reading, the
predominance of simple or complex sentences had little effect
on either speed or comprehension.

351. Kerr, M. "Use of Readability Formulas in Selecting Textbooks," *Elementary School Journal,* **49**:411–14, March,
1949.

The formulas of Dale, Lorge, and Flesch are described to show
how they can help teachers select textbooks. The limitations
of each formula are discussed and suggestions made for using
the formulas. Kerr concludes that the formulas are not and
cannot be the whole answer but merely a point of departure
for more thorough analysis and comparison of books.

352. Kinzer, J. R., and Cohan, N. R. "How Hard Are the Simplified Classics?" *English Journal,* **40**:210–11, April, 1951.

To determine the reading difficulty of 38 editions of the
adapted classics, the Flesch and Dale-Chall formulas were
applied to samples drawn from the books. Tabulated results
of the examination are presented as an aid to teachers in removing some of the guesswork from this phase of remedial
reading.

353. Larrick, N. "Try It On for Fit," *Library Journal,* **79**:729–
33, April 15, 1954.

Investigating the problem of finding the right book for the
right child, the author examines two books with five readability
formulas and compares the results for uniformity. Results
showed that there was no uniformity between formulas in the
grade placement of a book. The formulas measured at least one
of the following: hardness of words, average sentence length,
difficulty of sentence structure, number of syllables per 100
words, and human interest.

354. Lostutter, M. "Some Critical Factors of Newspaper Readability," *Journalism Quarterly*, 24:307–14, December, 1947.

The Lorge and Flesch formulas are applied to 180 newspaper articles. It was found that the Flesch formula was most convenient and effective for newspaper copy; attainment of readability is a conscious process independent of the newsman's education and experience; and the traditional newspaper lead will bear further inspection as a factor contributing to the difficulty of news copy.

355. Selikson, W. "A Critical Study of the Grade Placement of Textbooks in a Sixth Grade by the Use of Two Readability Prediction Formulas." Unpublished Master's thesis, Ohio State University, 1951.

The Dale-Chall and Flesch readability formulas were applied to sixth-grade textbooks. Arithmetic, spelling, geography, and health texts were found to be beyond sixth-grade reading ability; reading, science, English, and history texts had occasional passages that were too difficult. The science, health, history, and geography texts rated *Dull* or *Mildly Interesting* according to the Flesch Human Interest formula. Dale scores were consistently lower than the Flesch scores.

356. Smith, R. I. "An Investigation of the Readability of Recently Published History and Geography Textbooks, and Related Materials for the Fourth Grade," *Abstracts of Doctoral Dissertations*, Vol. 27, University of Pittsburgh Bulletin, 48:521–27, June 5, 1952.

An analysis of fourth-grade history and geography texts, workbooks, and current events papers was made using the Dale, Lorge, and Yoakam formulas. Conclusions revealed that the books had a readability average of slightly less than fifth-grade level. The three formulas gave about the same evaluation; however, the Yoakam formula required less time, fewer exact arithmetical computations, and was just as accurate as the other formulas.

357. Swarts, M. G. "The Readability of Books Written for Teachers About Reading," *A Report of the Tenth Annual*

Conference on Reading. Pittsburgh: University of Pittsburgh Press, 38–48, 1954.

The readability of textbooks dealing with the teaching of reading was investigated with the Dale-Chall, Flesch, and Yoakam formulas. The Flesch and Yoakam formulas were found to measure adult reading material more adequately than the Dale-Chall formula. All three were fairly consistent in placing the books in the difficult, average, or easy classifications.

358. Terris, F. "Are Poll Questions Too Difficult?" *Public Opinion Quarterly,* **13**:314–19, 1949.

Statistical methods are employed to determine whether the wording of present poll questions is too difficult for all educational levels of the American population. Analysis of questions from three survey sources showed that elements of difficulty do occur in the language of the poll questions.

359. Yoakam, G. A. "The Reading Difficulty of School Textbooks," *Elementary English Review,* **22**:304–9, December, 1945.

A ten-year study of readers and other school materials was conducted on the premise that materials of school subjects can either aid or retard learning. Results showed that the readers of the early 1930's were more difficult than those of the early 1940's. In the early years of the study, publisher's placement was much lower than the Yoakam score; this difference was seldom noticeable in the 1940 materials. Some well-known children's books were found far too difficult for the ages intended by librarians and publishers.

See also 38, 49, 65, 340, 367, 369, 385, 392, 402, 411, 412, 414, 417, 418, 421, and 475.

2. Outside Criteria

Nos. 360–421

360. Allen, W. "Readability of Instructional Film Commentary," *Journal of Applied Psychology,* **36**:164–68, June, 1952.

The Flesch, Dale-Chall, and Lorge readability formulas are used to test the effect of selected film commentary variations upon the learning of factual information by sixth-grade students. Results showed that formulas can measure the difficulty of film commentaries and that the three formulas were about equal in predicting comparative difficulty of commentaries.

361. Association of National Advertisers, Inc. *The Measured Effectiveness of Employee Publications: The Readership, Penetration and Readability of Seven Leading Employee Publications.* New York: Association of National Advertisers, Inc., 1953.

Investigation of readership and readability levels of company publications showed that they were widely read and regarded as credible. Features most read were classified advertisements, employees in service, news in brief, and 25-year veterans. The average publication was written at the high school level. There was little relationship between readership and readability.

362. Bernberg, R. E. "An Empirical Study of the Flesch Formulae," *Journal of General Psychology,* **51**:193–98, October, 1954.

This study dealt with the effect of differences in written materials, socio-economic status, and sex upon individual judgments about the ease and interest of magazine articles. Ratings by individuals were compared with Flesch scores. Results showed that socio-economic levels were significant in determining variation between groups; sex was not. Generally, Flesch scores were more severe in evaluating the materials than were the subjects.

363. Blain, B. B. "Effects of Film Narration Type and of Readability Level on Learning of Factual Information." Unpublished Doctoral dissertation, Indiana University, 1956.

A study of the effect of (1) expository and personalized-dramatic types of film narration, and (2) varied listenability levels of narration, on learning of factual information showed that an informal, conversational, and personalized narration aided learning but that listenability levels had no measurable effect on learning.

364. Brown, J. I. "The Flesch Formula 'Through the Looking Glass,'" *College English,* **13**:393–94, April, 1952.

To determine the importance of differences in readability scores to students and teachers, results of Harvard Reading Course tests differing in difficulty were analyzed. It was found that teachers can check rate and comprehension with the aid of the Flesch formula. Students with reading problems can be helped by choosing materials at a desired level and then progressing to materials graded "more difficult."

365. Carter, R. E., Jr. "Cross-Cultural Application of Four Flesch Formulas," *Journalism Quarterly*, 32:487–89, Fall, 1955.

The relationships between ratings given material distributed by the U.S. Information Service and Flesch readability formula scores were examined. Results indicated that Flesch Reading Ease and Human Interest scores are efficient indicators of difficulty and interest of materials as judged by subjects. Human Interest scores can predict how interesting subjects feel material is, but cannot predict their difficulty ratings of such material.

366. Cartier, F. A., Jr. "An Experimental Study of the Effect of 'Human Interest' Factors on Listenability." Unpublished Doctoral dissertation, University of Southern California, 1951.

Investigating the applicability of the "personal words" element in the Flesch Human Interest formula to listenability, the author found that, among tenth-grade students, raising or lowering the HI score of stories had no significant effect on listenability, regardless of story difficulty. Sex differences did not influence the comprehension level, which was generally low.   •

367. Chall, J. S., and Dial, H. "Predicting Listener Understanding and Interest in Newscasts," *Educational Research Bulletin*, 27:141–53, 168, September 15, 1948.

In a study to determine how well Dale-Chall and Flesch readability formulas could be applied to newscasts, it was found that predictions of readability can be applied fairly well to listening difficulty. A definite relation was found between interest and comprehension. Finally, it was found that readability formulas can predict interest of newscasts.

368. Clarke, L. K. "The Effect on Comprehension of Simplification of Social Science Reading Material in a Second Grade." Unpublished Master's thesis, State University of Iowa, 1933.

The effect on comprehension of simplified social science reading matter at the second-grade level was studied. Results indicated that simplification of vocabulary resulted in faster comprehension; however, the findings were not significant.

369. Dunlap, C. C. "Readability Measurements: A Review and Comparison." Unpublished Doctoral dissertation, University of Maryland, 1954.

Fifty-six techniques for measuring readability are surveyed in order to acquire a better understanding of the measures and the factors determining readability. Twelve of the measures are applied to samples from Rourke's *Davy Crockett;* results show that the book is too difficult for eighth-grade students.

370. Feld, B., Jr. "Empirical Test Proves Clarity Adds Readers," *Editor and Publisher,* 81:38, April 17, 1948.

Comparison of stories with high and low readability (as measured by the Flesch formula) from a single issue of the *Birmingham News* revealed that stressing Flesch's principles to make stories easier to read will increase readership as much as 75%. *Birmingham News* writers felt that their style of writing had improved as a result of using Flesch's principles.

371. Figurel, J. A. "Relative Difficulty of Reading Material for Ninth Grade Literature," *Pittsburgh Schools,* 16:125–38, January–February, 1942.

The difficulty of literature for ninth-grade pupils was studied. Application of the Yoakam formula to seven classics used in ninth-grade literature classes showed three of them to be of twelfth-grade difficulty. Pupils rated the easiest classics most popular and the same was true for library books chosen for free reading. Magazines read by the pupils averaged sixth-grade difficulty.

372. Flesch, R. F. "New Facts About Readability," *College English,* 10:225–26, January, 1949.

Lorna Doone, a novel, and *The Wealth of Nations,* Vol. II, a book about economics, are analyzed for readability. Results show that the average student reads difficult materials much slower than easy fiction. Usually, habitual reading rhythm is not changed when reading difficult material; however, blinking and right-to-left eye-movements are increased.

373. Flesch R. F. "Reader Comprehension of News Stories: Further Comment," *Journalism Quarterly,* **28**:496–97, Fall, 1951.

    Application of Flesch's new readability formula to two versions of a news story used by P. F. Griffin in an earlier study revealed that rewriting, based on developing a new lead, tightening the organization, and rearranging the structure, raised the Reading Ease score slightly and the Human Interest score considerably. The increase in "human interest" increased reader comprehension and approval.

374. Foster, C. "The Effect Upon Reading Comprehension of Paraphrasing Elementary Historical Material into the Spoken and Written Vocabulary of Children." Unpublished Master's thesis, State University of Iowa, 1931.

    Results of a study to determine how reading comprehension is affected by paraphrasing elementary historical material into a preschool vocabulary indicate that comprehension is not always facilitated by simplifying the material. Those who read the simplified version finished the comprehension tests more rapidly, although the reliability of the tests was low.

375. Gibbons, H. D. "Reading and Sentence Elements," *Elementary English Review,* **18**:42–46, February, 1941.

    This study investigated, among third-grade pupils, the relationship between parts of a sentence and the ability to understand the sentence, and the relation between this ability and the ability to read. Results showed that the ability to see relationships between sentence parts is an essential factor in understanding the sentence and is related to the ability to read.

376. Gilinsky, A. S. "How Valid is the Flesch Readability Formula?" *American Psychologist,* **3**:261, July, 1948.

    The validity of the Flesch readability formula against a scale of judged readability was tested by having college students and laboratory members rate samples of prose, and applying the the Flesch formula to the samples. The correlations between readability judgments and Flesch counts ranged from .61 to .84.

377. Griffin, P. F. "Reader Comprehension of News Stories: A Preliminary Study," *Journalism Quarterly,* **26**:389–96, December, 1949.

    Measurement of the effectiveness of two versions of a news story as communication instruments in terms of reader comprehension and interest indicated that less than half of the readers comprehend news stories well enough to repeat them in detail. This was due to careless structure, and irrelevant and unintegrated detail, which caused loss of interest. Awkwardness and monotony rather than sentence length were at fault.

378. Griffin, P. F. "Reader Comprehension of News Stories: A Note on the Comment by Dr. Flesch," *Journalism Quarterly*, **28**:497, Fall, 1951.

Speculating on whether increased Reading Ease and Human Interest as measured by the Flesch formula is the cause of increased comprehension, the author says the increase is probably due to better organization. Appropriate words and well-constructed sentences do not necessarily mean short or common words, or sentences simple in structure and shorter in words.

379. Guckenheimer, S. N. "The Readability of Pamphlets on International Relationships," *Educational Research Bulletin*, **26**:231–38, December 10, 1947.

Difficulty of international affairs pamphlets was determined by subjecting them to the Dale-Chall formula and the judgment of experts in the field. It was found that 75% of the material was at or above the college level, 14% at the senior high school level and 11% at high school freshman level.

380. Harvey, J. F. "The Content Characteristics of Best-Selling Novels." Unpublished Doctoral dissertation, University of Chicago, December, 1949.

Content characteristics of best-selling novels were isolated in order to determine combinations of these which can be used to predict sales. Sixteen variables emerged as most important; the first three were "emotion," readability, and "moralizing theme," in that order. The best formula included readability, sentimental theme, affectionate attitude of main character, and total strong emotion.

381. Herrington, R. L., and Mallinson, G. G. "An Investigation of Two Methods of Measuring the Reading Difficulty of Materials for Elementary Science," *Science Education*, **42**:385–90, December, 1958.

Judgments of grade levels of elementary science books made by readability formulas and reading experts were compared. The judgment based on the formulas was found more consistent than that of experts not using formulas. It is concluded that formulas should be used by teachers in judging difficulty, in conjunction with their judgments of interest, format, etc., and that teachers should be given training in the selection of texts.

382. Hites, R. W. "The Relation of Readability and Format to Retention in Communication." Unpublished Doctoral dissertation, Ohio State University, 1950.

A theory is proposed interrelating the readability elements used by Lorge with context and format. Hypotheses borne out by testing the theory among Air Force R.O.T.C. freshman were: paragraphing increases retention; the mean of reading comprehension scores of a group of people who have intelligence test scores above the median is significantly higher than the mean of a group whose scores are below the median.

383. Jackman, M. E. "The Relation Between Maturity of Content and Simplicity of Style in Selected Books of Fiction," *Library Quarterly,* 11:302–27, July, 1941.

One hundred works of fiction were rated by three methods to determine how closely the simple forms of written fiction are associated with simple ideas and the more complex forms with relatively more mature ideas. Results showed that the correlation between maturity and readability indicated an almost pure chance relationship between the two factors.

384. Klare, G. R. "Understandability and Indefinite Answers to Public Opinion Questions," *International Journal of Opinion and Attitude Research,* 4:91–96, 1950.

A series of questions taken from the *Public Opinion Quarterly* was analyzed by the Flesch formula in order to determine understandability. For the most part, when the formula indicated greater readability, indefinite percentages (Don't Know, Can't Say, No Opinion, etc.) for poll questions were found to be less. Questions rated as hard to understand by the formula were responded to with a larger percentage of indefinite answers on the average than those rated as easy.

385. Klare, G. R. "Measures of the Readability of Written Communication: An Evaluation," *Journal of Educational Psychology,* 43:385–99, November, 1952.

In order to evaluate them, five readability formulas were applied to samples drawn from 52 books on the list in Gray and Leary, *What Makes a Book Readable.* Results ranked the formulas in order of highest grade-level rating given: (1) Washburne, (2) Flesch, (3) Dale-Chall, (4) Lewerenz, and (5) Gray-Leary. The data indicated that the formulas probably measured essentially similar elements of difficulty.

386. Klare, G. R., Mabry, J. E., and Gustafson, L. M. *The Relationship of Verbal Communication Variables to Immediate and Delayed Retention and to Acceptability of Technical Training Materials.* Research Bulletin AFPTRC-TR-54-103. San Antonio: USAF Personnel & Training Research Center, Lackland AFB, December, 1954.

The influence of "style difficulty," "patterning" (underlining), and "human interest" upon immediate and delayed retention of Air Force Study Guide material was investigated, using trainees as subjects. Standard, Easy, and Hard readability versions of the material were prepared, and it was found that the three versions produced significantly different scores. "Patterning" produced higher scores for more able readers, while "human interest" increased the amount read slightly, without improving retention, and also was disliked by readers.

387. Klare, G. R., Mabry, J. E., and Gustafson, L. M. "The Relationship of Human Interest to Immediate Retention and to Acceptability of Technical Material," *Journal of Applied Psychology,* 39:92–95, 1955.

"Human interest" was related to "content" and "style difficulty," and to acceptability by airmen of Air Force technical materials. It was found that high "human interest" produced no significant difference in immediate retention and was consistently judged less acceptable, though it did tend to produce a greater amount of material read in a given time.

388. Klare, G. R., Mabry, J. E., and Gustafson, L. M. "The Relationship of Style Difficulty to Immediate Retention and to Acceptability of Technical Material," *Journal of Educational Psychology,* 46:287–95, May, 1955.

To study the relation of style difficulty to immediate retention, amount read in a given time, and acceptability of material, Easy, Standard, and Hard versions of an Air Force technical manual were prepared, holding content and technical terms constant. Results showed that with easier style, greater and more complete retention was effected, a greater amount was read, and material was judged more acceptable by airmen subjects.

389. Klare, G. R., Shuford, E. H., and Nichols, W. H. "The Relationship of Style Difficulty, Practice, and Ability to Efficiency of Reading and to Retention," *Journal of Applied Psychology,* 41:222–26, 1957.

The relation of "style difficulty," "practice" and "ability" to efficiency of reading and retention of technical material was studied, using subjects of high and low mechanical ability reading before an eye-movement camera. The Easy style produced higher scores than the Hard on words per fixation, words per second, and recall measures, as did repeated readings of the material.

390. Knauft, E. B. "Measured Changes in Acceptance of an Employee Publication," *Journal of Applied Psychology,* 35:151–56, June, 1951.

Content analysis, Flesch counts for Reading Ease and Human Interest, and a readership survey were used to evaluate a house organ. Changes made in the publication on the basis of the evaluation included a more balanced content and improvement in Reading Ease and Human Interest. The changes resulted in a significant increase in favorable employee attitude toward the publication.

391. Kueneman, H. "A Study of the Effect of Vocabulary Changes on Reading Comprehension in a Single Field." Unpublished Master's thesis, State University of Iowa, 1931.

Fourth-grade geography material was examined to determine whether it would be more comprehensible with the content written in a preschooler's vocabulary. No significant difference was noted between comprehension of the original and simplified material. Individual portions of the test showed a greater difference in favor of the rewritten material, but it was not significant.

392. Latimer, E. H. "A Comparative Study of Recent Techniques for Judging Readability," *Abstracts of Doctoral Dissertations,* Vol. 23, University of Pittsburgh Bulletin, 44:246–56, April 10, 1948.

The value of the Yoakam, Flesch, and Lorge formulas for judging readability of 12 religious textbooks at the elementary level was studied. Results indicated that existing techniques can be used to predict reading difficulty of religious material. The Yoakam formula seems most valid and reliable. A high correlation between general pupil reading ability and the ability to read and comprehend religious material was found.

393. Lockman, R. F. "A Note on Measuring 'Understandability,' " *Journal of Applied Psychology,* **40**:195–96, June, 1956.

An experimental rating scale for measuring the understandability of prose is presented. Results of an application of the method using Naval Aviation Cadets showed relatively little spread between the Lockman method and the Flesch formula. It was shown that Reading Ease scores and understandability ratings do not measure the same thing.

394. Lorge, I. and Kruglov, L. "The Relationship Between the Readability of Pupils' Compositions and Their Measured Intelligence," *Journal of Educational Research,* **43**:467–74, February, 1950.

An investigation of the relationship between the readability of high school pupils' compositions as measured by the Lorge formula and the pupils' measured intelligence showed no significant relationship between the two measures. High school students write, on the average, at least two levels below their understanding level.

395. Lorge, I., and Kruglov, L. "The Relation Between Merit of Written Expression and Intelligence," *Journal of Educational Research,* **44**:507–19, March, 1951.

The hypothesis that structural and conceptual aspects of written composition are indicative of general intellectual level was tested, using ninth-grade students. Significant relationships between structure and intellectual ability, merit of the compositions and intellectual ability, and structure and merit were found.

396. Ludwig, M. C. "Hard Words and Human Interest: Their Effects on Readership," *Journalism Quarterly,* **26**:167–71, June, 1949.

Investigation of the effect of vocabulary simplification and increased human interest in a farm magazine upon readership revealed that vocabulary difficulty is related to readership. It was also found that human interest does not necessarily attract readers and that when content interest is high, hard words and human interest tend to have less effect than content on readership.

397. Lyman, H. B. "Flesch Count and Readership of Articles in a Midwestern Farm Paper," *Journal of Applied Psychology,* **33:**78–80, February, 1949.

The effect of reducing the Flesch count to increase subscriber readership of articles in two farm magazines is reported. The study showed that increases in readership for the majority of the low-count articles ranged from 7.3% to 66.0%.

398. Macfadden Publications, Inc. *A Study of What Makes It Hard or Easy To Read.* New York: Macfadden Publications, Inc., 1947.

This report to businessmen, particularly those writing for mass audiences, concludes that attention to length of sentences, word complexity, and amount of human interest can bring writing to desirable readability levels. A subsidiary conclusion is that readable ads attract more readers.

399. MacKinney, A. C., and Jenkins, J. J. "Readability of Employees' Letters in Relation to Occupational Level," *Journal of Applied Psychology,* **38:**26–30, February, 1954.

The propositions that readability level of employee-written letters reflects the effective literacy level of the employees, and that literacy level increases with higher occupational levels, were tested. Four hundred letters in a General Motors letter-writing contest were analyzed. Results showed a gradation of mean Reading Ease scores ranging from *Fairly Difficult* for skilled salary groups to *Fairly Easy* for unskilled hourly employees.

400. Manion, O. G. "An Application of Readability Formulas to Oral Communication," *Speech Monographs,* Abstracts of Theses, **21:**151, June, 1954.

Some of the existing structural indices of readability were studied to determine whether they could be utilized to measure accurately and predict listener difficulty with oral communications. It was found that the procedures, population, and coding used in the readability indices were useful, but that no significant relationship existed between the criteria of listener understanding and the indices of difficulty.

401. Marshall, J. S. "The Relationship Between Readability and Comprehension of High School Physics Textbooks," *Dissertation Abstracts,* **17**:64, January, 1957.

The relationship between readability and comprehension of high school physics texts was investigated, using original and rewritten versions of the material. High school students who read the rewritten passage did not show better comprehension of the material than those who read the original passage. It was also found that the Flesch Reading Ease formula did not predict difficulty in the comprehension of high school physics textbooks.

402. Miller, L. R. "Reading–Grade Placement of the First Twenty-Three Books Awarded the John Newbery Prize," *Elementary School Journal,* **46**:394–99, March, 1946.

The minimum reading grade level of 23 Newbery Prize-winning books was determined by subjecting each to a comprehension test given to sixth- and seventh-grade public school pupils. It was concluded that the books were too hard for elementary school students and should be used in junior and senior high school. Tabulations are presented to aid teachers, parents, and librarians in selecting books suitable to the reading ability of specific children.

403. Moldstad, J. "Readability Formulas and Film Grade-Placement," *Audio-Visual Communication Review,* **3**:99–108, 1955.

A study was made to determine the effectiveness of film narrations of different listenability levels on learning of scientific information and vocabulary and the influence on vocabulary growth of narrations using an increased number of difficult, nonscientific words. No differences in ability of subjects to learn scientific facts or vocabulary were shown. The author concludes that repetition may have erased the effects of readability on learning and that commentary may merely supplement visual elements in teaching.

404. Murphy, D. R. "Test Proves Short Words and Sentences Get Best Readership," *Printer's Ink,* **218:**61–64, January 10, 1947.

A split-run experiment was conducted to ascertain whether simplification of the reading style of a farm journal would increase readership. The results showed that the simplified version had a reader-interest score substantially higher than the original copy. It was found also that the number of male readers increased for the simplified material.

405. Murphy, D. R. "How Plain Talk Increases Readership 45 Per Cent to 66 Per Cent," *Printer's Ink,* **220:**35–37, September, 1947.

The rewrite methods used by two farm journals to reduce their Flesch readability scores and obtain additional readers are explained. Reducing the readability level resulted in a significant reader increase; younger people responded more than older people to the easy version. The author states that employing readability measures should not result in mechanistic writing because a simple article can get poor reader response as easily as a more difficult article.

406. Nolte, K. F. "Simplification of Vocabulary and Comprehension in Reading," *Elementary English Review,* 14:119–24, 146, April, 1937.

The effect of vocabulary simplification upon reading comprehension was tested by presenting original and simplified reading materials to sixth-grade students. No statistically significant conclusions could be drawn from the study; no significant differences were found between comprehension of the original selections and the simplified versions.

407. Orndorff, B. A. "An Experiment to Show the Effect of Sentence Length Upon Comprehension." Unpublished Master's thesis, State University of Iowa, 1925.

To study the effect of sentence length upon comprehension, selected articles and revisions (changed in sentence length only) were presented to elementary school subjects. The results failed to show any significant difference between long and short sentences in their effect upon comprehension.

408. Peterson, M. J. "Comparison of Flesch Readability Scores

with a Test of Reading Comprehension," *Journal of Applied Psychology*, **40**:35–36, February, 1956.

In order to test the validity of the Flesch Reading Ease formula against reading comprehension tests using "popular" material, fifty anecdotes from the *Reader's Digest* were rewritten according to Flesch Reading Ease levels. The ten rated highest were used in final testing with high school students. Results showed that Reading Ease scores do estimate the comparative difficulty of "popular" adult reading materials adequately.

409. Pitcher, R. W. "An Experimental Investigation of the Validity of the Flesch Readability Formula as Related to Adult Materials." Unpublished Doctoral dissertation, University of Michigan, 1953.

The validity of the Flesch readability formula in relation to adult reading material was tested by having college students read passages of different levels of difficulty. Results showed that within a given content area the formula is valid and measures degrees of increasing difficulty. The formula is not valid when evaluating material containing different kinds of content.

410. Robinson, F. P. "Comprehension Difficulty and Inspirational Value," *Pedagogical Seminary and Journal of Genetic Psychology*, **56**:53–65, March, 1940.

Although the results were not significant, simplification of selections from the Bible, the Kellogg-Briand Peace Pact, and Gibbon's *Decline and Fall of the Roman Empire* did not decrease their inspirational value or their value as an indication of the author's knowledge of a topic. Robinson concludes that well-written simplifications of many pieces of literature will increase comprehension.

411. Russell, D. H., and Merrill, A. F. "Children's Librarians Rate the Difficulty of Well-Known Juvenile Books," *Elementary English*, **28**:263–68, May, 1951.

The difficulty ratings of 60 juvenile books as judged by children's librarians and six readability formulas were compared. Results showed that the librarians did not agree in their ratings; as a group, they generally gave a range of three or four grades for which they felt the books were suitable. The librarians rated the books slightly easier than did the formulas.

412. Russell, D. H., and Fea, H. R. "Validity of Six Readability Formulas as Measures of Juvenile Fiction," *Elementary School Journal,* **52**:136–44, November, 1951.

     In order to determine their validity, the ratings given twelve juvenile books by six readability formulas and children's librarians were compared. Results showed that three of the formulas are about equally good measures of the difficulty of children's books. The mean ratings of difficulty by the formulas were fairly close to those of the librarians; however, more divergence was noted when grade placements were compared.

413. Schramm, W. "Measuring Another Dimension of Newspaper Readership," *Journalism Quarterly,* **24**:293–306, December, 1947.

     This newspaper readership depth study revealed that a news story loses readers rapidly in the first few paragraphs; thereafter, the curve of loss flattens out. The average reader tends to read between a third and a tenth of the total news content of a paper. A formula combining initial readership with average depth of readership provides the most accurate index of news reading yet available.

414. Swanson, C. E. "Readability and Readership: A Controlled Experiment," *Journalism Quarterly,* **25**:339–43, December, 1948.

     Hard and easy versions of a prepared story were published in an experimental newspaper to determine whether increased readability produces more readers. The results showed that increased readability yielded an increase in total paragraphs read, median number of paragraphs read, and number of respondents reading every paragraph.

415. Swanson, C. E., and Fox, H. G. "Validity of Readability Formulas," *Journal of Applied Psychology,* **37**:114–18, April, 1953.

     To discover whether readability formulas can predict retention, readership, and comprehension of material, easy and hard versions of articles were presented to employees of a midwestern company. The results indicated that the samples used did not differ in retention or readership, but did differ in comprehension. It is suggested that the lack of differentiation in retention and readership indicates that the study of motivational factors need to be combined with the techniques used in construction of formulas.

416. Vancura, R. H. "Flesch Readability Formula Applied to Television Programs," *Journal of Applied Psychology,* **39**:47–48, February, 1955.

    Analysis of the audible vocabulary of television, using the Flesch readability formula (1951) and comparing Flesch scores and Telepulse ratings, yielded a nonsignificant correlation between the Flesch scores and Telepulse ratings of both daytime and evening programs at the .05 level. The rank-order correlation between Reading Ease and Human Interest scores for both daytime and evening programs was significant at the .01 level.

417. Vernon, P. E. *The Intelligibility of Broadcast Talks.* British Broadcasting Corp., 1950.

    The extent to which informational talks given to the British Armed Forces were understood and the qualities which distinguish intelligibility were examined. Objective analysis of scripts with readability factors gave unsatisfactory reliability coefficients; the author attributed this to the small sample.

418. Walther, C. "The Reading Difficulty of Magazines," *School Review,* **51**:100–105, February, 1943.

    The relative structural difficulty of 12 magazines commonly read by or recommended for high school freshmen was analyzed. It was found that the composite judgment of experts about the cultural level of magazines corresponds closely with structural difficulty of the magazines and that the Winnetka chart may be used to determine appropriate magazine reading for high school freshmen and sophomores.

419. Wert, J. E. "A Technique for Determining Levels of Group Reading," *Educational Research Bulletin,* **16**:113–21, 136, May 19, 1937.

    A technique is offered for evaluating the quality of reading material, as measured by college aptitude, English proficiency, and knowledge of contemporary affairs. The author believes the technique to be a reliable measure of quality of reading matter and superior to reading difficulty measures for measuring quality.

420. Wyant, R. "Voting Via the Senatorial Mailbag," *Public Opinion Quarterly,* **5**:359–82, 1941.

    The results of a study to investigate the wide differences between senators' mail and Gallup poll results regarding the conscription issue are presented. The greatest influx of mail came from towns of 2,500 to 25,000 population and from cities of over 250,000 people. More people write to criticize than to commend, and people of high or middle socio-economic status write more frequently than those of low status.

421. Young, J. R. "Understanding Radio News: The Effect of Style," *Journalism Quarterly,* **27**:19–23, March, 1950.

Results of a study to discover whether readability formulas can be used to predict listening difficulty of radio news stories gave no evidence of decreasing comprehension with increasing difficulty. This suggests that the factors measured by reading-difficulty formulas are not sufficient to determine listenability and comprehension of oral communications.

See also 23, 68, 97. 115, 300, and 327.

G. *Basic Considerations in Readability Measurement*

Nos. 422–467

422. Brinton, J. E., and Danielson, W. A. "A Factor Analysis of Language Elements Affecting Readability," *Journalism Quarterly,* **35**:420–26, Fall, 1958.

A factor analysis of data from Gray and Leary's *What Makes a Book Readable* is presented to describe the factors underlying the language variables producing intercorrelations reported in that work. A vocabulary factor and a sentence factor were discovered. These two factors involve elements which have been traditionally included in readability formulas for adults.

423. Carnap, R., and Bar-Hillel, Y. "An Outline of a Theory of Semantic Information," *Technical Report No. 247,* Research Laboratory of Electronics, Massachusetts Institute of Technology, October 27, 1952.

The mathematical theory of communication treats amount of information as a measure of the statistical rarity of a message. The theory of semantic information proposed in this paper considers content and amount of semantic information to be based upon logical probability functions. Two major types of amount of information are investigated, "inf" and "cont." The former is formally analogous to the customary information measure; the latter is a measure of content additive with respect to sentences. The authors suggest that semantic information and related concepts are the more adequate to psychological investigations.

424. Chall, J. S. "This Business of Readability," *Educational Research Bulletin,* **26**:1–13, January 15, 1947.

Reviewing the work done thus far on readability, the author cites the need for better communication through increased readability and for an objective standard of measurement. Further work needs to be done in application of results, in searching for reliable methods for dealing with adult material, and in discovering the limits, if any, of the use of readability formulas in technical and abstract fields.

425. Chall, J. S. "The Measurement of Readability," *A Report of the Tenth Annual Conference on Reading.* Pittsburgh: University of Pittsburgh Press, 26–37, 1954.

The Winnetka formula is discussed and the development of other formulas summarized. The Winnetka formula employed four basic elements: different words, prepositions, unfamiliar words, and number of simple sentences. The other formulas that followed developed in a similar manner. All of the formulas widely used today measure vocabulary difficulty.

426. Chall, J. S. "The Measurement of Readability," *Education Digest,* **21**:44–46, November, 1955.

Summarizing the methods used thus far in readability research and suggesting areas for further study, the author stresses that readability research is directed toward matching reader and material and that the measurement of objective factors of difficulty has been the main concern of research. It is recommended that these methods be extended and research on qualitative aspects be emphasized.

427. Chall, J. S. "This Business of Readability: A Second Look," *Educational Research Bulletin,* **35**:89–99, 111–12, April, 1956.

Reviewing the work done in readability, the author notes that applications of readability have been made in a wide range of areas including textbooks, newspapers, and psychological materials. The article recommends that the quantitative methods usually employed be refined and extended; that research into qualitative measures be more extensive; and more surveys of reader and expert opinion, experimental studies, analyst studies, cross validation studies, and experimental validation studies be made.

428. Chall, J. S. "A Survey of the Users of the Dale-Chall Formula," *Educational Research Bulletin,* **35**:197–212, November, 1956.

    A survey of the users of the Dale-Chall formula to ascertain the applications made of the formula revealed that it was most widely used by university people and the armed forces. It was often used with other formulas. The chief weaknesses seemed to be the time required and the absence of specialized terms in the word-list. Uses included analysis of manuscripts, research, teaching general guides for writing, editing and rewriting, and reference.

429. Chall, J. S., and Dale, E. "Familiarity of Selected Health Terms," *Educational Research Bulletin,* **29**:197–206, November, 1950.

    The results of a study of the familiarity of health terms showed an 11% discrepancy between words the subjects said they knew and words they could accurately define. The methods used in the study are reported, with the suggestion that they be used to obtain further data on familiarity of health terms as well as other terms.

430. Chapanis, A. "The Reconstruction of Abbreviated Printed Messages," *Journal of Experimental Psychology,* **48**:496–510, December, 1954.

    The purpose of this study was to examine some of the practical consequences of redundancy in English text. The method of measuring redundancy followed Shannon's procedure of deleting letters from texts and asking subjects to restore them. It was found that (1) the typical subject supplies the correct number of items only when the amount deleted is 25% or less, and even then much of the material supplied is incorrect, and (2) passages which are easiest to complete are not necessarily those with the highest readability scores.

431. Dale, E. "The Problem of Readability," Bureau of Educational Research, Ohio State University, *The News Letter,* February, 1954.

    In a general review of the problem of how to improve reading materials, it is remarked that readability formulas will give a rough indication by grade level of the difficulty which readers of varying degrees of ability will experience in reading material.

Formulas will not account for specialized vocabularies or provide rules for writing.

432. Dale, E. "The Problem of Vocabulary in Reading," *Educational Research Bulletin,* **35**:113–23, May, 1956.

Reviewing the past work on the vocabulary factor in reading and writing and discussing needs in this area, the author notes that the frequency-count of words does not correlate highly with familiarity and thus is theoretically defective, although practically useful. Emphasis should be put on studies of technical fields. Children may learn words more rapidly than previously supposed but not enough to suggest the neglect of vocabulary control.

433. Dale, E., and Chall, J. S. "The Concept of Readability," *Elementary English,* **26**:19–26, January, 1949.

It is shown that three common meanings of "readability" — format and organization, interest of content, and comprehensibility — are interrelated and that each is necessary to an adequate definition of readability. Such a definition is offered. It is also concluded that current research neglects the factors of conceptual difficulty and semantic variability, and overemphasizes others.

434. Dale, E., and Chall, J. S. "Developing Readable Materials," Ch. IX of *Adult Reading,* Part II, The Fifty-fifth Yearbook of the National Society for the Study of Education. Chicago: University of Chicago Press, 218–50, 1956.

In a discussion of reading ability, readership, and readability formulas, it was concluded that specialized information must be simplified for all the public and particularly for those with limited ability. Writing at approximately the seventh-grade level will reach a great majority and levels can be predicted and "written to" through the use of formulas. Help is needed in locating materials already available at various levels.

435. Dale, E., and Chall, J. S. "Reply" (reply to Dawkins, John, "A Reconsideration of the Dale-Chall Formula," in same journal), *Elementary English,* **33**:520–22, December, 1956.

In reply to John Dawkins' critical analysis of the Dale-Chall formula, statistical results and references are presented, rejecting his claim that mechanically shortening sentences and substituting easy words for hard will improve readability. The authors also reject the definition of reading attributed to them by Dawkins and discuss multiple-meaning words and the findings about organization.

436. Dawkins, J. "A Reconsideration of the Dale-Chall Formula," *Elementary English*, **33**:515–20, December, 1956.
Criticizing the Dale-Chall readability formula, the author argues that sentence length is only one of many factors affecting organization. Paragraph organization can produce difficult reading but the formula does not recognize such problems. It doesn't matter what meaning a word may have since its level of difficulty does not change. If this is the case, readability formulas show no awareness of the nature of language.

437. Fitzgerald, S. E. "Literature by Slide Rule," *The Saturday Review*, **36**:15–16, 53–54, February 14, 1953.
Protesting the use of readability formulas to make literary writing more readable, the author argues that a clear idea may be expressed in long form, while some brief explanations may be unclear and incorrect; avoiding foreign and complex words would eliminate some of the best-known words in the language, and it appears more important to improve ideas than words.

438. Flesch, R. F. "A Dissenting Opinion on Readability," *Elementary English Review*, **26**:332–34, 340, October, 1949.
To correct wrong impressions given in articles by Dale and Chall, Dolch, and Lorge, Flesch denies that the syllable count in his formula can be taken as a use of vocabulary load and calls it a measure of abstractness. He points out research showing that word-list formulas have poor reliability and relates his own formula to Gestalt psychology insofar as it emphasizes the frame of mind of the reader.

439. Gunning, R. "Some Misconceptions About Readability," *Editor and Publisher*, **80**:38, September 13, 1947.
Three misconceptions about readability are outlined: the short sentence mania caused by the impression that only short sentences can improve readability; the moronic phobia that makes people claim newspaper readers have 12-year-old minds; and the lack-luster lament which says readability principles tend to restrict writing to a stereotyped technique.

440. Haagen, C. H. "Synonymity, Vividness, Familiarity, and Association Value Ratings of 400 Pairs of Common

Adjectives," *The Journal of Psychology,* **27**:453–63, January, 1949.

To develop materials for use in studies of verbal learning, 480 two-syllable adjectives were selected and incorporated into series of six words related in meaning. These were then scaled in terms of similarity of meaning, closeness of associative connection, and vividness of connotation and familiarity, thus forming 80 sub-scales. A sample of the word-list is presented and its possible uses in learning research described and illustrated.

441. Hall, J. F. "Learning as a Function of Word-Frequency," *American Journal of Psychology,* **67**:138–40, March, 1954.

To determine more extensively the relation between word frequency and recall, over 200 college students were presented word-lists and later tested for recall. Four lists, representing four levels of frequency count, were used. Results showed that a significant, positive relationship exists between word frequency and recall.

442. Haseley, L. "The Relationship Between Cue-Value of Words and Their Frequency of Prior Occurrence." Unpublished Master's thesis, Ohio University, 1957.

Results of a study of the relationship between cue-value of Turkish and English words and their frequency of prior occurrence indicated a significant difference between mean scores of two extreme frequencies in both English and Turkish words. For Turkish words a linear relationship existed between the logarithm of frequency and cue-value while for the English words the relationship diverged a great deal from a linear function.

443. Holland, B. F. "The Effect of Length and Structure of Sentences on the Silent Reading Process," *Psychological Bulletin,* **30**:668–69, November, 1933.

To determine the effect of the length and structure of sentences on the silent reading process, complex and simple versions of geographical prose were presented to college freshmen and pupils in Grades 4, 5, 6, 7, and 9. The subjects were then tested for comprehension. Results showed that the effects of complexity and length vary with sentence patterns, with individuals, and with groups of subjects.

444. Howes, D. H., and Solomon, R. L. "Visual Duration Threshold as a Function of Word-Probability," *Journal of Experimental Psychology,* **41**:401–10, June, 1951.

Two experiments were conducted to investigate the relationship between the familiarity of words and the visual duration threshold necessary for correctly identifying such words. Experiment I revealed that a strong inverse relationship existed between word frequency and duration threshold. The effect of increased practice in Experiment I resulted in more low thresholds than the distribution for a word with the same frequency in Experiment II.

445. Hunt, C. W. "Protest Against Winnetka Lists," *The Library Journal,* **59**:470, June 1, 1934.

In opposition to graded reading lists for children's literature, the author cites her experience as a primary teacher and gives a sample of grade-listings of a few titles. She feels that open shelves of ungraded books do more to whet curiosity and teach vocabulary, and that the Winnetka list ignores subject interest, and grades books quite contrary to her experience.

446. Kearl, B. "A Closer Look at Readability Formulas," *Journalism Quarterly,* **25**:344–48, December, 1948.

Examination of the two Flesch formulas and the Dale-Chall formula in particular to determine their strong and weak points led to the conclusions that stylistic elements, which may be important, are rarely of major concern; that formulas cannot predict over-all readability, or be considered cure-alls in the field of readability; and that, like most statistical tools, they must be used wisely and with discretion.

447. King-Ellison, P., and Jenkins, J. J. "The Durational Threshold of Visual Recognition as a Function of Word-Frequency," *American Journal of Psychology,* **67**:700–703, December, 1954.

In this experiment, the relationship between the tachistoscopic recognition threshold of five-letter nonsense words (paralogs) and the frequency of prior usage of the words was examined. The correlation between the mean tachistoscopic exposure-time and the logarithm of the frequency of presentation was found to be −.99, confirming the results of previous studies. The results were also converted into information-theory terms, showing that as the amount of information per symbol increases, the durational threshold increases linearly.

448. Lorge, I. "Readability Formulae — An Evaluation," *Elementary English,* **26:**86–95, February, 1949.

Comparing and contrasting the most reliable readability formulas showed that measuring vocabulary burden results in the most reliable method of testing readability. Organization has been grossly neglected in all formulas. However, despite their weaknesses, most formulas do a relatively thorough job in classifying materials.

449. McGinnies, E., Comer, P. B., and Lacey, O. L. "Visual-Recognition Thresholds as a Function of Word Length and Word Frequency," *Journal of Experimental Psychology,* **44:**65–69, August, 1952.

In this study tachistoscopic recognition thresholds were determined for 20 neutrally toned English words varying in length and frequency. The results showed that duration thresholds for these words were a linear, decreasing function of word frequency and a linear, increasing function of word length. It was also found that subjects' hypotheses (wrong guesses) tended to be words of greater frequency than the experimental words themselves.

450. Marks, M. R., and Jack, O. "Verbal Context and Memory Span for Meaningful Material," *American Journal of Psychology,* **65:**298–300, April, 1952.

Suggesting several objections to an article by Miller and Selfridge, "Verbal Context and the Recall of Meaningful Material," the authors repeated the work with modifications designed to meet the criticisms. Results showed that order of approximation significantly affects the ability to recall. Recall appeared to be a function of the *a priori* relative meaningfulness of the materials used.

451. Miller, G. A. *Language and Communication.* New York: McGraw-Hill, 1951.

In an attempt to bring together the more important approaches to the study of communicative behavior in a way that makes sense to a modern psychologist, the author tries to suggest the breadth of the spectrum of linguistic studies. Of greatest interest for readability are pp. 131–39 and 233–35. The former is a brief presentation of readability in general and the 1948 Flesch formula in particular; the latter is a discussion of the notion of "recoding," or the coding of information in a new, more useful form than that in which it was originally encountered.

452. Miller, G. A., and Selfridge, J. A. "Verbal Context and the Recall of Meaningful Material," *American Journal of Psychology*, **63**:176–85, April, 1950.

In a study to determine how well people can remember sequences of symbols that have various degrees of contextual constraint in their composition, it was found that the percentage of recall increased as the order of approximation increased, and decreased as the word length of the list increased. Meaningful material is easy to learn, not necessarily because it is meaningful, but because it retains short-range associations which are familiar.

453. Milton, H. H. "Let's Improve Our Writing, Not Measure It," *Informational Bulletin,* Scott AFB, Ill.: Training Analysis and Development Directorate, Deputy Chief of Staff Operations, Hq. ARTC, 4:13–17, Spring, 1953.

Six "do's" and three "don'ts" of good writing are suggested as ways to improve writing without using readability measures. These suggestions, coupled with shorter sentences and personal pronouns, will make writing more direct and readable. Completed writing, using these suggestions, can then be measured with a formula.

454. Moore, A. C. "Recoiling From Reading: A Consideration of the Thorndike Library," *Library Journal,* **60**:419–22, May 15, 1935.

To examine changes made in children's classics in the Thorndike Library editions, the altered versions were submitted to appraisal by comparison and report of the staff of Children's Work for the New York Public Library. Some of the changes made in several classics are described, and the author concludes that children cannot learn love and knowledge of literature by word changing and sentence re-construction.

455. Noble, C. E. "The Meaning-Familiarity Relationship," *Psychological Review,* **60**:89–98, March, 1953.

In a study analyzing familiarity in verbal material and investigating the functional relationship between meaning and familiarity, 200 airmen rated their familiarity with 96 words on a five-point scale. Results showed that meaning does not determine familiarity, but that familiarity may be represented as a correlate of meaning.

456. Noble, C. E. "The Familiarity-Frequency Relationship," *Journal of Experimental Psychology,* **47**:13–16, January, 1954.

Sixteen words low in frequency value were used in a study to determine the exact form of relationship between familiarity of verbal stimuli and frequency of stimulation. Plotting of the resulting statistics showed the familiarity-frequency function to be hyperbolic in form. These findings were consistent with the theory that familiarity is a learning attribute of stimuli.

457. Peters, H. N. "The Relationship Between Familiarity of Words and Their Memory Value," *American Journal of Psychology,* **48**:572–84, October, 1936.

Several experiments were conducted to ascertain the influence of relative familiarity upon the memory value of words. Words of differing levels of familiarity were tested on college students. Results showed that frequency of recall was greater for the words of either extreme of familiarity and that there was no consistent superiority of any degrees of familiarity.

458. Powers, R. D., and Kearl, B. E. "Further Directions for Readability Research," *Journalism Quarterly,* **35**:427–32, Fall, 1958.

The main conclusion of a study of some areas for further readability research was that what has been done in the past, for the most part, needs further investigation, possibly along allied lines, to help increase the validity of the tool. Research has taken a narrow path and now it is time to branch out to determine whether the experimenters in the field have been on the right track.

459. Rubenstein, H., and Aborn, M. "Learning, Prediction, and Readability," *Journal of Applied Psychology,* **42**:28–32, February, 1958.

Thirty experimental passages were used to investigate the interrelationship of passage readability, ease of learning, and degree of predictability of constituent words. Learning, prediction, and readability were found to be closely interrelated. The

Dale-Chall scores correlated more closely with learning and prediction than did the Flesch scores of the passages' readability.

460. Seashore, R. H., and Eckerson, L. D. "Measurement of Individual Differences in General English Vocabularies," *Journal of Educational Psychology,* **31**:14–38, January, 1940.

To construct and evaluate a set of recognition and use tests for the measurement of estimated vocabularies of college undergraduates, and to study the relation of vocabulary size to other intellectual abilities, word-lists and recognition and use tests were administered to undergraduates. The average undergraduate recognized 35% of the common basic words, 1% of the rare basic words and 47% of the derivative words. The range of total scores was 112,100 to 192,575 words.

461. Seyfert, W. C. "Perhaps the Greeks Had a Word for It," *School Review,* **62**:71–73, January, 1954.

Presenting factors other than frequency of words which contribute to reading difficulty, the author points out that unusual words are not the only unreadable words. Many are difficult because their range of possible meanings is not restricted; others are difficult because they are not given an operational definition. It is suggested that many abstract words might better be dropped from our vocabulary.

462. Shannon, C. E., and Weaver, W. *The Mathematical Theory of Communication.* Urbana: The University of Illinois Press, 1949.

This book is made up of two papers on communication (information) theory. The first, by Shannon, is a technical presentation of the mathematical bases of the theory; the second, by Weaver, is a nontechnical introduction to the theory, with suggestions for broad applications. Of interest for the study of readability is the estimation by Shannon of the redundancy of English text (p. 26). He finds it to be roughly 50% by several methods, one of which is restoration of deleted letters by a reader.

463. Solomon, R. L., and Postman, L. "Frequency of Usage as a Determinant of Recognition Threshold for Words,"

Journal of Experimental Psychology, **43**:195–201, March, 1952.

In a study of the relationship between tachistoscopic recognition thresholds for seven-letter nonsense (Turkish) words and the frequency of prior usage of the words, it was found that recognition thresholds vary inversely with frequency of prior usage. Either frequency of prior exposure or frequency of prior response, or both, may have been the determinant; the relative importance of each was not studied here.

464. Standlee, L. S., Fattu, N. A., and Auble, D. "Frequency Index of Words Appearing in Four Navy Publications," *Bureau of Naval Personnel Technical Bulletin,* No. 54-2, January, 1954.

This is a word-list based on a frequency index of words used in four Navy publications and designed to provide a basis for preparation of materials to meet the vocabulary requirements of enlisted men in the Navy.

465. Stolurow, L. M., and Newman, J. R. "A Factorial Analysis of Objective Features of Printed Language Presumably Related to Reading Difficulty," *Journal of Educational Research,* **52**:243–51, March, 1959.

An intercorrelation matrix, originally prepared by Gray and Leary and later reduced from 44 to 23 "variables," was submitted to factor analysis to isolate patterns of relationship among the style factors in printed material. "Word" and "sentence" factors accounted for the major amount of variance.

466. Zipf, G. K. *The Psycho-Biology of Language.* Boston: Houghton Mifflin Co., 1935.

The primary aim of the book is to formulate into tentative laws the forces behind linguistic expression; the secondary aim is to relate the laws to phenomena of meaning and emotional intensity in language. Chapter 2 (particularly pp. 20–29), develops and presents a "Law of Abbreviation," which states that the length of a word tends to bear an inverse relationship to its relative frequency.

467. Zipf, G. K. *Human Behavior and the Principle of Least Effort.* Cambridge, Mass.: Addison-Wesley Press, 1949.

The author attempts to establish the "principle of least effort" as a primary principle governing individual and collective behavior of all sorts. Of particular interest to a study of readability and reading is the application of this principle to human language behavior.

See also 3, 11, 14, 15, 16, 21, 32, 41, 87, 97, 104, 105, 119, and 386.

H. Review and Bibliographic References

Nos. 468–482

468. Betts, E. A. "Readability: Its Application to the Elementary School," *Journal of Educational Research,* **42**:438–59, February, 1949.

Summarizing 12 readability studies, the author concludes that readability is influenced by number and length of sentences, prepositional phrases, vocabulary, multi-syllable words, and human interest. Generally, easy material has short sentences, many common words, and many personal references, while difficult material has long sentences, many uncommon words, and many prepositional phrases.

469. Chall, J. S. *Readability: An Appraisal of Research and Application.* Columbus: The Bureau of Educational Research, Ohio State University, 1958.

In a review of the significant research in readability measurement and application, the author suggests that further refinement of readability measurement should be undertaken and that formulas should be more critically applied.

470. Cowing, A. G. *Readability Yardsticks,* U.S. Department of Agriculture, Printed Folder 1.913 S2R224, April 12, 1946.

The major contributions made by McClintock and Hopkins (1929), Dale and Tyler (1934), Gray and Leary (1935), Lorge (1939 and 1945), and Flesch (1942) are reviewed, and the similarities between Dale, Flesch, and Lorge indicated. It is stated that the work done on readability since 1929 can be used as a guide for writing and estimating difficulty of written materials but is not to be regarded as a rigorous determination.

471. Flesch, R. F. "A Readability Formula in Practice," *Elementary English,* **25**:344–51, October, 1948.

Attempting to show the utility of his formula for the measurement of readability and particularly for the measurement of readability in adult materials, the author concludes that the successful application of his formula reveals the utility of approaching problems of readability from the linguistic standpoint. He believes the avoidance of a vocabulary factor makes his formula preferable to those using one.

472. Flesch, R. F. *How To Write, Speak, and Think More Effectively.* New York: Harper and Brothers, 1960.

A compilation of the author's earlier articles and books on writing, this book is intended to provide a systematic way of improving the mind. It also contains directions for the use of the Flesch Reading Ease and Human Interest formulas and the new, quick Self-Test to measure the dimension of formality to popularity in writing.

473. Gray, W. S. "I. Sociology of Reading," 967–72; "II. Physiology and Psychology of Reading," 972–87; "III. Teaching of Reading," 987-1005, *Encyclopedia of Educational Research.* New York: Macmillan Co., 1950.

Discussing various aspects of reading, the author concludes that research in reading can continue to make notable contributions in the future at all levels of formal and informal education by progressive thought concerning the function of education and the rapidly increasing body of facts known about child growth and development.

474. Hotchkiss, S. N., and Paterson, D. G. "Flesch Readability Reading List," *Personnel Psychology*, 3:327–44, Autumn, 1950.

This article lists for workers in the field of industrial communications the Flesch formulas and the studies and articles on their use. A search was made of the literature from 1943 to early 1950 and 96 articles and books selected, classified by topic, and briefly annotated. These sources are listed under 12 different topics for reference guidance.

475. Klare, G. R. "Evaluation of Quantitative Indices of Comprehensibility in Written Communication." Unpublished Doctoral dissertation, University of Minnesota, 1950.

Assessing the readability formulas in use and pointing to directions for further research, the author notes that, despite inaccuracies, comparative judgments based on formulas can be made. Grade level estimates fail as anything but gross indices of probable adult levels but can and must be used for children's materials. The Gray-Leary, Dale-Chall, Flesch RE, Washburne-Morphett, and Lewerenz formulas were compared in this study.

476. Klare, G. R., and Buck, B. *Know Your Reader: The Scientific Approach to Readability.* Professional Writers Library. New York: Hermitage House, 1954.

This is a review of the available literature on readers, readability, and readability formulas, intended primarily for the professional writer of adult nonfiction and designed to help him communicate better. Writers can and should know more about readers than they do; this knowledge need not detract from the artistic nature of writing.

477. Leary, B. E. "Difficulties in Reading Material," *Reading in General Education.* Washington: American Council on Education, pp. 272–306, 1940.

Discussing some approaches to reading difficulty, the author finds that investigators specifically trained in analysis are more adept at grading reading difficulty than teachers, librarians, or publishers. A survey of available evidence showed that the most important factors making a book pleasant to read are content, style, format, and organization. A list of factors to consider when evaluating books is presented.

478. Painter, H. W. "A Synthesis of Research on the Placement of Reading Material in Secondary-School Literature," *English Journal,* 31:642–46, November, 1942.

A survey of the research studies on placement of selections in seventh- through twelfth-grade English literature texts (according to student interest and comprehension) indicated that common experience is the chief reason given by children for liking a selection. More studies are devoted to interests than to difficulty. Comparison of difficulty and interest median grade placements reveals almost 75% of the selections have the same or adjacent grade placements.

479. Painter, H. W., and Franzen, C. G. F. "A Synthesis of Research on the Placement of Reading Material in Secondary-School Literature," *Journal of Educational Research,* **39**:304–6, 1945.

An attempt to synthesize the findings of 144 studies on interest and difficulty led to the conclusion that such synthesizing gives aid in proper grade placement, permits observation of the main points of agreement and disagreement, and suggests where further work needs to be done.

480. "What Makes for Readable Writing and Reading Success?" Technical Memorandum No. 2, University of Illinois, Div. of Communications, HRRI, Under Contract AF18 (600) 335; 52-24, 670-07, October 1, 1952.

From a survey of the field of readability research, it was found that a total of 150 different language elements have been used to measure readability, 129 classify writing on the easy-difficult scale and the remaining classes using the interesting-dull scale. Study elements included vocabulary difficulty, length of words and sentences, difficulty relating to parts of speech, personal references, verb-adjective ratio, and picture words.

481. Witty, P. "Improving Readability of Printed Materials," *Elementary English,* **28**:392–401, 409, November, 1951.

After extensively reviewing readability literature for an account of the various factors involved in the improvement of the readability of printed materials, the author claims that the best use of formulas is to check material after it is written. The author strongly opposes use of formulas as canons for writing or as final authorities on readability, and stresses the principles of arousing interest and relating the writing to the reader's life experiences.

482. Yoakam, G. A. "Determining the Readability of Instructional Materials," *A Report of the Seventh Annual Conference on Reading.* Pittsburgh: University of Pittsburgh, 47–53, 1951.

After considering the readability of children's textbooks and comparing the Yoakam formula with other formulas, the study concludes that children will learn from readable materials and that textbooks must be carefully built to prevent retardation in learning through reading. The Yoakam formula is found easy to apply and more reliable when tested for grade placement than the Dale, Flesch, and Lorge formulas.

See also 5, 6, 41, 369, 424, 425, 426, 427, 433, 434, 446, 448, and 458.

Index

Index*

* Italic page numbers refer to entries (names or topics) listed in the Bibliography.